MW01194708

The Kingdom of Children

The Kingdom of Children

A Liberation Theology

R. L. Stollar

WILLIAM B. EERDMANS PUBLISHING COMPANY
GRAND RAPIDS, MICHIGAN

Wm. B. Eerdmans Publishing Co.
4035 Park East Court SE, Grand Rapids, Michigan 49546
www.eerdmans.com

© 2023 R. L. Stollar
All rights reserved
Published 2023

Book design by Lydia Hall

Printed in the United States of America

29 28 27 26 25 24 23   1 2 3 4 5 6 7

ISBN 978-0-8028-8283-7

Library of Congress Cataloging-in-Publication Data

A catalog record for this book is available from the Library of Congress.

Unless otherwise noted, Scripture quotations are from the New International Version.

To Jack Crabtree—for teaching me to love theology

The most significant challenge before us is to recapture in our own particular contexts the radicalness of Jesus' teaching on children. Children are not only subordinate but sharers with adults in the life of faith; they are not only to be formed but to be imitated; they are not only ignorant but capable of receiving spiritual insight; they are not "just" children but representatives of Christ. What makes that challenge so difficult is that it would entail changing not only how adults relate to children but how we conceive of our social world. Jesus did not just teach how to make an adult world kinder and more just for children; he taught the arrival of a social world in part defined by and organized around children. He cast judgment on the adult world because it is not the child's world. He made being a disciple dependent on inhabiting this "small world." He invited the children to come to him not so that he might initiate them into the adult world but so that they might receive what is properly theirs—the reign of God.

—Judith M. Gundry-Volf[1]

Contents

CONTENTS

Foreword

As both a child advocate and a parent, I'm always trying to learn and implement strategies of giving more power to children when I interact with them. This is because of my inherent power as an adult. Recently, I learned to tell a child my age before I ask them theirs. "I'm 44, how old are you?" Children frequently get asked how old they are, as if they owe us this private information by virtue of being children. By offering my age, I volunteer my personal profile before requesting theirs.

Another trick I've learned is getting down on eye level with children when speaking with them. Instead of literally speaking over them, I can squat down, intentionally shrinking my body smaller to embody a more equal power stance when I'm engaging in conversation with kids. One time, I did exactly this and gained more than connection with the child. I lowered my body to eye level to speak to a young child. Like many young children, their attention shifted quickly after engaging for a short while. They skipped off to play with something apparently more interesting than me.

But instead of getting back up, I stayed down there at the child's eye level for a little while longer. What I saw from that vantage point was a very intimidating world. All the objects around me appeared so much larger. I couldn't see over the countertops. Many things became inaccessible to my reach. The adults around me didn't even notice me because, from their perspective, I became invisible beneath them. I felt instantly powerless and I didn't like that feeling at all. However, I also noticed things I never noticed before: the dirt on the ground and the little critters that inhabited these spaces. It's no wonder toddlers often interrupt their adult's errand running in order to satisfy their curiosity about critters. They are fascinating!

I wondered: How much of the beauty of this world was I missing because I did not see through a child's eyes? I thought I was giving my power away to help a child feel more comfortable. But instead, that experience changed me more than it did them.

We live in a deeply anti-child world. From violent physical and sexual abuse of vulnerable children—who are often at the intersection of various other oppressions such as race, class, and disability—to microaggressions committed in the ways we speak to and about children, kids are enduring unspeakable indignities. Even the most benign, responsible citizens—liberal, educated progressives, loving mothers, caregivers—can be heard joking casually about children in subhuman ways. To advocate for equal dignity for children today, to demand basic human rights for children that have long been denied, is to be at the forefront of a revolutionary fight for progress—one that will undoubtedly transform society as we know it.

What would happen if the adults of our world collectively gave away our power in board rooms, at Congress, in church leadership meetings, at the voting booths, in our family living rooms? What if we got down on our knees, not just to make the kids feel more at ease and included, but to fundamentally change the core of who we are as a civilization—one that strives to honor the dignity of every human being? Because *that's* who our kids are! They are humans who do not yet have the rights they deserve.

Every time I choose to get on my knees at a child's level, I become more conscious of anti-child prejudices. While this makes me more aware, the fact is that I don't always choose to do it. It requires effort to squat down, it takes time out of my busy schedule, and it removes me from the interesting "adult" conversation I'm currently having. It is within my power to make this choice. I can also ignore children, shush them, and even berate them without consequence because of my adult privilege.

There are a few instances when I cannot ignore the voices of children demanding that I treat them with dignity. One of them is my highly sensitive child, who cried for hours on end as a baby and vomited frequently as a young child because of their sensitivities to the world. This child never fails to let us know we have to do better at hearing children's voices—to see and to believe their experience of this shared planet. As Ryan says in this book, children can be prophets—and indeed my child is one, calling us to forge a better world, one where children are seen and heard and treated with respect.

Another instance is whenever I interact with Ryan. I can count on one hand the number of people I've known who have persistently, thoroughly, and passionately advocated for the liberation of children. Ryan isn't a parent of a child. But he, like all of us, was a child. Like all of us, he is now a parent of society's children.

Ryan beckons me to get down to a child's eye level and to pay attention. It can be tricky to find a term to describe children that affords them equal dignity as adults since terms like *children*, *kids*, and *minors* all carry some pejorative connotations of the anti-child biases we've internalized. One of my favorite alternatives is borrowed from my mother tongue. In Mandarin, we call children "xiao peng you"—which translates literally to "small friends." I am honored to call Ryan my friend, and I am relieved and grateful that my small friends have a friend in Ryan.

Ryan and I also have in common a shared history of toxic conservative evangelical influences in our upbringing. We both know how adverse religious experiences in childhood can inflict profound harm that takes a lifetime to repair. It is such a gift to our world that Ryan has chosen to bring the full experience of his own childhood to explore liberation for all children through child liberation theology. His meticulous exegesis of biblical narratives is transformative and should be required study for all who care about justice at every intersection. In the following pages you will become well equipped to advocate for children and in the process, I hope, discover that our adult liberation is bound together with children's. You will find that in seeing the Bible, theology, and the world from a child's perspective, you'll experience transformation for yourselves, too.

Cindy Wang Brandt

Acknowledgments

Three individuals have especially inspired my thoughts regarding child liberation theology and have influenced and shaped the way I have written this book. Those individuals are: Janet Pais, the original creator of child liberation theology; Cindy Wang Brandt, the visionary author of *Parenting Forward* and the creator of the *Unfundamentalist Parenting* blog that originally hosted my thoughts on child liberation theology; and Marcia J. Bunge, one of the founders and primary thought leaders of the child theology movement. I am greatly indebted to these individuals' work, thoughts, and passion for children. To me, these people are heroes of the faith.

I am also grateful not to be the only person developing the field of child liberation theology today. Rebecca Stevens-Walter, Craig Nessan, and Samantha Field are all making vital contributions.

Additionally, I am deeply indebted to Jonathan Carraher, who first introduced me to liberation theology while I was an undergraduate student at Gutenberg College.

I would like to thank everyone who gave me feedback on original drafts of this book, including Michelle Panchuk, Eve Ettinger, Lillia Munsell, Heidi Sandoval, Giselle Palmer, David Chapman, Eric Zwierzynski, Robin Benedict, Samuel Burns, Melanie Bozzay, Sarah Rice Duterte, and Scarlettah Schaefer.

Shout-outs go to those friends who helped me obtain the books I needed to complete this project, including Michelle Panchuk, Adam Arthur, Kevin Timpe, Becky Rouzer Northcutt, Kathi Bonham, and Giselle Palmer.

Many thanks to my agent, David Morris, for helping me make this book a reality. Thanks as well to Bradley Onishi for introducing me to

David, and to Chrissy Stroop for encouraging me to write more. Thanks to Trevor Thompson and everyone at Eerdmans for taking a chance on me and this idea. To my copyeditor, Rachel Martens: thank you for both seeing and bringing out the best in me. I am grateful for your guidance and wisdom. This book would not be the same without you.

Thanks to *Patheos* and Cindy Wang Brandt for first hosting my thoughts on child liberation theology on the *Unfundamentalist Parenting* blog and giving me permission to reprint and rewrite several of my blog posts for this book.

Finally, I would like to thank my partner, Scarlettah Schaefer, for everything she has done and continues to do for me. She is my rock and I love her to the moon and back.

* * *

Portions of the following chapters draw upon and rework the following writings of mine.

Chapter 1: from "We Live in an Anti-Child World," *Unfundamentalist Parenting* (blog), *Patheos*, February 17, 2017, https://tinyurl.com/42cs7prm.

Chapter 2: from "Towards a Child Liberation Theology," *R. L. Stollar* (blog), June 21, 2015, https://tinyurl.com/4sxbbczu.

Chapter 3: from "7 Ways to Read the Bible That Lift Up Children," *Unfundamentalist Parenting* (blog), *Patheos*, March 24, 2017, https://tinyurl.com/4fuyj3zv.

Chapter 4, "Isaac's Binding: An Example of a Cautionary Tale": from "The Binding of Isaac as Cautionary Tale," *R. L. Stollar* (blog), May 23, 2016, https://tinyurl.com/3uex9bf7.

Chapter 4, "Lot's Daughters: An Example of Victim Blaming": from "The Lot of the Abused: How We Shift the Blame onto Victims," *Unfundamentalist Parenting* (blog), *Patheos*, April 21, 2016, https://tinyurl.com/7wb59nxr.

Chapter 4, "Including Children": from "Reading Violent Bible Stories through a Child Protection Lens," *Unfundamentalist Parenting* (blog), *Patheos*, March 24, 2016, https://tinyurl.com/3mf6j9ua.

Chapter 5, "Miriam, Child Critic of Anti-Child Patriarchy": from "Miriam, Child Prophet," *R. L. Stollar* (blog), November 4, 2015, https://tinyurl.com/yc88z7tb.

Chapter 5, "The Enslaved Servant Girl, Child Savior of a Mighty Man": from "The Little Girl Who Saved the Mighty Man," *Unfundamentalist Parenting* (blog), *Patheos*, June 2, 2016, https://tinyurl.com/2jashxsd.

Chapter 6, "Jesus as Child": from "Jesus as Child," *Unfundamentalist Parenting* (blog), *Patheos*, June 14, 2017, https://tinyurl.com/yckktenv.

Chapter 7: from "God as Child," *Unfundamentalist Parenting* (blog), *Patheos*, April 28, 2017, https://tinyurl.com/yc4yzwsr.

Chapter 8, "Innocents": from "Children Are Not Angels," *Unfundamentalist Parenting* (blog), *Patheos*, May 3, 2017, https://tinyurl.com/2p8cmpyn.

Chapter 9: from "The End of Child Liberation Theology," *R. L. Stollar* (blog), October 16, 2015, https://tinyurl.com/542t7fvj.

Chapter 10, "Implications for Child Liberation Theology": from "Give Children Space to Be Conscientious Objectors," *Unfundamentalist Parenting* (blog), *Patheos*, May 24, 2017, https://tinyurl.com/4xtat2xc.

Chapter 11, "A Little Child Will Lead Them": from "A Little Child Will Lead Them: Child Protection and the Kingdom of God," *Unfundamentalist Parenting* (blog), *Patheos*, July 28, 2016, https://tinyurl.com/mrx57w2z.

Chapter 11, "Understanding Children's Existential Struggles": from "Understanding Children's Existential Struggles," *Unfundamentalist Parenting* (blog), *Patheos*, June 9, 2017, https://tinyurl.com/4u3ct5be.

Chapter 12, "Implications for Child Liberation Theology": from "Children, Disobey Your Parents in the Lord, for This Is Right," *Unfundamentalist Parenting* (blog), *Patheos*, May 9, 2016, https://tinyurl.com/33brhjcc.

introduction

Suffer the Children

What does it mean for me to be a theologian?
It means that I must use the fruits bequeathed
to me to help create a perspective on religion
that is liberating.

—Chung Hyun Kyung[1]

We live in extreme times. COVID-19 has killed over six million people around the world and over one million of those deaths have occurred in the United States.[2] Millions of children globally have become orphans in the wake of COVID-19[3]—and more continue to every day. At the height of the pandemic, a child lost a parent or primary caregiver to COVID-19 every six seconds.[4] The United States was not spared in this regard: over two hundred thousand American children have become orphans due to the pandemic.[5]

In many ways, the US government's response to COVID-19 illustrates one of the messages of this book: children experience systemic abuse and oppression just like any other vulnerable group of people. As many child advocates and researchers have pointed out, the US response to COVID-19 revealed that our world is an anti-child world from top to bottom.[6] Children—and their needs and concerns—have consistently been deprioritized throughout the pandemic.

While the pandemic persists, we have also witnessed the rapid ascendancy of the Christian Right in the United States—an ascendancy marked by an attempted insurrection and increasingly common mass shootings.[7] (Many of these shootings are directed toward children at schools.)[8] With this increasing political power, the Right has successfully engineered the fall of reproductive rights with the overturning of *Roe v. Wade*. Among conservatives, this reversal is celebrated as the ultimate act of child advocacy. What could be more noble than securing a child's right to life? Yet the same Christian Right that orchestrated the restriction of reproductive rights is also responsible for the United States being the only country in the world that has not ratified the United Nations Convention on the Rights of the Child.[9] This is not a coincidence. As I explore in this book, the Christian Right—long portrayed in the media as a movement driven by family values—is responsible for spreading deeply harmful ideas regarding children, families, and parenting. Many children have suffered greatly because of how the Christian Right views and treats children.

It is not only the Christian Right that needs to be held accountable for the fact that we live in an anti-child world, though. It is not only evangelicals; it is not only Christians; it is not only Americans. Child abuse and neglect are universal problems. While this book focuses on anti-child issues relevant to the United States, I hope readers worldwide can find ideas here to apply to their own contexts. Children experience abuse and oppression everywhere, and hopefully the ideas I present will be applicable just as broadly.

Because this introduction is long and covers a lot of ground, let me begin by mapping what I will discuss: First, I will present an overview of why I wrote this book—the facts about the world we live in today that motivate me to advocate for children. Second, I will explain what *liberation theology* is and what a *child liberation theology* should look like. Third, I will discuss some textual choices I made when writing this book. Fourth and finally, I will explain my point of view as an author.

Why I Wrote This Book

Consider a few statistics about the world American children live in today. A report of child abuse is made every ten seconds in the United States.[10] As many as one hundred thousand American children are trafficked for the purpose of labor and sexual exploitation each year.[11] Globally, one in three victims of human trafficking is a child.[12] The United States has one of the worst child abuse records among industrialized nations—losing on average five children every day to child abuse and neglect.[13] The United States also incarcerates more of its children than any country in the world.[14] In the United States, African American children comprise 59 percent of all prostitution-related arrests for those under the age of 18, the vast majority of whom are girls.[15] Around the world, 160 million children between 5 and 17 years old are engaged in child labor each year—79 million of whom are engaged in hazardous labor.[16] Even in the United States, hundreds of child labor law violations are identified annually.[17] Thirty-four percent of LGBTQIA youth suffer physical violence from their parents because of their sexual orientation.[18] Suicide has become the second-leading cause of death among teenagers in the United States, recently surpassing homicide deaths.[19] Nearly 20 percent of high schoolers report having serious thoughts about suicide and 9 percent report a suicide attempt.[20] Living through the COVID-19 pandemic has only exacerbated children's mental health struggles.[21] Sixty-seven percent of all sexual abuse reported to law enforcement in the United States each year is perpetrated against children.[22] One in four girls and one in six boys are sexually abused before the age of 18.[23]

If you're like me, you will be overwhelmed by these facts. When I read them, they make me angry. I am angry that children experience such things every day and I am angry that we live in a world that allows these conditions to continue. But I also believe that anger should inspire us to create change. These facts cannot remain abstract statistics; they cannot just be discouraging news that we post about on Facebook and then forget about a week later. These facts must motivate us to act. They must stir our hearts to do better for children in our local communities and around the world. As human beings, this is our duty.

For those who are Christians, doing better for children is also a matter of following Jesus. Jesus was clear that a primary Christian duty is loving and protecting children: "Whoever welcomes one of these little children in my name welcomes me" (Mark 9:37). This raises two questions: Do we welcome children into our families, faith communities, and religious organizations? And if we do welcome children, what messages do we communicate to them on a daily basis?

These are important questions because more than half of the children in the United States attend a religious service on a weekly basis.[24] They make up almost 25 percent of the average church population.[25] And the vast majority of these children are being raised in the *Christian* faith.[26] So Christians must ask: What messages do these millions of children hear— week after week—about God and their relationship to the world? What messages do those children's parents hear—week after week—about how to properly relate to, discipline, and love their offspring?

Central to this book is the argument that the American church must radically rethink the messages it communicates to children and their parents. We must do better to model those messages after the spirit of Jesus. The church's record on children is not one to be proud of, especially in the United States. The church has engaged in or justified horrific practices toward children such as the enslavement of African American children,[27] the forced conversion of Native American children,[28] and death-by faith-healing.[29] The early American church revered preachers who spread anti-child messages like "Your Children, are the Children of Death, and the Children of Hell"[30] and "[Children] are young vipers—and are infinitely more hateful than vipers."[31] Today, churches—whether Catholic[32] or Protestant (all denominations)[33]—are facing repeated child sexual abuse tragedies.

American lust for freedom has also created a "parental rights" movement that turns parents into gods, instead of listening to God's command to protect and value children.[34] This parental rights movement has bubbled over from the Right into the Left, filling a vacuum where the Left has lacked practical resources for parents and educators on caring for and empowering children.[35] This happened because, while rightly fighting for women's equality and autonomy, the Left neglected to intersect their work with children. As a result, many conservative evangelical resources for parenting and child training saturated liberal and progressive faith communities.[36] So it is unfair to say one group or one movement or one political party is solely to blame when it comes to how children are mistreated in the United States.[37]

In response to my questions above about whether we welcome children and what messages we communicate to them, this book exhorts us to revisit the messages of Jesus as well as the voice of God as transcribed by the ancient Hebrew prophets and poets.[38] This book hopes to reclaim the message of children being liberated from the pain and suffering forced upon them by abusive principalities and powers—many times powers within the American church itself. In the sense that this book reclaims the Christian message of children's liberation, this book is *child liberation theology*.

What I Mean by Liberation Theology

American Christians have all sorts of opinions about liberation theology. Some love it; some hate it; many have no idea what it is. The easiest, shortest definition of liberation theology is this: it is a theology of *self-determination*. Liberation theology is about equipping and empowering groups of people to discover and speak about God on their own terms and with their own language.

There are many types of liberation theology. There are liberation theologies for Black people, for women, for Pakistani Christians, for Native American Christians, for LGBTQIA Christians, and so forth. Each specific liberation theology revolves around a central image and issue that is deeply important to the group the theology aims to liberate. Each is "really an attempt to rediscover the liberation that Christ has already accomplished and of which we should be aware."[39]

At its heart, liberation theology is a call to realize both that our ideas impact the world and that the world impacts our ideas. It is a reminder that what we believe can really make a difference in people's lives—for good or for evil. It is also a reminder that what makes a difference in people's lives should influence what we decide to believe. Since Jesus calls us to love our neighbors as ourselves, we should make sure that our love for our neighbors is the foundation of how we construct our theology and that we evaluate our theology according to whether or not it empowers us to better love our neighbors.[40] That is liberation theology in a nutshell.

Every liberation theology is also unique. Every liberation theology "is a way of speaking prophetically and contextually to a particular situation."[41] And the theology I want to talk about in this book is similarly unique and context-driven. At the same time, it has a few areas in common with the other liberation theologies—after all, those shared common areas are what make it "liberation" theology and not some other type.

Speaking generally, liberation theology—in all of its various forms—involves five themes. These themes are: (1) theology needs to be practical, applicable to the here and now;[42] (2) theology is at its best when the people doing the theology are empowered to do it on their own terms and for their own sake;[43] (3) theology should highlight and value everyday, personal experiences;[44] (4) theology should focus on the human community that is created by knowing and loving God;[45] and (5) the theological ideas of sin and injustice are best understood as keeping our neighbor at arm's length—when we fail to obey God's command to love our neighbor as ourselves.[46]

These are the common themes of the many different liberation theologies. I think Mercy Amba Oduyoye wonderfully summarizes these themes: "I do my theology always asking, 'What difference does it make?'"[47] This question—*What difference does it make?*—and the five themes outlined above will serve as the guiding lights to our present task of building a child liberation theology.

Traditionally, liberation theology has focused on the image of God as *suffering*: the suffering of the poor,[48] of people of color,[49] of specific nations,[50] of women,[51] of LGBTQIA people,[52] and of people with disabilities.[53] But then why is there little focus on the image of God as the suffering *child?*

It certainly is not the case that children and youth are better off than some of these other people groups. In fact, while marginalized groups experience increased risk and rates of abuse, the children and youth in those groups are even more at risk. Most sexual assaults, for example, occur against children: out of all reported sexual assaults, nearly 70 percent are inflicted upon children. But when children are also members of other marginalized groups, their risk and rates of abuse increase. Girls are five times more likely to be abused than boys, Black children face twice the risk of sexual abuse compared to white children, children in poverty are three times more likely to be abused, and children with disabilities are almost three times more likely to be victims of sexual violence.[54]

Childhood itself also bears a unique disadvantage, one that is particularly difficult to overcome: "Unlike minority groups and the poor, children can never gain equal access to power as children. . . . As long as a child is a child, she or he will never have access to power or resources equal to adults. . . . The disadvantaged status of children can never be erased, although its significance in relationships can be transformed."[55]

As far as I am aware, there is only one book on the topic of child liberation theology: Janet Pais's *Suffer the Children: A Theology of Liberation by a*

Victim of Child Abuse, written over a quarter of a century ago.[56] Pais is the first—and only—theologian to dedicate an entire book to a child liberation theology to date. While various individuals and organizations have explored a theology of childhood[57] or advocated for child theology,[58] the specific topic of child liberation theology has received very little attention. My goal with this book is to change that and bring the vital conversation about child liberation theology forward to a new generation.[59]

Why I Wrote the Book This Way

A number of choices I have made regarding how I wrote this book may surprise or frustrate readers. Allow me to explain.

First, I want this book to be accessible to everyone. I take seriously Ada María Isasi-Díaz's point that the everyday experiences of people deserve to be lifted up as theologically valuable. Isasi-Díaz argues that "the 'stuff' of our reality," or "daily experiences," reveal to us truths about God as much as the "stuff" of the academy.[60] To put this another way, "If your liberative praxis is something that your mother, your grandmother, your aunts, cannot understand because it's full of technical jargon, then it is bullshit."[61] So while a significant amount of scholarship underpins this book, I aim to explain my points using nonacademic language and without overwhelming the reader with lengthy footnotes. Be assured that appropriate credit will be given. Indeed, a lot of credit is due to many wonderful, challenging thinkers, but I will try to keep the main text of this book as simple and digestible as possible.

Second, I believe that the image of God presented in the Bible is overwhelmingly diverse. God takes on many forms throughout history. I want to honor a broader vision of God than a gendered pronoun. The Bible speaks of God as a father, yes, but also as a mother, a son, a child, a neighbor, and even a lover. So to capture the biblical message itself of God's diverse representations, I will be referring to God in the plural third person: they. And I refer to Jesus of Nazareth—a specific person within history who identified himself as a son of Mary (and Son of God)—as he.

Third, I will not be using the phrases "Old Testament" and "New Testament." Those distinctions are dismissive and offensive toward Jewish people. I will refer to what Christians call the "Old Testament" by its

Jewish terminology, the Tanakh. When I refer to what Christians call the "New Testament," I will be specific as to what part (such as the Gospels, a particular epistle, etc.). Most of my focus will be on the Christian Gospels since those specifically feature the words and actions of Jesus.

Fourth, I will not debate the truth or accuracy of the Bible in this book. Such discussion is important. But to engage in those conversations here would conflict with the purpose at hand: to reclaim the theme of better loving and caring for children that the Hebrew prophets, poets, and Jesus himself promoted. Whether you consider yourself a Christian or not, it's important that we collectively encourage one another to lift up messages that lead to a better world. Fanatical pursuit of religions has led to hurt and pain in our world, yet those religions have also given rise to some of the most important voices for equality and liberation. My goal here is simply to amplify such voices in the context of children.

Who I Am as the Author

An important value in liberation theology is recognizing there is an "I" doing the theology. I am not simply *discovering* biblical truths. I am doing my best to understand biblical truths as a subjective, biased human living in a particular time in history and in a particular place that undoubtedly shades how I understand the Bible. So, I want to be up front with you about my personal point of view. I want you to know my life experiences that have shaped me and made me want to write this book.

My particular point of view is that of someone who was sexually abused as a child. As a result of the abuse and other factors, I suffer from major depressive disorder, anxiety disorder, bipolar disorder, and post-traumatic stress disorder. While I am disadvantaged by both abuse and mental illness, I am nonetheless privileged in many ways. I am white, I was assigned male at birth, and I was born into a middle-class family in the United States. My skin color, sex, class status, and nationality unfairly grant me many social and political privileges others do not have.

Additionally, I was born, raised, and homeschooled by conservative, evangelical parents from kindergarten through my high school graduation. And my undergraduate education was similarly religious and right-wing. These experiences with conservative evangelicalism in the United States shades the way I view Christianity.

Growing up in the conservative, evangelical homeschooling world is what first inspired me to become involved in child advocacy and child protection. I observed significant amounts of child abuse and neglect among my peers who were homeschooled. While my own experience was generally positive, I saw firsthand how homeschooling can be used to control and harm children as well. When I became an adult, I decided something needed to be done. My friends' stories deserved to be told. So, I cofounded Homeschoolers Anonymous, a website that shared the stories of my homeschooled friends and peers. It provided them with a platform to speak about the abuse and neglect they suffered, and it created a community for them to connect with one another and realize: there are so many of us out here.

Homeschoolers Anonymous went viral. It racked up millions of views and garnered profiles in national and international media, including *The Guardian*, *The American Prospect*, *Christian Science Monitor*, *The New Yorker*, and *Pro Publica*. We received hundreds upon hundreds of stories from homeschool alumni around the world—all sharing very similar, heart-breaking stories. And we quickly built a large, online community of thousands of survivors of abuse in the context of evangelical homeschooling. Together, this community founded multiple national nonprofit organizations to fight for the rights of homeschooled children and alumni, including the still-existing Coalition for Responsible Home Education.

As my advocacy for homeschooled children and alumni grew and I became increasingly responsible for shepherding people's stories of abuse and neglect, I realized I needed to better equip myself to help my peers and friends. I went back to school, earning a master's in child protection. And the more I learned about child protection, the more I realized that the world I grew up in follows some truly dangerous and harmful beliefs and practices when it comes to children, families, and parenting. There are so many ways in which the Christian Right encourages and sanctions the anti-child aspects of our world. Surely there must be another way!

A friend had introduced me to liberation theology back when I was an undergraduate student. I was immediately drawn to it and inspired by its passionate advocacy for improving life in the right-here and right-now for those at the margins of society. Ever since my first exposure, I have studied different liberation theologies and learned much from them. But in all my studies, I have noticed the same thing: the absence of children in the discussion. I started to think, *there has to be a liberation theology for children, right?* That is what led me to the work of Janet Pais initially—and what ultimately inspired this book.

These experiences are running right under the surface of this book. They are the lenses through which I view child advocacy and children's rights. I have seen and heard the cries of many hurt children who grew up in the conservative evangelical world, especially those who were homeschooled. I write this book with the hope that it can improve that world's conditions.

I also write this book with the hope that it can lead to a better future for all children. The more I learn about child protection and child liberation, the more I understand that child abuse and marginalization are not unique to conservatives, evangelicals, or homeschoolers. These evil actions transcend political and religious beliefs. Everyone everywhere must make child protection and child liberation a priority if we are to break from our anti-child thoughts and actions. Some of the most anti-child language I hear these days comes from liberal and progressive "child-free" circles.[62] This needs to change.

INCLUDING CHILDREN

It would be disingenuous and hypocritical if this book—a book about making our world and faith accessible and relevant to children—was itself not accessible and relevant to children. Because of this, I have chosen to write this book for lay readers (people who are not professional theologians or ministers). Furthermore, I end every chapter with a section titled "Including Children." These sections feature actionable ways in which the content of each chapter can be made applicable and life-giving to children.

As I explain in chapter 9, liberation theology is a theology of *self-determination*. That is, it hopes to give the subjects of liberation—in this case, children—the power to take hold of their God-given right to discover, love, and share about God on their own terms. While this book is addressed to adults to encourage them to lift up and radically love children daily, children also have a right to be a part of and lead that process themselves. The "Including Children" sections are my attempt to bring adults and children together to work creatively for children's liberation.

In this first "Including Children" section, I introduce an exercise that will help parents, educators, and faith communities assess where they currently stand with relationship to children. This exercise involves a self-assessment for child inclusivity.[63] I invite you and the other adults in your faith community to take the self-assessment. I also invite the children and youth in your community to take it. For children with disabilities, be sure to provide any needed assistance so they can participate fully. Be sure as well to define the larger words so that children of all ages understand the questions.

Step One: Reviewing Motivation

The first step in this self-assessment exercise is to consider your motivations for making your family, faith community, or religious organization more inclusive of children. By answering the following questions honestly, you will learn more about your motivations:

1. Why, in general, do you want to engage children? Why do you want to engage children *specifically* at this current time?
2. How important is engaging children to your (personal and organizational) vision and goals?
3. Have you tried to engage children in the past? If so, what worked well and what worked poorly? Why?
4. What would your family, faith community, or religious organization look like if you successfully engaged children?
5. What obstacles are keeping you from fully committing to engaging children?
6. Who in your family, faith community, or religious organization will you need to persuade before you can commit to engaging children?

Step Two: Taking Stock

For each of the following issues, have individuals write down (1) what works well within your family, faith community, or religious organization, and (2) what needs improvement.

1. Your understanding of what "engagement" is
2. Your engagement of children
3. Your engagement of adults
4. Your vision and goals, as they relate to children
5. The roles adults play
6. The roles children play
7. The amount of access children have to your decision-making process
8. How you make decisions
9. How you establish priorities
10. How you communicate with children
11. What motivates children to get involved
12. The public image or identity you reflect to children
13. How you recruit caregivers who are involved with children (For families, this could be babysitters or tutors; for faith communities and religious organizations, this could be volunteers and staff members.)

If you are answering these questions within a multiage group setting, collect everyone's answers. Once the answers are compiled, compare the adults' answers and the children's answers. Pay special attention to when and how the children's answers differ from the adults' answers. When it comes to children's answers regarding what needs improvement, ask the children to further organize their answers according to their felt priorities. As a family, faith community, or religious organization, and as adults and children, start addressing those areas in need of improvement together.

one

The World We Live In

Children's lives—how they are treated, the
quality of their lives—indexes how far Israel
is from embodying God's will. The fate of
the children, the orphans in particular, is a
barometer that indicates how far Israel is
from keeping the Torah, from living as God
would have them live.

—Jacqueline E. Lapsley[1]

We live today in a world that does not value children like it should.
We live, in many ways, in an *anti-child* world. Our world uses
children and abuses children. Our world reduces children to political
fodder. Our world objectifies children. Our world forces children to serve
as battlegrounds for debates about God instead of respecting them as
image bearers of God.

This is the world we live in, and it is no wonder that God calls this
world of ours fallen. Our world treats children in broken, sinful ways. "In
many ways we treat children as almost subhuman."[2] It is all the ways in
which we do not value children and mistreat children that make up the
idea of *childism*.[3] Childism is prejudice and discrimination against children. Childism is both passive and active hatred of children, whether due
to their smallness or their neediness or their loudness. Like other forms
of oppression, childism can take a personal form—like one specific adult
hurting one specific child—or a structural form—like laws that systematically treat children unfairly.

The idea of hatred of children is different from another negative force in our world. The other force I call *adultism*.[4] Adultism is behavior that comes from the idea that adults are better than or more valuable than children—that the adult experience and point of view are superior, more important, and more worthy of our attention than the child experience and point of view. While adultism and childism are two distinct forces, they are related. Valuing adults and their feelings and thoughts over and against children provides legal and moral cover for prejudice and discrimination against children. Prejudice and discrimination against children also make over-valuing adults and their feelings and thoughts feel natural and right.

Before I continue, I want to make something clear. While the world we live in mistreats children, we should not pretend like it is worse today than any other time in history. I often hear Christians in the evangelical homeschooling world do this. They make claims like *The world has never been so godless before!* or *It's never been more dangerous to raise a family than it is now!* None of these claims are true; none of them stand up to a quick review of history. But they sound "good" in the sense that they sound terrifying and are therefore good for motivating customers. They make people want to buy books from whoever wrote the so-called solution to living in such perilous times. Unfortunately, the solution presented is nothing but snake oil.

Thus, it is really important that we avoid this particular panic. It is especially important for those of us who care about children's rights, because certain episodes of moral panic have unfortunately surfaced during the children's rights movements of the last two centuries. The Satanic Panic of the 1980s and '90s involving day cares and alleged ritual abuse is a good example of this.[5] So is the recent #SaveTheChildren campaign, which was hijacked by QAnon conspiracy adherents.[6] Such moments of panic do not help fight against child abuse and neglect. They do not promote child liberation. Instead, they misdirect potential child advocates by conjuring up fake monsters and encouraging people to chase after windmills. Moments of moral panic also make people who might be allies to children's issues suspicious of legitimate efforts to protect children.

Yes, there is significant abuse and pain inflicted by our world upon our children. Yes, "without risking hyperbole, one can say that the visible situation of the child today frequently is grim."[7] But no, we should not exaggerate or resort to hyperbole. There is enough work to be done on behalf of children within the confines of reality. We do not need to fabricate additional work to motivate us.

Setting aside false conditions, what *is* the world we live in when it comes to children? It is the right-here and right-now. This is what liberation theology calls the "social context." It is all the good things and all the bad things that surround us and motivate us to seek after and study God—to do *theology*, in other words. Theology is, after all, *logy*, which means "study of," and *theo*, which means "God." Theology is the study of God. We never study God in a vacuum.[8] If we do theology in a comfy armchair while smoking a cigar, we are doing theology *somewhere*, during *sometime*, and *someone* is doing that theology. That is the world we live in, the right-here and right-now, the social context. So as we explore child liberation theology, we must ask the following questions: What world do we live in? What sort of world are our children growing up in? What are the challenges and troubles they are facing and will face?

The shortest answer to these questions is that we live in an *anti-child* world. The current American environment stacks the deck against children even before they are born. Compared to other wealthy nations, the United States has the worst child mortality rate, especially infant mortality.[9] Worse still, our infant mortality rate reveals systemic racism in action: African American and Native American babies are twice as likely as white babies to die during their first year.[10] The United States also has the highest mortality rate for pregnant people among developed countries[11] and is the only industrialized nation in the world where that mortality rate is rising.[12] Our mortality rate for pregnant people similarly reflects systemic racism, with Black people over three times as likely to die in pregnancy and postpartum than white people.[13]

Despite these facts, "the federal government mandates *only 12 weeks of unpaid leave* for employees in companies with at least 50 workers. Most women, however, work in smaller businesses, and many of those who work in large enough companies cannot afford to take this much unpaid leave."[14] As a result, most pregnant people in the United States only take six weeks of childbirth leave (119). And make no mistake, this has an impact on families: "When a family is stressed by a baby's arrival, leaves of six weeks or less are linked to increased maternal anxiety, depression, conflict between work and family responsibilities, and negative interactions with the baby" (119).

The stress felt by a pregnant person can impact the health of an unborn child "above and beyond the impact of other risks, such as maternal smoking during pregnancy, low birth weight, postnatal maternal anxiety, and low family income" (106). A pregnant person's stress can lead to a child's anxiety, anger and aggression, short attention span, and lower mental performance (106). But despite those negative outcomes, the United States makes no effort to ensure pregnant people have stress-free pregnancies—even though studies have shown that something as simple as paid parental leave can reduce infant mortality rates by an impressive 13 percent![15] From the moment of conception in the United States, children are being brought into an American world that demonstrates little care for their health and well-being.

Although many conservative Christians claim to be "pro-life" because they denounce abortion, there is a drastic inconsistency with and failure to follow through on that stated belief. For those who say they care about getting a child out of a womb safely—yet do not make every effort to care for the health and well-being of that child both inside and outside of that womb—the child is an abstract ideal. Children in the real world have real needs, and those needs are woefully unmet, even by those who claim to be pro-life with their rhetoric.

The world we live in is not kinder to children once they grow beyond infancy, either. Children are born into a world where abuse is a significant risk. I mentioned this in the introduction yet it is worth repeating: The United States has one of the worst child abuse records among industrialized nations—losing on average five children every day to child abuse and neglect.[16] Child abuse takes many forms in the United States, including neglect, physical abuse, sexual abuse, emotional abuse, sibling abuse, and even religious abuse. Yes, even churches—churches that purport to follow Jesus, who commanded us to welcome the little children—are responsible for child abuse. Many churches have protected adults who prey upon children by not reporting the abusers to authorities and allowing the abusers to remain in close proximity to children. Many churches have taught parents that God wants them to hurt their children by using corporal punishment and the threat of eternal damnation to force obedience. And many churches have told children that they are gross, disgusting people who deserve this abuse and pain because of their inherent sinfulness and unworthiness.

The abuse of children in the United States also connects with international mistreatment of children, including evil forces like human trafficking. Between 2007 and 2016, the National Human Trafficking Resource Center hotline received tips on more than four thousand cases of child labor trafficking inside the United States.[17] Child laborers are found in a number of American industries. One example is tobacco farms, where children "are exposed to nicotine, toxic pesticides, and other dangers. Child tobacco workers often labor 50 or 60 hours a week in extreme heat, use dangerous tools and machinery, lift heavy loads, and climb into the rafters of barns several stories tall, risking serious injuries and falls."[18] Beyond domestic examples, consider as well the many products we buy in the United States that are made overseas by child laborers,[19] potentially even enslaved children.[20]

Child sex trafficking is even more prevalent than child labor in the United States. Between 2007 and 2016, the National Human Trafficking Resource Center hotline received tips on more than 14,500 cases of child sex trafficking inside the United States.[21] The National Center for Missing and Exploited Children reports that one in six endangered runaways they encountered were likely sex trafficking victims, 86 percent of which were in the care of social services or foster care before running away.[22] We are clearly failing not only many children, but also many children who were specifically entrusted to our government for protection.

International forces additionally impact US children in unexpected ways. While Americans often claim they live in a country that is not "barbaric" like their stereotypical idea of a less developed country,[23] this view is racist and incorrect. Regressive, violent practices against children, like the mutilation of young girls' genitals, happen right here in the United States. As of 2021, the number of American girls who underwent or are at risk for genital mutilation reached over half a million.[24] Eleven states and Washington, DC, have no laws criminalizing the practice at all, leaving girls in those states vulnerable.[25] Female genital mutilation has occurred in Christian homes.[26]

Other evil practices that objectify young girls and reduce them into sex objects, like child marriage, also happen right here in the United States. These practices are not limited to extremist religious groups like the Fundamentalist Church of Jesus Christ of Latter-day Saints (FLDS).[27] Child marriage has happened in the United States in families of many different faiths, including Buddhist, Christian, Hindu, Muslim, and Sikh.[28] Child marriage happens in the evangelical homeschooling world in which I grew up.[29] In fact, efforts to ban child marriage in the United States are frequently opposed by evangelicals who want to preserve the option.[30] Consequently, the legality of child marriage persists in US law; children as young as twelve can be married off to adults in certain states.[31]

But early marriage is not the only area where children have no say. Children have no voice in all sorts of matters: from their medical care to immigration rights to education to government representation. In several states, parents can legally allow their children to die by denying them medical care—provided those parents have "religious reasons" for doing so. Children have no authority in the matter. The rights of the parents supersede children's rights.[32] In fact, most US states—thirty-four of them—allow parents and other caregivers of children numerous religious exemptions from child abuse and neglect laws.[33] This includes exemptions from liability for abuse, liability for neglect, and liability for the failure to report abuse and neglect. It also includes exemptions from misdemeanor or felony criminal charges for inflicting injury to a child.[34]

The United States has been known to force many immigrant children—often fleeing to the United States because of abuse or violence in their home countries—into deportation proceedings with no legal representation. In the 2010s, 42 percent of twenty thousand immigrant children facing deportation had no attorney one year. Children five years old and younger have had to defend themselves in court.[35]

In the public schools, corporal punishment remains legal in nineteen states.[36] Those punishments are distributed in racist and ableist ways. Teachers physically punish Black children at disproportionate rates compared to white children.[37] Teachers physically punish Native American children at disproportionate rates as well.[38] (Setting aside their current physical endangerment, Native American children also face complete erasure of mentions of their people and history from public school textbooks.)[39] Teachers also physically punish children with disabilities at disproportionate rates.[40] Children with disabilities face additional threats from educators, such as being brutally restrained and thrown into "scream rooms" as punishment.[41]

In the homeschooling community, there is virtually no oversight or regulation to protect children, despite homeschooled children facing a greater risk of dying from child abuse than other children[42] and despite there being hundreds of documented cases of severe abuse and death since the 1980s.[43] In fact, *only two states* ban convicted sex offenders from keeping their kids at home and out of public school (thus away from adults who are legally obligated to report possible abuse and neglect to authorities, known as mandatory reporters).[44] *Only two states* have background-check processes in place for parents who choose to homeschool.[45] Eleven states do not require parents to notify any government entity if they decide to homeschool.[46] Seventeen states have no required subjects for home-schooled students.[47] In forty states, homeschooling parents are not required to have even a high school diploma.[48]

Despite being forced to pay taxes[49] and treated in courtrooms as adults,[50] youths under the age of eighteen in the United States are unable to vote. With reference to taxes, the situation youths face is literally taxation without representation—a cornerstone reason for the founding of the United States. Yet we subject teenagers to the same oppression America's so-called founding fathers once so loudly denounced. With reference to the criminal justice system, most states set the minimum age at which children can be tried, convicted, and sentenced as adults to fourteen (before said children can even obtain a driver's license).[51] Yet even younger children can face this fate since "fourteen states have no minimum age at which children can be prosecuted as adults," leading to cases where "children younger than 10 have been prosecuted as adults."[52] Sentences as severe as life without the possibility of parole have befallen these children.[53] The government treats such children as mature enough to condemn them to life imprisonment, but they are not deemed mature enough to participate in the electoral process.

Another category of children requires consideration here. LGBTQIA youth daily face rejection and pain. While LGBTQIA youth make up only 5 percent of the general youth population, they make up around 40 percent of the entire homeless youth population. Indeed, the number of LGBTQIA youth in the United States who are homeless is between 320,000 and 400,000—40 percent of whom were rejected by their families, often for religious reasons.[54] Transgender children are particularly vulnerable: nearly 80 percent of transgender youth report experiencing harassment at school[55] and 12 percent report being sexually assaulted in K–12 settings by peers or educational staff.[56]

Intersex children are often stripped of their agency with regard to medical decisions. Their parents put them through life-altering surgeries when they are infants. These surgeries have immense ramifications for them for the rest of their lives, sometimes even prompting them to commit suicide.[57] Even though one in one thousand newborns are intersex,[58] religious leaders have been known to callously dismiss their very existence.[59] Intersex people's lives have become collateral damage in US culture wars.[60]

No discussion about anti-child sentiments in the United States would be complete without returning to the controversial subject of abortion. Approximately one million abortions are conducted every year in the United States—which means more than one in five pregnancies ends in elective abortion.[61] Pro-life individuals would argue that abortion is murder, and thus the act of abortion itself represents how our society does not value children. Pro-choice individuals, on the other hand, would argue that abortion is a necessary medical procedure because we live in a society that does not support pregnant people and families, making it difficult for many pregnant people to have children. Regardless of which side you take, both sides agree on this core point: abortion reveals that we live in a world that does not adequately lift up children, parents, and families. Whether you support or condemn reproductive rights, abortion's perpetual existence— that so many people feel they have no other choice but to end the life of a fetus or child—means we have significant societal deficiencies in how we value both children as well as the people who bear and care for them.

One might be tempted to look at all these different categories of children experiencing anti-child forces as separate problems, but that would be a mistake. These problems considered together indicate that there is a *systemic* prejudice in our world against children. Anti-childness is wound up in the very way our world, and particularly our American world, is structured.

A parallel situation can be seen in the book of Isaiah in the Tanakh, where the prophet Isaiah "excoriates the people [of Israel] for failing to execute justice for the widow and the orphan, the most vulnerable members of society."[62] Isaiah does this on numerous occasions. He first exhorts the Israelites, "Learn to do right; seek justice. Defend the oppressed. Take up the cause of the fatherless; plead the case of the widow" (Isa. 1:17). Then he condemns the leaders of the Israelites for not heeding his exhortation: "Your rulers are rebels, partners with thieves; they all love bribes and chase after gifts. They do not defend the cause of the fatherless; the widow's case does not come before them" (Isa. 1:23). Later he issues a warning to the same leaders: "Woe to those who make unjust laws, to those who issue oppressive decrees, to deprive the poor of their rights and withhold justice from the oppressed of my people, making widows their prey and robbing the fatherless" (Isa. 10:1–2).

Note that Isaiah does not simply condemn the *people* of Israel for failing to care for children. Rather, Isaiah lays the blame for how Israel fails children at the feet of the people's leaders and specifically, the laws they make. "Your rulers are rebels," he proclaims, "who make unjust laws." "Those who issue oppressive decrees" are the ones "making widows their prey and robbing the fatherless." In other words, the anti-child attitude prevalent during Isaiah's time was not simply a matter of individual failure, but a *systemic* deficiency.[63]

This chapter's opening quotation from Jacqueline E. Lapsley deserves special mention here: "Children's lives—how they are treated, the quality of their lives—indexes how far Israel is from embodying God's will."[64] God established codes of behavior and ethics for the Israelites as individual people and also for Israel as a *nation*. Those codes included requirements for how children—orphans specifically—were to be treated. When children are allowed to suffer, that is not only a personal failure. It is a wholesale failure on the part of the nation. The nation's laws—in the case of Israel, laws established by God—have been perverted or neglected. So when the Israelite children suffer, Isaiah's prophetic critique "is leveled not at ordinary folk for their refusal to lend a hand to the widows and orphans but at Judah's rulers, the people who lead, who set policy and make decisions. . . . The issue is not the occasional refusal by ordinary people to lend a helping hand to a neighbor in need but the wholesale abandonment of the widows and orphans to a corrupt legal system."[65]

While Isaiah was speaking prophetically against a particular government centuries ago, his words remain just as relevant today. They are joined by current ringing condemnations of any society that does not value children. Like Isaiah, we live in a country that abuses children from individual to systemic levels—a country that presses a boot to children's heads to keep them down. We live in a country where it is perfectly legal to teach children they must be trained like animals, corralled like beasts, and punished as the worst members of society. This country is, in every sense, an ungodly world. It is the very sort of world that Jesus so prophetically spoke against when he invited children into his midst instead of keeping them away. It is the sort of world that Jesus asked us to tear down when he said to love children like we love him (Mark 10:14).

This is the true meaning of child liberation theology: that as we study and know God and learn to love God better, we understand that our right-here and right-now needs to change. Our right-here and right-now is broken. It hurts children. This is the starting point for further discussion. It is the point of departure. If our theology does not help children break free from the evils imposed on them by this country and the broader world, then it is not the right theology. If our theology does not lift up, love, and protect children like Jesus did, it is fraudulent.

The world we live in is where we begin.

INCLUDING CHILDREN

Ask the children in your family, faith community, or religious organization to pick a problem they know other children in your community or city are dealing with—for example, child hunger, child bullying, or child homelessness. Have the children think about these two questions: (1) Who is being hurt? (2) What does the Bible say about helping children in need?

In response to your conversation, have the younger children do a creative project (drawing, collage, etc.) to inform people about the problem.

Have the older children research the problem and answer these two questions: (1) What are some of the causes of the problem? (2) How can we as a church help?

Plan a Sunday—either during your normal worship service or during a special service after your normal one—where the children get to run the service and tell the adults what they discovered. And really let the children run the service. Let them pick the songs. Let them pick the Scripture. Let them design the bulletin. Let them present their findings instead of a sermon. Adults can still be involved, guide the children, and give them feedback on the structure—but make this Sunday about honoring the children and their vision and voices.

two

The Questions We Must Ask

One of the most important work[s] we can do
is to advocate for justice for children. In every
intersection of oppression, children exist.

—Cindy Wang Brandt[1]

Is there hope for saving the many children who seem doomed to abuse and pain? What can we do to improve their lives? What can we do to make our churches places of safety and refuge? How can we lift up and better love children in our homes and communities? These questions are at the heart of child liberation theology.

Child liberation theology begins with God the Child: the God-Child named Jesus. The God-Child is like any other child: born into a dangerous, abusive world. I think it is remarkable that the God of Christianity chose to reveal themselves not merely through a human being, but through a human being conceived in a human womb, brought forth to earth from a grueling birth process, and beginning life as all children do—a vulnerable, naked infant screaming with confusion and shock. How amazing and strange is that? How extraordinarily *ordinary*!

We often marvel that God chose to "lower" themselves to the position of a human being. But less often do we marvel that this "lowering" was to the lowest possible version of a human being in Jesus's time: a *child*. By becoming a child, Jesus was born without rights and was subject to the anti-child attitudes of Greco-Roman society.[2] Additionally, Jesus was born during an especially dangerous time for children; his birth inspired the Massacre of the Innocents, King Herod's deadly campaign against children in his effort to find and murder the infant Jesus (whom Herod perceived to be a political messiah). God, who created all human beings with the majesty and power of their own image, reduced themselves to the *one* version of humanity least recognized as being made in that image. Again, how amazing and strange is that?

Child liberation theology also begins with all human children: the children throughout history who bear the image of God. Not only the white children, not only the children of Western civilization, but all children. Children of all races, sizes, abilities, genders, and sexualities. Children of the United States and children of China, children of Guatemala and East Timor and Papua New Guinea and South Africa. Children who grew up in suburbs segregated by classism and racism and children who grew up in foster care or homeless. Children who have everything and children who have nothing. Children from the Warring States period and children from the Middle Ages and children of the postmodern now.

Child liberation theology thus begins with God the Child and the children of all histories and locations who bear God's image. It places these children at the center of religious texts. It asks us to consider religious texts from the vantage point of those children—from the vantage point of Jesus as the God-Child and all children as God's image bearers. Thus we must read our texts using the interpretive lens of these children. Children become the point from which all our thoughts and actions relating to theology must begin and end.

While versions of Christian theology have been used for centuries to justify the abuse of children, there are others that can help us invert abuse-laden interpretations and identify places of revelation that signify the liberation found in Jesus. Child liberation theology should not whitewash, diminish, or excuse the fact that Christianity has been and can be used to oppress children. However, those who embrace child liberation theology will dedicate themselves to also finding ways in which Christianity can liberate children.

true

And liberate it can. Jesus the God-Child did more than welcome children into his midst. He welcomed children into the very center of how he acted. He raised children up from the margins. He said one must welcome children to welcome him. In the same way, child liberation theology must

*Actually
by putting
Jesus center this
should be
autism*

free children from the margins of our thoughts and actions and place
children at their very centers. We must understand Jesus's call to welcome
children in a way that radically reprioritizes our thoughts and actions. By
placing children at the center, we can reimagine our world's powers and
principalities in a way that liberates those children.

Reimagining our world's powers and principalities requires an understanding of *intersectionality*—the idea that our response to injustice needs
to include *everyone* who is hurt.[3] No wrong happens in a vacuum. So if
the liberation of children is to be truly liberating, it must liberate not only
the middle class, cisgender, heterosexual, white male child from suburban
America. Certainly, the suburban white American child is made in the image of God. Yet the image of that particular child is not the defining image
of childhood, nor is it in any way superior to any other image of childhood.
The image of God as Child—as seen through Jesus the God-Child—
extends to and includes every single child everywhere. Thus child liberation
theology must also extend to and include every single child everywhere.

Child liberation theology must preach freedom not only for the children in white suburban churches but also the children of Black churches,
the children of progressive churches, the children who do not go to
church, and even the children who hate church. The message of child
liberation theology seen in the words of Jesus is clear: "Do not hinder
[the children]," a commandment that transcends boundaries and is without qualifications. It is a universal, all-encompassing, and all-welcoming
command. Do not hinder *any* of the children. And let *all* the children be
welcome in the God-Child's arms.

If these are the criteria child liberation theology must meet, what
then are the questions it seeks to answer? Questions that child liberation
theology must answer include:

1. What sort of *hermeneutics* (method of interpreting the Bible) does a
    child liberation theology require? How do we read the Bible in a way
    that better liberates, loves, and protects children? What does it mean
    to center children in the way that we read the Bible? Is it sufficient
    that we center the *idea* of children in how we read the Bible, or do we
    need to read the Bible with actual children?

2. What is the significance of the fact that the very first story involv-

ing children in the Bible—the story of Cain and Abel—is a story of abuse? How can the Bible promote a message of child liberation when it contains this and other stories of similarly shocking brutality and violence toward children?

3. What do biblical stories tell us about the power and impact of children in our world? Why does God frequently choose children—often a younger or the youngest sibling in a family—to bring their message and plans to fruition?

4. Considering other religions around the world that feature child deities or child saviors, what can we say is unique about Christians' claim that God became a human child through the incarnation? Does Jesus's infancy and childhood give us a key to understanding the meaning of the salvation he brings?

5. What is the full theological significance of Jesus identifying himself not simply as God the Human but rather as God the Child? What does it mean that "the Father judges no one, but has entrusted all judgment to the Son," the God-Child (John 5:22)? How ought that meaning invert or transform our concepts of eternal justice as well as social justice? What does it mean that our concepts of justice should derive from the justice in the heart of a child, the God-Child? If God takes on and identifies with the suffering of the world, as other liberation theologies contend, what does it mean for God to take on and identify with the suffering of children?

6. What does Jesus (Immanuel, God-with-us) mean when he says that in order to welcome him, one must welcome children? In what way do children function as God-to-us?

7. If liberation theology is a theology of self-determination and if the point of liberation theology is to give a group of humans the right and power to learn and speak about God on their own terms, then would not child liberation theology require children to create and lead the theology themselves? A liberation theology for the poor would be inauthentic if it is developed by the rich. Would not a liberation theology for children be similarly inauthentic if it is controlled and dictated by adults? If this is the case, how do we create the space in our families, faith communities, and religious organizations for children to be active agents in their own spiritual lives?

8. How should we interpret the rich narrative tradition of children possessing divine insight and speaking prophetically within Judaism? Do we take seriously the biblical narrative in the Gospel of Matthew that it was unruly children, not the educated adults, who first recognized Jesus for who he was and unabashedly began "shouting in the temple courts, 'Hosanna to the Son of David'" (Matt. 21:15)? Do we grasp the full implication of Jesus's affirmation of the Psalmist's declaration, "From the lips of children and infants you, Lord, have called forth your praise" (to which Jesus points in Matt. 21:16)? Or do we dismissively pat children on the head and say their ideas are simply cute or funny rather than recognizing those ideas as apocalyptic, prophetic, and transformative?

9. Do we believe and understand that children have deeply profound inner lives, meaning that they ask existential and spiritual questions just like adults do? If so, are we willing to allow children to teach and lead us in spiritual and other matters?

10. Can we see theology in a new light so that children can be viewed as theologians? Can we rethink what play is such that play itself can be seen as a form of theology?

11. While exploring the questions being asked in this list, how do we consider and respect children's developmental stages simultaneously? How do we avoid going too far in the other direction, toward adultifying or parentifying children?

12. How do we prevent child liberation theology from remaining abstract? How do we ensure that this theology becomes concrete, practical, and relevant to the everyday lives of children and those who care for them? How do we make sure that the liberation we preach for children is something *all* children can participate in, regardless of who they are, what they look like, who they love, where they live, and what they believe?

13. What is the full meaning of Jesus's bold declaration that the kingdom of God is "at hand" (Mark 1:15 ESV) and it "belongs to" children (Mark 10:14)? Does child liberation theology mean that we should worship children and let them do whatever they want? How do we avoid unhelpful extremes?

These are but a few of the many questions to which child liberation theology must seek answers. Each question corresponds to an upcoming chapter. As we pursue the answers, we must constantly remember that it is through the perspective of the God-Child—as well as all children—that we must view the world. Only through this lens can we truly understand as well as hear and see from children how we can be participants in their liberation.

INCLUDING CHILDREN

As a family, faith community, or religious organization, identify a pressing issue children face in either your faith community or local community—for example, child hunger or racism in the local public schools. (If you completed the "Including Children" exercise in chapter 1, select one of those issues.) Depending on the time available, ask adults in your community to generate five to ten significant questions they have about the issue. Then ask the children in your community to come up with their own five to ten questions. Next, with the adults and children together, compare the two lists of questions. Explore as a group the similarities and differences between the adults' and children's lists, why the similarities and differences exist, and what the adults and children, respectively, can learn from the others' questions. Finally, commit as a whole group to answering all of the ten to twenty questions over the next few weeks or months—whatever time frame best works for your community. Ask for volunteers or groups of volunteers to work on each question.

After everyone has had adequate time to answer their question(s), schedule another meeting for everyone to gather and share their answers. If you have time during this follow-up meeting, create an action plan for addressing the pressing issue as an entire community as well.

three

Loving Children in How We Read the Bible

> This child is like a lens through which some
> aspects of God and his revelation can be seen
> more clearly. Or, if you like, the child is like
> a light that throws existing theology into
> new relief.
>
> —Keith J. White and Haddon Willmer[1]

How should we approach the Bible? How should we read it? What should we be thinking about and to what should we be paying attention? Christians have asked these questions for centuries and will probably continue asking them for many more. I am not going to suggest this chapter provides the definitive answers. But I do want to suggest that we need to rethink how we approach the Bible if we are going to better love and protect children. We need to radically change how we read the Bible if we want to liberate children.

In a liberation theology, the subjects of liberation are supposed to be placed in the center of why and how we read the Bible. In the case of child liberation, those would be *children*. Why are we reading the Bible in this moment in time? Because we want to liberate, love, and protect children. How ought we to read the Bible? With a mind and eye toward liberating, loving, and protecting children. Professional theologians call the science of why and how we read the Bible *hermeneutics*. We will borrow the terminology here: our hermeneutics will be centered on children.

When we center why and how we read the Bible on children, that can and should take a number of forms:

1. We need to focus on how children's roles are featured in any given story.
2. We need to pay attention to how children are excluded from or glossed over in many biblical stories.
3. We need to think about how stories that do not explicitly involve children might implicitly say a lot about children.
4. We should maintain sight of the goal: that we want to make a difference in the right-here and right-now with regard to children.
5. We need to read the Bible with actual children.
6. We need to focus on actual children's worlds (their cultures, stories, aspirations) as vehicles for Christian truths.
7. We need to give children the freedom to actively construct their own theologies and not force them to passively accept ours.

These are the seven elements of what it means to love children in how we read the Bible. They are the seven cornerstones of child liberation theology's hermeneutics. Note that child protection is included in the idea of child liberation. This is because I believe child protection is a key part of, as well as an effective way to achieve, child liberation. Liberation theologians discuss how the right-here and right-now—what they call the social context—should be the starting point for how we read the Bible.[2] The Bible itself is never the starting point because *we*—specific people in a specific time and place—are always the ones starting. We approach the Bible with our own experiences and our own struggles in view.[3] As a survivor of child abuse, for example, I approach the Bible because of my current role in the struggle for child protection. The right-here and right-now for me is resisting an anti-child world. That is *my* personal starting point.

Saying the Bible is not the starting point might alarm some of you. Please know that this does not mean we should be disinterested in what is true or that we do not care about what the Bible says.[4] Liberation theologians are not making up things because we want them to be true.

What it means, rather, is that we approach theology from our personal experiences. When something makes sense to us and when we believe something is true, it is because it resonates with our own experiences in life. When we read a Bible story and think, "I believe this is telling me X," we think that because it makes sense *to us*. We cannot scrub ourselves out of the equation.[5] Our experiences "cannot be pushed aside."[6] It is OK, in other words, to bring our own unique questions and issues to the table when we approach the Bible—*everyone* does that, even if they claim they do not.

So how do these seven elements work? What exactly does it mean to love children in how we read the Bible? To answer these questions, we will look at each element in turn.

The First Element: Children's Roles in Stories

Children play many roles within biblical stories. They complete many good, brave acts. For example, think about the cleverness of Miriam in saving Moses's life (Exod. 2:1–10), the courageous speech of Samuel to the prophet Eli (1 Sam. 3), and the faith of Naaman's enslaved servant girl speaking up to her master (2 Kings 5:1–19). Children also do much evil. Consider the sibling abuse Cain inflicts on his brother Abel (Gen. 4:1–16), the money-lust of the servant boy Gehazi (2 Kings 5:20–27), and the spoiled children of Eli (1 Sam. 2:12–25).

In many American churches, stories in the Bible featuring children are valued less than stories about adults. The stories are often reduced to the status of "just stories for children" and then they are kept out of the "adult church." They are relegated to "children's" Bibles and flannelgraph displays.[7] Yet these stories are just as much a part of the Bible as stories featuring adults!

The starting point for loving children in how we read the Bible, then, is to seek out, study, and value every story about children within the Bible, no matter how short. Focus in particular on the *agency* and *action* of children in those stories.[8] We must also promote these sorts of conversations at every possible occasion. We should ask our pastors to preach sermons on children in the Bible. We should have mid-week Bible studies that focus on children in the Bible. We should celebrate with liturgy reflecting on children in the Bible. Stories about children are not inherently easy-reading or light material; they are the keys to understanding what Jesus meant when he said to become like children. How will we understand Jesus's command if we neglect to study the children in the very scriptures Jesus taught?

Notice children's presence in the Bible. Then center their stories.[9]

The Second Element: Making Sure Children Are Included in Stories

While children do play many roles in the Bible, those roles are often anonymous. Sometimes children are mentioned only in passing in a story and kept at arm's length by the text. Take the example of Naaman's unnamed, enslaved servant girl, whose prophetic witness to Naaman regarding the prophet Elisha sets in motion the events recorded in 2 Kings 5, the end result of which changes world politics. The child shows up only once, in the beginning of the story. Then she disappears from the narrative and the adult men are featured. The little girl remains nameless; we never find out what happens to her. Despite arguably being the most important person in the story, she is abandoned instead of maintaining the reader's attention.

Instead of skimming over a child's role in a story, we need to include that child in the storytelling and the story's message. We need to feature the child in the front and center of the story. When pastors or theologians do not do this, when they exclude the children mentioned in Bible stories, we need to challenge them. We need to say, "Hey, it's not right to keep the child in this story on the sidelines. How about we spotlight the child?"[10]

Another key part of making sure children are not excluded from their own Bible stories is to make it a priority to examine the right-here and right-now of the children in the stories. What were their social contexts? What issues were they facing during the stories?[11] Asking questions like these will change the sorts of answers we will look for when we read the Bible (thus potentially the answers we find as well). If we do not know, for example, that Naaman's enslaved servant girl risked her life by speaking up, then we will miss a big part of the story. We need to ask questions like, What was it like to be a child in ancient Syria? What was it like to be an enslaved person in ancient Syria? What was it like to be a girl or a woman in ancient Syria? And finally, what was it like to be an enslaved female child?

The Third Element: Learning about Children from Stories without Children

There are many Bible stories that do not involve children. These stories can still have a big impact on how we as Christians should think about children. In fact, child liberation theology suggests that *all* Bible stories and *all* of Jesus's teachings have a significant impact on how we should think about children. Our major theological ideas—notions like free will, the nature of sin, and how justification and salvation work—if these ideas are not relevant to children, if they are not discussed in a way that includes children, then we have missed the mark.[12] We have instead generated ideas that exclude children and encourage people to think that the adult's way of thinking and doing things is more important than the child's way. And that is counter to the messages of Jesus.

What should we do instead? What we need to do is weave the theme of children in and out of all our theological notions, no matter how big or small those notions are. We need to consider how every Bible story impacts children and influences how we think about children, whether or not the story stars children.

One example of how this can be done comes from the story about Philip the evangelist and the Ethiopian eunuch (Acts 8:26–40). No child is featured in this story. Even though the eunuch is an adult, we can discern applicable truths for how we should interact with children based on how Philip acts toward the eunuch. Philip loves the eunuch as they are, accepts them as they are, and does not attempt to change their identity. In this case, Philip's treatment of the eunuch can be read as a model for how the American church should interact with LGBTQIA children. Like Philip, the church should embrace LGBTQIA children as they are and rejoice with them as they learn and share the gospel.[13] By making stories like this a launching point for understanding how we can better liberate, love, and protect children, we are expanding the impact the Bible can have on our lives and the lives of children around us.

The Fourth Element: Applying Everything to the Right-Here and Right-Now

Child liberation theology is false if it only engages children in the abstract—meaning if our ideas remain in our heads and do not catalyze changes in our lives. After all, "Faith without deeds is useless" (James 2:20). Any theology—especially a liberation theology—that does not offer practical help in the right-here and right-now is also dead.[14] Jesus never said that penning fancy theologies is how we show our love for God. Jesus said loving our neighbors is how we do that. Who are our neighbors if they do not include the children in our families, our churches, our schools, and our world?[15] If our theologies are not spurring us to help those same children in the right-here and right-now, then we are not loving God.

Jesus tells us in Mark 1:15 that "the Kingdom of God has come near." Child liberation theology needs to embrace the right-here and right-now where the Kingdom of God is. We must be faithful to our Lord and Savior in transforming our anti-child world into the kingdom of God.

How we read the Bible is a part of this transformation. How we read the Bible needs to be entirely oriented toward transforming our anti-child world into a world that loves and respects children. Into a world that places children in the center of our conversations and says, like Jesus did, "Let the little children come to me, and do not hinder them" (Mark 10:14). If our theology does not lead to the liberation of children, then we are "like whitewashed tombs, which look beautiful on the outside but on the inside are full of the bones of the dead" (Matt. 23:27). In Matthew 18:6 (ICB), Jesus said, "If one of these little children believes in me, and someone causes that child to sin, then it will be very bad for that person. It would be better for him to have a large stone tied around his neck and be drowned in the sea."

Our current theologies may be rational or impressive, yet if they are hurting children, Jesus cares little for them. He would rather such theologies sink to the bottom of the ocean. Instead, we need a theology that liberates, that brings faith, that breathes life into our world, and most especially a theology that lifts up children and values them and fights on their behalf.

The Fifth Element: Reading with Children

The fifth element of loving children in how we read the Bible is to read the Bible with actual children. By this I am not suggesting that you read your children a Bible passage as a bedtime story—though if you do that, that is an excellent way to increase your child's literacy. I would encourage all caregivers to read to children, whether from the Bible or from other books. It is a healthy practice that stimulates a child's brain development and promotes language skills.[16]

What I mean by reading the Bible with children is more than just reading *to* children. Reading *with* children means that we approach the Bible with children as learning partners. It means that when we study the Bible with children, we consider those children to be sources of revelation just as much as adults would be. It means we consider children's interpretations to be just as important as our own. Reading the Bible with children, in other words, means accepting children as capable of providing revelation.[17] It means intentionally asking children, "What do *you* think?"—and then listening to their responses.[18]

When we read the Bible with children, we are not simply accepting children's presence. We are also "joining children in their world."[19] Their world is a new vantage point from which we can know and learn—and children become our guides. When we adopt the children's perspectives, we are strangers in an unfamiliar land. Instead of adults guiding children, the powers are reversed: children take us by the hand and show us what a given passage means to *them*. In this way child liberation theology is not simply a theology *of* children; it is a *with* theology. It is a theology with children in the lead.[20]

The Sixth Element: Seeing Children's Worlds as Vehicles for Truth

The sixth element in loving children in how we read the Bible is to view children—their selves, their worlds, their experiences, and their stories—as vehicles for truth. In many Christian communities, what can be an acceptable vehicle for truth is limited. For example, in certain fundamentalist faith communities, the Bible and the Bible alone is considered a source of truth. Science, psychology, geology, and any other source of knowledge are considered flawed because they are not the Bible. In some Eastern Orthodox communities, tradition is also considered a source of truth alongside the Bible. The thoughts of the early church fathers and the many creeds throughout history inform Orthodox Christians about the nature of the universe. Even so, the sources of truth are defined in a limited way.

Similar to other liberation theologies, child liberation theology points us to *people's experiences and stories* as sources of truth.[21] In the case of child liberation theology, we are specifically interested in children's experiences and stories. This means we need to expand our view of what can give us truth. If we limit the sources of truth to only the Bible and tradition, all of which have been written by adults, we are necessarily excluding children's points of view. For example, male adults recorded all the images and metaphors used in the Bible. Might this explain why God so often is described as a male adult, too?[22] What might happen if children described God in writing instead—and if we took their descriptions seriously?

Part of loving children in how we read the Bible, therefore, involves taking children seriously in how they talk and think about the Bible and how their experiences and stories influence their words and thoughts. We need to accept children's words and thoughts as vehicles for better knowing God.[23] "In a community a person's word must be heard and evaluated alongside that of others."[24] This includes children.

The Seventh Element: Letting Children Create Their Own Theologies

Taking seriously children's words and thoughts about the Bible also necessitates something else: that we have confidence in children's ability to create their own theologies. Children are not meant to simply memorize and assent to traditions established by adults; children are to be active participants in knowing God.[25]

Why do we think that theology is solely the domain of adults? Theology is the study of God. Can children not study God in the same way that adults do? Child liberation theology says they can, and thus we must create spaces for children to do their own theologizing.

Children will have questions and struggles that are unique to their respective ages. It is important, therefore, that we give children the space and support to wonder theologically about those questions that are unique to them. We do not want children to be "busy solving other people's theological puzzles"—namely, the theological puzzles of adults that have limited bearings on the real problems and challenges children face today.[26] Children must be given freedom to develop "their own way of speaking about God" and to "generate new symbols, concepts, and models that they find congenial for expressing their religious vision."[27]

These are the seven elements of loving children in how we read the Bible: focusing on how children's roles are featured in any given Bible story; paying attention to how children are excluded from, or their roles are glossed over in, biblical stories; thinking about what stories that do not involve children might actually say about children; keeping sight of the goal to make a difference in the right-here and right-now with regard to children; ensuring that we are not simply reading the Bible *to* children, but *with* children, and thereby considering children to be partners in learning; recognizing children's words and thoughts as vehicles for truth about God; and giving children the freedom to create their own theologies relevant to their own lives and struggles.

In the next two chapters, we will see these principles applied to two types of stories about children. In chapter 4, we will examine stories involving children in the Bible that revolve around violence, specifically stories where children are abused or hurt by adults or other children. In chapter 5, we will look at uplifting, inspiring stories in the Bible, particularly stories where children perform revolutionary acts that show how brave, thoughtful, and prophetic children can be. We will compare how both sets of stories can be read with children and with child liberation theology as a lens.

INCLUDING CHILDREN

Read the story of Jesus, the little boy, and the loaves and fish in John 6:1–15 with children in your family, faith community, or religious organization. (Better yet, ask a child who is comfortable reading aloud to read it.) Afterward, instead of telling the children what to think about the story, ask the children to explain to you what they think. Have the children consider and discuss the following questions:

1. What role does the little boy play in this story?
2. Why do you think the little boy had so much food with him that day?
3. What happens to the little boy after the disciples take his food?
4. Why do you think John mentions the little boy in this story?
5. What can we learn from this little boy that would apply to our lives today?
6. Does this story remind you of any situation, experience, or person from your own life?
7. What does this passage tell you about God?

Give the children space to wonder both quietly and aloud. Do not judge their answers. Give them freedom to interpret the passage on their own terms and using their own words.

four

Loving Children in How
We Read the Bad Stories

Imagine what might happen if we were to
start thinking about these children who are
victims of literary and theological exploitation,
if we were to start looking for these children
who are hidden between the lines, if children
were allowed to surface and reshape the
meaning of the biblical text?

—Danna Nolan Fewell[1]

There is a theme running through the Bible about how we can better love and care for children. It begins in the Tanakh, where God gives the Israelites standards for protecting children and their rights.[2] It then keeps going through the Christian Scriptures, where Jesus himself develops the theme—arguing that children should be defended (Matt. 18:6) and centered (Mark 10:13–16) in our lives.

There is also a problem: the Bible does not only tell us how to better love and care for children. The Bible also includes many stories where children are hurt; they are abused, raped, and murdered. Some of the stories are so horrible it is hard to read them. And sadly, a lot of the evil acts recorded involve people who claimed to love God. This mirrors behavior we see today. Today, many people who claim to love God harm children. Sometimes they even use the Bible to defend or justify their actions.

To take Jesus's words about defending and centering children seriously means we must seriously wrestle with the violence against children as seen in the Bible. If Jesus truly is the fulfillment of a theme of liberation for all people and especially children, then we must understand that theme within the context of violence and oppression—elements from which children and all people must be liberated.

I believe that one of the best ways to understand these stories of violence against children in the Bible is to engage in the practice of *flipping*. Flipping means turning a story on its head: looking at it from the child's point of view, for example, instead of the adult's; or looking at the story as if the adult is fallible instead of her actions being ordained by God. Often when we read disturbing passages in the Bible, our instinct is to read these passages positively, either because one of God's chosen leaders is the one engaging in the disturbing practice or because we assume that if a story is in the Bible, it must be sanctioned by God. However, I would urge readers to consider how the abuse and maltreatment of children is consistently evil across cultures and times. If an action is wrong today, it was likely just as wrong two thousand years ago—even if God's "chosen" representative is perpetrating it.

Thus when we read stories of violence against children in the Bible, I think that our first instinct should be to flip the stories and to figure out how we can read the stories in a way that edifies us in our current contexts. This means we should be plumbing the depths of each story to discern what it teaches us about better protecting children today. When a story seems to be approving violence against children, we need to flip the story to harness the opposite message: violence against children is always wrong and is something against which we must consistently and courageously fight.

To understand how to flip the stories, let us consider three of the most troubling passages in the Bible together: the story of Abraham binding and almost killing his son Isaac, the story of Lot impregnating his daughters in the cave, and the story of Elisha sending bears after forty-two children. I will consider each story in isolation, and afterward, I will look at three themes shared by all three stories.

Isaac's Binding: An Example of a Cautionary Tale

The binding and near-sacrifice of Isaac (Gen. 22:6–10) is one of the most disturbing and confusing passages in the Bible. Abraham whisks his son

Isaac off to a mountaintop, binds him with rope, and raises a knife to kill him; these actions are intended as a sacrifice to his God, Yahweh. Only at the last moment is Isaac's life spared when Yahweh calls out to Abraham and provides a ram in the bushes for the sacrifice (Gen. 22:11–14). This passage has bewildered, troubled, and provoked all sorts of interpretations from readers. Defenses have been developed, critiques have been levied—yet full understanding of the passage remains elusive.[3] Is it the penultimate example of religiously justified child abuse, only eclipsed by Yahweh's actual sacrifice of his own child Jesus?

The passage confounds me. I am not going to suggest I have found the true interpretation. I do want to consider how perhaps many interpretations have missed the point by focusing so much on Abraham, and thus neglecting to consider the point of view of the child, Isaac. Most interpretations consider whether Abraham was doing the right thing, whether Abraham *really* meant to kill his son, whether Yahweh *really* would have let Abraham follow through, or whether Abraham is a model of faith. Little attention is given to Isaac—not only the role he played in the near sacrifice, but more importantly, how he experienced the events in question. The famous Christian philosopher Søren Kierkegaard, for example, argued in *Fear and Trembling* that Abraham placed religious concerns over ethical concerns, thereby proving his faith in God.[4] But we are left wondering: What about *Isaac's* religious concerns? Does Isaac's relationship to God mean nothing simply because he is a child? Interpretations such as Kierkegaard's consider the likely agony Abraham went through during his test, but neglect to center the overwhelming terror Isaac likely experienced.

As stated previously, the goal of our current theological pursuit is to approach biblical passages with an eye toward child liberation and child protection. Looking at this passage from the vantage point of Isaac will help us discover what this passage can tell us today about children. How can we interpret this passage in a way that better protects children today? How can we think about the ramifications of Isaac's experience such that we can better liberate children in our contemporary faith communities?

The first question we must consider is the age of Isaac at the time of the binding and near-sacrifice. Some scholars believe Isaac to be an adult during this time, around the age of thirty-two. Others place him at the age of a toddler or a late teenager. I agree with Terence E. Fretheim, who argues Isaac was likely twelve or thirteen. Fretheim says, "On the one hand, he was old enough to carry wood and ask questions that assume a capacity to analyze a situation and potential problems relating to it (Gen. 22:6–7). On the other hand, God refers to him as a 'boy' (22:12), and he calls out 'Father' to Abraham (22:7)."[5] Isaac certainly does seem old enough to recognize that Abraham is making a trek to offer a sacrifice without the required animal. However, Isaac also seems to completely trust his father, despite the ominous foreboding of the story; he seems young enough to have a childlike faith in his father's promise that God would "provide the lamb" (22:8). While Abraham clearly hoped that would be the case, he did not give an entirely honest answer to Isaac.

This childlike faith of Isaac's is an entry point into the story. Isaac trusts that his father has his best interests in mind and is telling the truth that God will provide an animal to sacrifice. Isaac does not hesitate when tasked with carrying the firewood. When Isaac asks Abraham where the animal will come from, he accepts his father's answer without question. What is notable here is that Isaac is vocal at this point—he voices his doubts freely. This is notable because later, when Abraham binds Isaac to the wood, Isaac's voice is no longer heard in the recorded narrative.

For me, the disappearance of Isaac's voice suggests that Isaac knows he has been betrayed. Note that Isaac openly asked Abraham where the animal will come from—but Abraham was not entirely honest in response. Abraham knew full well what God said, and that God was asking him to sacrifice his son. Whether or not Abraham trusted God would provide an alternative, and whether or not "Abraham reasoned that God could even raise the dead" (Heb. 11:19), seems irrelevant at this point. If Abraham thought either of those thoughts, he did not share them with Isaac. Instead, the text leads us to conclude that he kept Isaac at arm's distance and was not forthright with him about the possibly traumatic outcome (or Abraham's conviction that God would indeed provide for the sacrifice). In his fervent commitment to God, Abraham missed a chance to walk alongside his child as a partner in faith. Contrast this with how the story is told in the Islamic holy book, the Qur'an, where Abraham fully informs his child about God's command, asks his child his perspective, and they move forward as a team.[6]

The actual binding moment appears brutal in the Tanakh. We are not told whether Isaac struggled or fought back against his father, but the narrative moves ahead quickly and bluntly, with Isaac "bound," placed "on top of the wood," and then watching as his father "took the knife to slay" him (Gen. 22:9–10). One moment Isaac is a talkative, trusting, and inquisitive child; the next moment he is silent, unmoving, and restrained. One moment Isaac is a subject, a human being pursuing knowledge about God's ways; the next moment he is reduced to an object, a *thing* to be sacrificed in order for an adult to better himself with God. Indeed, after Isaac is bound, Isaac's voice disappears entirely from the text. The rest of the text concerns Abraham and an angel who tells Abraham that God will "bless" him "because you have done this and have not withheld your son, your only son" (22:16–17).[7]

I wish I could explain away the whole event. What is made clear in the text, though, is that God commends Abraham's faith to some extent. This is why many people make parallels between Abraham nearly sacrificing Isaac and Yahweh sacrificing Jesus. Nonetheless, I think that the binding of Isaac is a cautionary tale. This is because, despite God's recorded commendations of Abraham's faith (Gen. 22:15–18, Heb. 11:17–19), the near sacrifice of Isaac actually is the *very opposite* of Jesus's sacrifice.

Jesus came willingly to our world. Despite Jesus saying in John 3:16 that God "gave" their "one and only Son," his later words in John 5:16–23 indicate that it was also his own choice to enter our world and be in relationship with us. Jesus *chose* his path, to "have life in himself" (5:26) and to give "life to whom he is pleased to give it" (5:21). In short, he *chose* to be the God-Child and walk among us, as Yahweh once walked in the garden with Adam and Eve. As a human child and later an adult, Jesus remained a subject and an active agent in his spirituality and in how he engaged with God as his divine Parent—to the point that some people became angry that he was "making himself equal with God" (5:18). As the God-Child, Jesus assumes the power in his relationship to the God-Parent. God "loves the Son and has placed everything in his hands" (3:35). And it is ultimately Jesus the God-Child who "comes in his glory and all his angels" and "will sit on his glorious throne" and judge humankind, separating "the sheep from the goats" (Matt. 25:31–33).

In contrast, Isaac did not go willingly to his own slaughter. Isaac was not offered a choice to be a sacrifice. Abraham not only gave Isaac no choice in the matter; Abraham also erased his child's agency. He treated his child as an object and a means to an end instead of treating his child as a subject with his own thoughts, relationship to God, and rights to determine his own life. While God commends Abraham's faithfulness, note that God never commends any other aspect of how Abraham put his faith into practice. In fact, we are later told by the prophet Jeremiah that God considers child sacrifice "a detestable thing" (Jer. 32:35).

If God finds child sacrifice detestable, but Abraham's faith is commendable, it seems reasonable to separate Abraham's faith from how he let his faith make him act. This is not an uncommon event in the Bible. For example, in Judges 11:29–31, "the Spirit of the Lord came on" Jephthah the Gileadite and he "made a vow to the Lord: 'If you give the Ammonites into my hands, whatever comes out of the door of my house to meet me when I return in triumph from the Ammonites will be the Lord's, and I will sacrifice it as a burnt offering.'" But "when Jephthah returned to his home in Mizpah, who should come out to meet him but his daughter, dancing to the sound of timbrels! She was an only child'" (Judg. 11:34). Jephthah's faith caused him to act in a stupid, rash way.

Devout faith does not necessarily result in moral acts. If we apply this idea to the passage in Genesis, it would suggest that the text might condemn how Abraham as a parent valued his own spirituality over and against his child's safety and well-being. As religious scholar Carol Delaney asks about this passage, "Why is the willingness to sacrifice rather than the protection of the child the model of faith in these traditions?"[8] Note that when Abraham and Isaac ascend the mountain, "the *two* of them went on *together*" (emphasis added). But when the descent is made, the story reports, "*Abraham* returned to his servants" (emphasis added). It appears that Isaac does not return alongside his father.

Not only does Isaac not return alongside his father, Isaac is never again reported as being in a relationship with his parents. Fretheim notes, "Abraham and Isaac never again converse in the narrative that follows, not even in connection with the search for a wife for Isaac (Gen. 24). While Isaac attends Abraham's funeral (25:9), he does not attend Sarah's or even return to her death bed (Gen. 23). Moreover, why would God, but not Abraham, bless Isaac (23:11)?"[9] Fretheim then asks, "Might these textual details, even if in subtle ways, recognize that a child has been abused?"[10] I think the answer is yes—though I do not think the details are subtle in that regard. The answer is unequivocally yes, a child has been abused. A child was restrained without his consent, was tied to firewood, and then had to watch his own parent lift a knife with the intent to kill him. Full stop: that *is* child abuse. Whereas Jesus chose to sacrifice himself, Isaac was not given a choice. Whereas Jesus was respected as a subject, Isaac was reduced to an object.

This is why I read the binding of Isaac as a cautionary tale about parents who value their own faith over and against their children's lives. Yes, Abraham showed immense faith by obeying what he understood God to be asking of him. But that faith came at a steep cost: the silence and alienation from his beloved child. God commends Abraham's faith but God never commends how Abraham withheld details from his child and gave his child no choice in the matter.

If Abraham's lonely descent from the mountain and implied later distance from Isaac indicates anything, it is that faith without love and relationship is dead. Extreme faith kills people, sometimes literally. I cannot help but think of parents who believe fidelity to God means they must throw their own LGBTQIA children out on the streets. Or parents who allow their children to die because of their commitment to faith healing instead of allowing medical intervention. Or parents who beat their children because of their myopic interpretation of Proverbs 13:24 ("Whoever spares the rod hates their children, but the one who loves their children is careful to discipline them"). Surely their religious fervor is astounding, but they entirely miss the point of faith: to better love both God and neighbor. This is why Jesus said loving one's neighbor is "like" loving God (Matt. 22:34–40). The gospel is found in relationship, in loving one's neighbor and seeing one's neighbor as a fellow subject before God, not as an object to sacrifice in the name of purity. When one sacrifices one's neighbor in the name of faith, one loses the very heart of the gospel.

Lot's Daughters: An Example of Victim Blaming

As a child, I did not understand the story about Lot and his daughters in Genesis 19:30–36. Lot's daughters were nameless and faceless characters used to move along the larger story. We are told only three things about them. First, the daughters were of betrothal age[11] during Abrahamic times, which means they likely were recently pubescent.[12] Second, these two young girls had been offered up to a mob for gang rape by their father: "Look, I have two daughters who have never slept with a man. Let me bring them out to you, and you can do what you like with them" (Gen. 19:8). And third, despite their likely youth, vulnerability, apparent disposability to their father, and their later isolation in a cave, the daughters were eventually accused of raping Lot when they became "pregnant by their father" (19:36).

Even as a child who did not understand the dynamics of abuse at play, this story did not make sense to me. I came away from the story with the message I *felt* the narrative's author intended—that Lot's daughters were licentious and depraved. That they took advantage of their poor, drunk father, just like Ham sexually assaulted his father, Noah.[13] But I also was confused. How did these young girls, who were just moments prior about to be thrown out to be sexually assaulted themselves, become—seemingly overnight—active and machinating sexual criminals?

As an adult, I have studied the dynamics of child abuse and sexual abuse. And when I examine the story of Lot and his daughters today, I cringe. I cringe because I know this story has been taught to children in a way that communicates that Lot was a victim and his daughters—*who were likely still children*—were the abusers. I mourn the error of many adults who miss how this story can and should be a powerful demonstration of how our world shifts the blame for abuse onto victims.

Before discussing the story further, I want to address three potential objections to this interpretation. First, I realize people have interpreted the story in diverse ways for many years.[14] I am not claiming this is an authoritative exegesis. Second, I realize the story itself is questionable—whether it is historical fact, revisionist fiction, or tragicomic morality tale. Third, nothing I say should be construed to mean that it is impossible for women to drug and rape people. I am a survivor of child sexual abuse at the hands of a woman and I have been sexually assaulted as an adult by a woman as well. So yes, the traditional reading of the story of Lot's daughters—that they were women who raped a man—represents an evil that can and does happen.

At the same time, this case rings false, whereas the story about Potiphar's wife falsely accusing Joseph (Gen. 39:6–20), for example, rings true.

Joseph's story rings true because Potiphar's wife, the woman in question, held the power in that situation. In Lot's case, the daughters were powerless in multiple ways. Additionally, their actions were unnecessary. Lot was not the only man left on earth contrary to what the daughters say: "There is not a man on earth to come in to us after the manner of all the earth" (Gen. 19:31). Right before Lot "lived in a cave" (Gen. 19:30) with his two girls, he lived in Zoar—the city he specifically asked the angel to save so he would not have to go to the hills (Gen. 19:17–22). The angel granted Lot's request, and God spared the city of Zoar as they rained sulfur and fire onto Sodom and Gomorrah for the sins of opulence and ignoring the oppressed (see Ezek. 16:49). But after a brief stay in Zoar, Lot decided to leave because he "was afraid to live" in the city (Gen. 19:30).

To summarize: Lot and his family were fully aware there were other human beings and cities in existence after the destruction of Sodom and Gomorrah. They lived in one such city. Furthermore, the tribe of Lot's uncle Abraham was close by—close enough to witness the destruction of Sodom (Gen. 19:27–28). There were plenty of options other than Lot for partners to meet the need to procreate, such as the residents of Zoar or members of Abraham's tribe.

This observation causes me to have a different take. Reading the text with an eye toward child liberation and child protection means I place the children at the center of the story. When I do that, here is the story I read: two young girls are offered up by their father for gang rape—a father prone to drinking, who cares little about his daughters' protection or objects to their sexual violation. The poor girls are dragged from one city to another until they are forced to live in isolation with their drunken father in a cave. Shortly thereafter both daughters are pregnant. A child liberative and protective lens would color this story as child sexual abuse.

I first discovered this alternative interpretation in the work of Ilan Kutz. Kutz argues that this view dates back to at least the 1400s and has found resonance among artists:

> How is it that father-daughter incest is universally perpetrated by the father, while in Genesis the roles are reversed? In my view, some painters, such as Dürer (1555), Francesco (1600–46), and most strikingly

Goltzius (1558–1617), suggest that the roles were not reversed, and that it was Lot who abused his daughters. In Goltzius' painting, the naked Lot is not in a deep alcoholic daze but is fully coherent and cunningly sizing up his prey, a far cry from "and he knew nothing of her lying down or her rising up" repeated after each daughter lies with him. In this painting, alcohol is not dulling his senses but probably disinhibiting his frontal lobes, which is precisely what happens to many abusive fathers when they drink.[15]

But then why does the biblical narrative tell us that Lot's daughters raped *him*, not that he raped *them*? Because that is how child abuse and sexual abuse stories often work in our world: the victims are cast as the victimizers. Look no further than the recent story of child rapist Thomas Hopper and his pastor Michael Orten. Orten defended Hopper's placement on Orten's church's ministry staff, saying, "It takes two to tango, okay? So if that girl chooses to sleep with him, she's just as guilty as he is."[16]

The story of Lot's daughters is just another example of this kind of victim blaming. As Elizabeth Breau writes, "The story of Lot's daughters in the Old Testament blames daughters for incest instead of fathers, legitimating theories of 'seductive daughters' centuries before Freud (Gen. 19:31)."[17] One can imagine the author(s) of this biblical narrative, living in patriarchal and adultist times similar to (or arguably worse than) ours, deciding it was impossible for the girls to become pregnant without them seducing their father. *It takes two to tango, okay?*

A glaring example of this can be seen in Christian publisher Zondervan's 1988 commentary on the story:

> The two daughters born to Lot in Sodom were as shameless as they are nameless. Their father, righteous though he may have been in contrast to the godlessness around him, exercised no influence over them. . . . The lack of any true morality whatever in Lot's daughters is evident by what happened in that cave once all three were clear of the smoking Sodom. There is no mention of any remorse on their part over the sin occasioning the destruction of the city, and the tragic death of their mother. Their utter degradation ending in Lot's intense shame is the most dreadful part of his story. How revolting was the conduct of the

daughters when they made their father drunk in order to make him the unwilling father of their children.[18]

Note that author of this commentary appears to revel in the namelessness of the children, contrasting their alleged shamelessness with Lot's alleged righteousness. Zondervan's commentator partially blames the *children* for the destruction of Sodom ("their part over the sin occasioning the destruction of the city"), but not Lot. The commentator argues "the most dreadful part" of the story is that Lot experienced "intense shame" after his daughters end up pregnant, yet Lot's offer of his daughters for gang rape somehow goes unmentioned. And the daughters are "revolting" for "making" their father drunk—entirely excusing Lot for his drunkenness. There is not a single reference to the age of children or discussion of the possibility that the daughters were raped by their father.

This is how child abuse and sexual abuse stories work in our world.

The adult claims the child wanted it—or the child deserved it—or the child masterminded it—or the child needed it—or the child was sinful. Abusers constantly try to shift blame for abuse onto the victims of their abuse. While there are significant differences between Lot's world and the United States today, there are also some important similarities. Both worlds are patriarchal and men are the most common recorded abusers in both. In both worlds we see people justify the abuse, excuse it, or suggest reasons why it was not the abuser's fault—or people decide the abuse was a sinful but mutual decision. Then people repeat these stories and justifications and excuses and rationales any time the cycle repeats. These efforts to shift blame have been so successful that so many Christians hardly blink an eye when this biblical narrative is interpreted by our faith leaders in favor of the adult abuser.

Here are the current facts about incest and child sexual abuse: Almost 70 percent of all reported sexual assaults (including assaults against children) occur to children aged 17 and under.[19] Someone known to the victim, like a family member, commits 90 percent of those assaults.[20] Even more heartbreaking: The younger a sexual abuse victim is, the more likely it is that their abuser is family.[21] Children cannot consent to sex with adults, including their parents. Adults or parents who claim otherwise are trying to deflect attention from their crimes.

Here are the facts about a one-time sexual encounter and pregnancy, which is what is purported to have happened to both of Lot's daughters. According to medical reports, the incidence of pregnancy for one-time unprotected sexual intercourse is between 3.1 to 5 percent.[22] The likelihood of Lot's daughters both becoming pregnant from a one-time sexual encounter is slim. What is more likely based on common sense, then, is that Lot raped his daughters until they were pregnant. This would not be the only time a father has attempted something so horrific and used alcohol to ply his guilty soul. Kutz notes,

> That incest is usually repeated is supported by modern research. Once he starts, the incestuous perpetrator often continues for years. As the daughter reaches an age when she is able to resist or flee, the activity may be repeated with a younger sister. Though the profiles of incestuous families may vary, the father-perpetrator is typically an immature individual with low self-esteem, while the wife-mother is depressed, helpless, or otherwise emotionally absent. The father often uses alcohol to allay his inhibitions before molesting his daughters.[23]

Parents need to know these facts and use them to protect their children. Even within such a small world as the Christian homeschooling world (which is where I used to conduct my advocacy work), situation after situation like this can be found.[24] Painting victims as the abusers is one of the oldest tricks in the abuser's book, and I am suggesting it is entirely possible Lot wrote the page himself.

As an adult, if I were to now share this story with children, this is what I would teach: our world is sinful in many ways, and one of those ways is that we shift blame for abuse onto abuse victims. We automatically assume victims are at least somewhat to blame; we automatically side with those who have power and against the powerless; we automatically side with men and against women and children. I would encourage children to disrupt these assumptions and automatic instincts. And I would instruct children that if anyone, even one of their parents, touches them in inappropriate ways, to tell an adult they trust immediately.

This is what I would teach to not only children but also adults, about Lot's daughters. Though the daughters remain nameless, I would name them *survivors*. The daughters should be praised for their resiliency, as they raised their children to eventually become the forbearers of many significant biblical characters, including Ruth the Moabite and Jesus himself.[25]

The Forty-Two Children and Elisha's Bears: An Example of Adultification

Second Kings 2:23–24 is another difficult and troubling passage. The story it recounts, one where the prophet Elisha unleashes several bears on a group of children who are taunting Elisha's baldness, has provoked all sorts of interpretations. Due to its sensational nature, it has become a favorite story among atheists and evangelicals alike. Atheists use the passage to argue that Judaism and Christianity are religions that sanction child abuse.[26] Evangelicals, on the other hand, like to use the passage as an apologetics opportunity to refute the atheist interpretations by suggesting imminent divine punishment for those who mock servants of the Lord—or worse, simply to scare children into obedience.[27]

I was struck by a few facts that I uncovered during my research. First, most of the articles you can find about the story of Elisha and the bears online are written by evangelicals.[28] This is interesting for a number of reasons, but most relevant is this fact: because many evangelicals interpret the Bible literally, they are particularly invested in explaining away or justifying troubling Bible passages such as 2 Kings 2:23–24.[29] Due to the constraints this literalism imposes, many evangelicals find nuance in their exegesis either a threat or a challenge. So they are forced to defend this story as if it happened exactly as written. But a literal, face-value reading seemingly renders Elisha a child abuser who uses the power of God to assault children.

Being forced to believe God would allow their own prophet to summon bears to maul forty-two children is not a pleasant position. To lessen the cognitive dissonance this interpretation necessitates, many evangelicals rely on the exact same thing: they appeal to the Hebrew language to argue that the words used in 2 Kings 2:23–24 for "little children" really do not mean *little* children, but rather *teenagers* or *young adults*.[30] This explanation is the second fact that surprised me from my research.

The apologetics organization Answers in Genesis, for example, says, "The vital question of concern to most here is the age of these 'little children,'" also noting, "We recoil in horror at the idea of bears mauling a gaggle of preschoolers." The organization then goes on to argue that the children were likely older adolescents or young adults (as if that should somehow lessen our horror). Together as a group these older youth formed a threat to Elisha. Answers in Genesis continues, "The events of that day in Bethel involved an unprovoked, verbal assault by a group of young hoodlums." Not only that, but "they were old enough to know better."[31] In short, the children reaped what they sowed.[32]

But I would argue the age of the group heckling Elisha is irrelevant. Even if these children were actually fully grown adults screaming obscenities, Elisha's decision to summon bears to maul them is extreme. In fact, it is the very opposite sentiment we see on display three chapters later in 2 Kings 5, where Naaman's enslaved servant girl wishes that Naaman be free from the pain of leprosy. The kind and brave nature of that little girl is what sets in motion a dramatic chain of events, culminating in *Elisha*, of all people, healing Naaman. Yet here, three chapters prior, Elisha does not express even a fraction of that little girl's goodness or forbearance. Rather, he lets his anger and pride get the better of him, the end result of which is that forty-two young people made in the image of God are violently maimed.

Third, many evangelical interpreters of this passage employ racist language and tropes to explain away or justify the passage. That is to say, for many evangelicals, the biblical story of Elisha unleashing bears against forty-two children seems to be a projective test[33] of their adultification bias against Black children. The evangelical authors I read frequently justify Elisha's actions by comparing the children to "hoodlums" or "gangs" in "the ghetto."[34]

Adultification bias involves stripping Black children of their innocence and forcing them into or perceiving them in mature, adultlike roles. It is a real, studied phenomenon that Black children experience in their everyday lives. Due to systemic, racist abuse recorded in the history of Black enslavement, segregation, and mass incarceration, Black children have been forced—and continue to be forced—into adult roles while still they are still children. They have been forced to shoulder emotional, physical, and social roles that children should not.[35]

Part of what contributes to adultification bias against Black children is seeing them as threats when in fact they are just children! How American police treat Black children is a prime example of this bias.[36] Law enforcement officers are not alone in this kind of response. White people frequently project our fears of Blackness onto Black children and we assume the worst about them. Thus Black children in "the ghetto" become so threatening that in the minds of white observers, they literally deserve to die a gruesome death.

You can see this adultification bias in the interpretations shared above: the assumption is that the children—"hoodlums"—posed a threat to Elisha's safety and potentially to his life. There is no biblical evidence to justify this assumption. Yet that does not stop the evangelical commentators I read from conjecturing. One author, Vance Bradley, writes, "There's no evidence that these young men were innocent and only intended to insult God's prophet. . . . Maybe these were not 42 innocent little kids. They were more likely a crowd of over 42 young men who wanted to do more than just insult God's prophet and then peacefully leave." In fact, Bradley goes so far as to argue that it was not Elisha who is responsible for the injuries or deaths of the children, but rather God themselves. And if God wants to take your life, Bradley says, you cannot object: "If He wants to take your life, He has the right and authority to do such an action whether directly or indirectly and for whatever reason He deems necessary." Bradley concludes, "Even if deaths or injuries occurred, there is nothing evil and unjust in what God or Elisha did in this scenario."[37]

Since these evangelical authors have already decided that God or Elisha cannot be in the wrong in this narrative, they therefore determine the children are entirely at fault. To establish cause for the fault, interpreters imagine crimes the children must have *intended* to commit; these fictitious crimes then justify Elisha's preemptive strike. They increase the age of the children and then compare them obliquely to Black teenagers—as if justification based on racist fears washes their hands clean. Considering how frequently white people justify violence against Black people because they "feel threatened," this really just makes the situation worse.

It became clear to me that the evangelical interpretations of this passage I read were insufficient and sometimes even sanctioning violence against children, especially Black children. I realized I needed to look elsewhere, so I did what I should have done first in light of the Hebrew origins of this text: I considered how Jewish people interpret the passage. Immediately I discovered that in the Talmud (the primary text in Rabbinic Judaism), God actually punishes Elisha because his anger and pride led him to harm the children. In the Talmud, it is written, "The Sages taught: Elisha fell ill three times. One was a punishment for inciting the bears to attack the children; and one was a punishment for pushing Gehazi away with both hands, without leaving him the option to return; and one was the sickness from which he died."[38]

While Jewish rabbis join evangelicals in quibbling about the age of the children, they do not do so to excuse Elisha's actions. They understand that the age of the child does not impact whether or not Elisha's actions are right and just.[39] Even if these children were (like in some evangelicals' most prejudiced imagining) a gang of Black eighteen-year-olds in the inner city, summoning bears to maul them because one feels threatened would be wrong. Black eighteen-year-olds are made in the same image of God as the rest of us.

So how do we read this passage through the lens of child liberation and child protection? I think we start by placing the children at the center of the story. We should place ourselves in the children's shoes and consider their lives and their stories just as important as Elisha's. Why were they walking the road to Bethel that day, just like Elisha? What were they thinking about? What was on their minds? What populated their dreams and life goals—dreams and life goals dashed or cut short as a result of Elisha's violent outburst? And what did their homes and communities look like, such that a large group of them felt it was OK to congregate and harass a solitary prophet together? The children were guilty of bullying Elisha. But children do not learn to bully in a vacuum. Bullying is a learned behavior.[40] Somewhere, adults in these children's lives were sanctioning this sort of behavior.

Children do act out in immature ways. Anyone who knows children knows they do this because children are just as human as adults are. Children need adult guidance to learn what is right and wrong. But in the case of Elisha, rather than him being the mature party and not taking the jokes personally, the adult allows his anger and pride to guide him. The adult lashes out and acts in an immature, dysregulated way. The result of this adult rage is forty-two abused children.

If we take our cues from the Talmud and believe that Elisha was punished for his bad behavior, then we must be clear in articulating that *Elisha* was the evildoer in this situation. Yes, the children should not have bullied Elisha. However, Elisha was the adult and Elisha chose to continue the cycle of abuse by reacting violently. Elisha chose not to transform the situation into a constructive lesson to improve the children's lives. Instead, he possibly ended their lives.

If we read the story by filtering it through child liberation and child protection lenses, it becomes—instead of a frightening morality tale about disrespecting one's elders—something very different. It becomes a grave reminder that we should never assume God's anointed people—pastors, youth group leaders, or celebrities—are safe people. They are just as capable of evil acts against children as anyone else. "Touch not God's anointed" is a lie. [41]

The idea that God's anointed people never do wrong is pernicious and pervasive in evangelicalism. [42] Unfortunately, many evangelicals use it to sanction all sorts of bad behaviors in the Bible, especially by adults toward children. Many children have been taught, as mentioned above, that 2 Kings 2:23–24 is a lesson about not disrespecting adult authority. The lesson is that if children disrespect adult authority, God might smite them with bodily harm as well. Accused child abuser and influential Christian homeschool authority Bill Gothard offers a prime illustration of how this misguided teaching plays out. Gothard's teachings instructed children to be silent about abuse they experienced. Children raised under Gothard's teachings were taught, "To question the anointed leader was to question God!" [43] When those same children were allegedly preyed upon by Gothard himself, they felt they could not report anything. As one survivor of Gothard's alleged abuse said, "You just do not talk against God's anointed, you know." [44] We must break the hold that deference to "God's anointed" has on so many American faith communities. It has caused so much suffering and covered up so much child abuse. It is time that we read against the grain of these stories that seem to justify and vindicate adults and impulsive, violent responses to children; it is time that we think about the children in the stories and give their lives and stories equal time and treatment.

This, then, is how I ultimately interpret the story of Elisha, the bears, and the forty-two children: it is a test of what we think children "deserve" when they act out—a test that unfortunately many of us fail. This is because we live in a world where children are not always respected. We live in a world where children are often blamed for the adult violence they experience. Instead of defending the children who are still learning how to make wise decisions, we invest our time and energy into defending the violent adults. We go to great lengths to explain why the adults were right to respond as they did, while we give the children no benefit of the doubt. We adultify the children, stripping them of their childhood innocence. We speak about them with racial tropes meant to justify that adultification. No more! We are changing this faulty interpretation right now through our act of reinterpreting this story.

Themes

There are three themes that I notice when I read these stories of violence (Abraham and Isaac, Lot's daughters, Elisha and the forty-two children). The first theme is the absence of the children's point of view from consideration. I am most struck by the fact that, when most people read these Bible stories, they automatically think about—and side with—the point of view of the adults in the story. We see this most clearly in just about every interpretation given of Abraham's near sacrifice of his son Isaac. Interpretation after interpretation considers Abraham's state of mind and his likely inner turmoil over the thought of sacrificing his son. So much ink has been shed over the point of view of Abraham.[45] Little thought is devoted to Isaac and what he experienced, yet is not the story almost more about Isaac than Abraham? For it is Isaac who has to deal with the possibility of murder by his father's hand. It is Isaac who has to reconsider his faith in a God who supposedly told his father to murder him.

The same applies to the story about Lot and his daughters. We hear so much discussion about Lot when people consider this story but we hear so little about the daughters themselves. When we consider the story from the daughters' point of view, I would argue that it is nearly impossible to walk away from the story accepting the traditional interpretation of the story. Instead, we see what results from two scared young girls who are isolated and alienated from their communities and who are living with a drunk, erratic father. The results are a nightmare.

The story of Elisha and the forty-two children, which elicits similarly nightmarish results, is just as notable for the absence of any representation of the children themselves. So we have to work against that lack of representation. Reading these stories with an eye and ear toward how the children themselves experience the narrative is key to better understanding the passages. This approach reveals new layers and potential interpretations that we might have missed previously.

The second theme I see present in these stories of violence against children is the fallibility of their parents and other adults. In each story, we see that the parents and adults are not perfect. Their actions hurt the children around them. Abraham pursues his faith with reckless abandon and alienates Isaac. Lot is willing to give up his daughters to be gang raped and instead later rapes them himself. And Elisha lets his pride and temper dictate his response to childish taunts, thus cursing forty-two children to a horrid fate.

These passages offer wisdom for adult readers today by demonstrating to us how adults can behave poorly around children. The passages offer insight into how adults should act (and should not act) around children. They reveal that adults are no better than misbehaving or ill-willed children at times. We, too, can be just as emotionally unregulated as a child, although we should know better and cannot use our age as an excuse for poor behavior.

The third theme, and the one I would argue is most important, is the theme of inspiration for measures of child protection. Stories about violence against children in the Bible are upsetting, yes. But they also point out to us ways in which adults will hurt children by reporting ways in which adults *have* hurt children. In doing so, these passages offer us an opportunity to learn about how we can better protect the children around us today. We can learn from Abraham, for example, the dangers of adults valuing their religious beliefs over and against the safety and well-being of children. We can learn from Lot some of the beliefs, techniques, and rhetoric employed by adult child molesters. And we can learn from Elisha the ways that adults can justify physical violence against children due to thinking those children are sinful or threatening. By approaching these stories with the goal of improving children's lives right-here and right-now, the stories become protective lessons instead of texts of terror.

INCLUDING CHILDREN

Growing up in a conservative evangelical home, I encountered these and other stories of violence against children in the Bible with little to no context provided to help me process them. Twice I read the entire Bible from Genesis through Revelation on my own. I also participated in the Bible verse memorization club AWANA,[46] memorizing a slew of verses simply to win prizes like plastic jewels and candy. Like many other children I knew, I was not encouraged to understand these violent stories as inspiration to equip, protect, and liberate myself as a child.

Stories about violence against children in the Bible should be more than disturbing anecdotes reduced to behavioral lessons taught in Sunday School. Children's interactions with scripture should not be limited to being a means of earning candy. Stories about violence against children in the Bible should (and must be) used to equip, protect, and liberate children from current and future violence.

To this end, I present the following suggestions as examples of how caregivers and teachers can do this with violent stories found in the Bible.

The Story of Cain and Abel, for Young Children

The very first story about children in the Bible is a story of child abuse. Specifically, it is a story of sibling abuse. Cain kills his younger brother Abel because Cain is jealous that God likes Abel's sacrifice more than Cain's (Gen. 4:1–8). I do not think this is a coincidence. Child abuse is a pervasive reality and this story highlights this reality for important reasons. The story demonstrates the vulnerability of children, especially younger children. It points to the failure of the archetypal parents, Adam and Eve, to protect their child against an aggressor. It also points to the fact that those who threaten children are not usually strangers but people close to the victim's family—in this case, the victim's very own sibling.[47] It illuminates the violence that can occur when parents neglect their children, as Adam and Eve are entirely absent from the recorded story apart from their act of sexual procreation. Additionally, parental absence makes one wonder where Cain learned such violent behavior.

The story of Cain and Abel can be a launching point for talking to children about the importance of expressing anger in nonviolent ways. After presenting the story to the children in your care, ask the children, "Have you ever been really mad at someone, like Cain was mad at Abel?" When the children say yes, ask them, "Were you ever so mad at the person that you wanted to hit them?"

Before you move on, stop and make sure that you really *hear* what the children say about their anger or other feelings. Make sure, too, that the children *feel heard*. As you engage them, sit or kneel so you are on the same level with them. Nod your head or use other affirmative body language to communicate you are *listening* to the children's full responses, not just waiting to proceed with the lesson. Listen with your whole body.

After the children have spoken, let them know that anger is itself OK. Anger is an emotion and emotions aren't bad; they just *are*. God made us in God's own image. In the Bible, we read that God shows all sorts of emotions: joy, sadness, jealousy, and even anger. We're made in God's image—that's *why* we feel such big feelings!

At the same time, sometimes our emotions become so big that we choose to do things we shouldn't, such as hit someone when we're angry. The anger is OK, but the hitting is not. Connect the children's answers to Matthew 26:52, where Jesus tells Peter to lay down his sword. Point out to the children that Peter had a real, big reason and right to be angry: Judas, one of Peter's and Jesus's best friends, betrayed Jesus. That was really mean of Judas. Even so, Jesus tells Peter that using his sword to hurt other people would not be the right response.

Reflecting on Jesus's example, ask the children, "How can you express your anger to the person who made you mad in a way like Jesus? What are ways to be angry without hitting?" If the children are enthusiastic and open to the idea, you can even role-play. Ask one child to come up to the front and interact with another child by pretending the other child is someone about whom they feel angry. Have the first child practice different ways of talking to the other child about the angry feelings that do not involve violence.

You can also talk to the children about how sometimes adults feel angry and hit other adults and children. Explain that this, too, is wrong. Adults are not allowed to hit other people just because they are adults. Tell the children that if they ever see an adult hit another adult or child, or if they are hit by a parent or sibling, they should tell an adult they trust: a teacher at school or a pastor or an adult relative. Everyone has the right to feel safe in their own bodies and no one deserves to be hit. To wrap up the session, go around the room and help each child brainstorm to identify one trusted person in their life they can talk to if they ever feel unsafe.

The Story of Tamar and Amnon, for Young Children

Teaching children about their right to feel safe in their bodies does more than help to equip and protect children against physical abuse, as we explored in the above story of Cain and Abel. It also helps to equip and protect children against sexual abuse, as we shall now see in light of the story of Tamar and Amnon.

Children should be taught as early as possible about the difference between safe touch and unsafe touch. Justin and Lindsey Holcomb's book *God Made All of Me* is a wonderful introduction to this topic that is geared toward young children and teaches them important lessons such as, "You are in charge of your body" and "You can say no."[48] Growing children should regularly hear empowering messages like these. They should know that their bodies belong to themselves and they have the right to feel safe and secure in their bodies.

Tamar's story (2 Sam. 13) provides a good place to begin discussing basic lessons about safe and unsafe touch. Without going into graphic detail, children can be told that Amnon, Tamar's brother, didn't respect Tamar or her body. He touched her in ways she didn't want to be touched. When she told him to stop touching, he didn't. This is wrong. If someone doesn't want to be touched, even if it's a quick hug, tell the children they need to respect that and refrain from touching that person. And if someone touches the children when they don't want to be touched, instruct them to say no firmly. Tell them to *yell* no if necessary. Remind them to always, always, always immediately tell an adult you trust about what happened if unsafe touch occurs. Having this conversation with children introduces them early to the idea of bodily autonomy, the importance of consent, and the value of body safety, which is a conversation that can be built upon for the children's entire lives.

The Story of Tamar and Amnon, for Older Children

We are told in 2 Samuel 13 that Tamar was "beautiful," so beautiful that Amnon was "ill" with desire for her. This is a good starting place for talking to older children and particularly teenagers about the finer details of consent. Teenagers should already have a basic understanding of sexuality and the importance of respecting other people's bodies. When they read that Amnon raped Tamar, they should know what that means and that rape is wrong. They should know that if they are ever assaulted sexually or if they know of a friend who is assaulted, they should report it to trusted adults immediately.

But what about so-called gray areas of consent? Tamar's story is a good way to talk about these areas and establish black and white boundaries for whatever instances teenagers might think are gray. For example, ask teens the following questions: If Tamar intentionally dressed beautifully (or in a sexy manner), would that have given Amnon the right to have sex with her? If Tamar intentionally dressed beautifully (or sexily) *for Amnon*, would that have given Amnon the right to have sex with her? If Tamar flirted with Amnon, would that have given Amnon the right to have sex with her? If Tamar kissed Amnon, would that have given Amnon the right to have sex with her? If Tamar said yes to sex with Amnon yesterday, would that have given Amnon the right to have sex with her today? If Tamar was drunk and murmured yes to Amnon's request to have sex, would that have given Amnon the right to have sex with her?

A resounding no should be the answer to each of these questions. However, it is likely that the teens in your care might have said yes to some of the questions or might have been unsure about how to answer. In those cases, talk about how no one has the right to have sex with someone without receiving conscious, enthusiastic, informed, and immediate consent from the other person. Sex without such consent is rape.

The above are merely three examples of how the discussion of stories about violence against children in the Bible can be used to equip, protect, and liberate children from current and future violence. Instead of avoiding these violent stories altogether, Christians should bravely face them. Ask the adults in your family, faith community, or religious organization to start thinking creatively about how these and other violent stories can become prompts for important and necessary conversations about liberating children in our midst from abuse and oppression.

five

Loving Children in How
We Read the Good Stories

Reading Scripture through the lens of child
abuse and neglect, we learn about God's hopes
for us in strengthening families and protecting
children. We find stories of Jesus blessing
and taking time for children. We find parents
valuing and protecting their children. We find
instructions for healthy family relationships.

—Jeanette Harder[1]

Throughout the Bible, God chooses children to serve divine purposes. God consistently elevates the smallest and lowest in order to reveal part of God's divine nature, a nature that privileges the marginalized and the oppressed.[2] Not only that, but God also frequently chooses the *younger* or *youngest* sibling in a family to bring God's message and historical plans to fruition. Consider, for example, how God allows the younger twin Jacob to receive the blessing over Esau; or how God chooses Joseph, the second youngest in his large family, to rule over Egypt during a famine.

We see God choose children to play all sorts of roles: prophets and prophetesses, rulers of kingdoms, and evangelists. Even children with small roles—like the boy who selflessly gives up his two fish and five small barley loaves to Jesus to feed the masses in John 6—ultimately have great significance because of how God uses them and blesses their efforts. As Judith M. Gundry-Volf points out, "Yahweh chooses children or youth as servants, highlighting the divine power at work through them (cf. 1 Sam. 3:1; 1 Kings 3:7; Jer. 1:6)."[3]

Surely, too, it is remarkable that many of those whom Jesus heals during his ministry are children. Considering that Jesus lived in a time and place where children had no rights and were considered on par with enslaved people (i.e., property), the fact that Jesus so focused on children holds great significance.

We have considered how the Bible contains many stories of violence against children in the previous chapter. The Bible also contains a multitude of stories where children are lifted up and treated in revolutionary ways. In this chapter we will be studying some of those stories.

There are certain Bible stories about children that are extraordinarily popular for usage in children's church. For example, the story of David, the child champion against the giant Goliath, has been repeated over and over in Sunday school so many times it is almost cliché at this point. So I will be avoiding those types of stories in this chapter. In this chapter, I want to model the hermeneutics—the method of biblical interpretation—that I discussed in chapter 3. I want to show you how we can zero in and zoom in on even the smallest biblical hints about mighty children in the Bible and coax out of the stories many great lessons for children today and also for adults: lessons about how we can lift up and liberate children in the same way that they were lifted up and liberated in these biblical passages.

The first story I want to look at is the story of Miriam, who I would argue is one of the world's first feminists—and a *child* feminist, even. After that we shall consider the child prophet Samuel, who spoke out as a young person against the high priest Eli. Finally, we shall look at the story of Naaman's enslaved servant girl, whose mighty acts saved Naaman.

Miriam, Child Critic of Anti-Child Patriarchy

Miriam is introduced at the beginning of the Book of Exodus. She is born to Amram and Jochebed. She is the older sister of Aaron and Moses, born four years before the former and seven years before the latter.[4] The context of her life is the tyrannical government instituted by a new Egyptian pharaoh as described in Exodus 1:8–22. In this passage, we read that the pharaoh decides that the people of Israel who are living in Egypt "have become far too numerous for us" (1:9). Thus he plans to enslave them, forcing them into slave labor "to oppress them" (1:11). However, his plan backfires, as "the more they were oppressed, the more they multiplied and spread" (1:12). This causes the pharaoh to double down on his oppression of the Israelites. He "made their lives bitter with harsh labor in brick and mortar and with all kinds of work in the fields" (1:14). His empire shows the Israelites no mercy in their enslavement; the biblical narrative twice describes the pharaoh's empire as "ruthless" (1:13, 14).

In a cruel act of desperation, the pharaoh decides that enslavement is not enough. He thus implements a systematic genocide of the male Israelite children. To do so he attempts to enlist the aid of two Hebrew midwives, "whose names were Shiphrah and Puah" (Exod. 1:15). Judaic tradition holds that Shiphrah is Jochebed and Puah is Miriam.[5] Pharaoh instructs them, "When you are helping the Hebrew women during childbirth on the delivery stool, if you see that the baby is a boy, kill him; but if it is a girl, let her live" (1:16). Jochebed and Miriam engage in civil disobedience, refusing to kill the male children.

The next time we encounter Miriam is after the birth of her youngest brother, Moses. Jochebed gives birth to Moses and "hid him for three months" (Exod. 2:2) in order to save him from the mandated infanticide. After the three months pass, Jochebed places the infant in a basket and puts the basket "among the reeds along the bank of the Nile" (2:3). Miriam watches from afar, standing "at a distance to see what would happen to him" (2:4). When Pharaoh's daughter comes to the river to bathe and discovers the child, Miriam creates an elaborate ruse to get Moses back to Jochebed. She asks Pharaoh's daughter, "Shall I go and get one of the Hebrew women to nurse the baby for you?" (2:7). When Pharaoh's daughter says yes, Miriam brings Jochebed to nurse Moses, thus reuniting mother and child (2:9). In this way Miriam not only saves the life of Moses, but also gives Moses's mother the chance to continue to be in his life.

The Tanakh describes Miriam as a prophet (Exod. 15:20). Jewish scholar Tamar Meir notes that the first time Miriam is mentioned by name in the biblical narrative is "in the Song at the Sea, where she is called (Ex. 15:20) 'Miriam the prophet, Aaron's sister.'" Meir explains that Judaic tradition takes the description of Miriam as "Aaron's sister" to mean that

"Miriam prophesied even before the birth of Moses, when Aaron was her only brother."[6] Jewish rabbi Nissan Mindel elaborates on this point: "Our sages tell us that the spirit of prophecy came to her when she was still a child. Her earliest prophecy was that her mother was going to give birth to a son who would free the Jewish people from Egyptian bondage. This is one of the reasons why she is said to have been called Puah, meaning 'Whisperer,' for she was whispering words of prophecy." Her prophecy regarding Moses occurred when she was five years old.[7]

Miriam, however, was not only a prophet in the sense of possessing divine insight. She was also a prophet in the sense of sociopolitical critique, issuing bold challenges to the authorities in her culture—most notably, her father, who was also a leading religious authority in the Jewish community ("the outstanding scholar and leader of his generation," according to Meir[8]). Judaic tradition holds that when the pharaoh instituted the systematic genocide of Jewish boys, Miriam's father Amram decided to separate from Jochebed, to no longer have children, and encouraged the rest of the Jewish community to do the same: "When he saw that Pharaoh had decreed that all the boys be cast into the Nile, he proclaimed: "Are we laboring in vain" [we give birth to sons who will eventually be killed], and so he divorced his wife. All Israel saw this, and in consequence they also divorced their wives."[9]

Miriam, just six years old at the time, courageously called out her father for betraying not only his own family, but also his culture's values. Jewish rabbinic literature records Miriam proclaiming, "Father, Father, your decree is harsher than that of Pharaoh. Pharaoh only decreed against the males, but you have decreed against both the males and the females. Pharaoh decreed only for this world, but you decreed both for this world and the next. It is doubtful whether the decree of the wicked Pharaoh will be fulfilled, but you are righteous, and your decree will undoubtedly be fulfilled."[10]

Miriam's prophetic critique of her father had a profound impact on not only her own family, but also the entire Israelite people. Maggy Whitehouse says, "[Miriam] made Amram realize that he was preventing girls from being born at all and that any baby that was born and died as a result of Pharaoh's decree would still reach the World to Come; but an unborn child would never exist. Amram heeded his daughter, and remarried his wife."[11]

By having the courage to speak up and out against her father, a power-holder in a patriarchal world, Miriam saved the well-being of all the Israelite women and also ensured the lives of all future Israelite children. This included Moses, who was born a year later and would eventually liberate the Israelites from the oppressive empire of the Egyptians. Through her brave prophetic critique as a six-year-old child, Miriam saved an entire nation.

While Miriam's story disappears from the biblical narrative after she successfully convinces the pharaoh's daughter to care for the infant Moses, it resurfaces years later during the Israelites' flight through the Red Sea. As the Red Sea envelops the terrifying military might of Egypt, completely engulfing them such that "not one of them survived" (Exod. 14:28), the Israelites begin rejoicing. Moses and all of the Israelites sing a song of praise to their God detailed in Exodus 15. And as their song comes to close, we are told that Miriam—the once-child prophet, now a courageous political leader in her own right—leads the women in music and dance. As she does so, the narrative of Exodus 15:19–21 reminds us that she is a prophet:

> For when the horses of Pharaoh with his chariots and his horsemen went into the sea, the Lord brought back the waters of the sea upon them, but the people of Israel walked on dry ground in the midst of the sea. Then Miriam the prophetess, the sister of Aaron, took a tambourine in her hand, and all the women went out after her with tambourines and dancing. And Miriam sang to them: "Sing to the Lord, for he has triumphed gloriously; the horse and his rider he has thrown into the sea."

This is an important anecdote because within the Judaic tradition there is a belief in the supernatural singing of children, a belief that dates back to Miriam's song and dance by the Red Sea. In fact, some scholars believe that Matthew 21:12–16, the passage where Jesus says that "the lips of children and infants" have "called forth the Lord's praise," refers to this moment. Gundry-Volf says, "The notion of children who uttered divinely inspired speech is not unparalleled in Greco-Roman antiquity. In fact, W. D. Davies and Dale L. Allison suggest that Matthew is alluding here to the tradition of the supernatural singing of Israelite children by the Red Sea when Moses led the people out of Egypt (cf. Wisd. 10:21)."[12]

The passage that Gundry-Volf references, Wisdom 10:21, is from the Book of Wisdom. For those raised in conservative evangelical circles who might be unfamiliar with this book, it is considered part of the biblical canon by both the Roman Catholic Church and the Eastern Orthodox Church. One of the greatest authorities of the early Christian church, Bishop Melito of Sardis (died ca. AD 180), considered it to be one of the books of the Christian canon.[13] However, most Protestants have rejected the Book of Wisdom as apocryphal. The following is the section from the Book of Wisdom that Gundry-Volf references, Wisdom 10:18–21:

> [Wisdom] carried them across the Red Sea and led them through deep waters. She drowned their enemies and caused the depths to boil up over them. The people who did what was right then stripped the ungodly of their weapons. All together they sang hymns to your holy name, Lord. They praised your hand, which had defended and fought for them. Wisdom opens the mouths of those who can't speak and puts clear words on the tongues of infants.

Clearly Miriam is a concrete and important example of how "Wisdom" or God does indeed open up the mouths of young children and puts clear words on their tongues. At six years old, Miriam's prophetic critique of her father is impressively mature and thoughtful as well as incinerating in its impact. She also—as nothing more than a young person, and a *female* young person in a patriarchal society at that—has the bravery to say what no one else did, thereby changing the fate of the Jewish people.

Samuel, Child Critic of a Corrupt Power Structure

Miriam is not the only child prophet who played a powerful, fate-changing role for the Jewish people. Like Miriam, Samuel played a vitally significant role in the history of Israel as a nation and Judaism as a religion. Also like Miriam, Samuel began that role as a young child. His story is first told in 1 Samuel. Samuel's mother, Hannah, is childless. She is the second wife to Elkanah, whose other wife, Peninnah, is blessed with children.

Peninnah takes advantage of her fertility's favored nature within a patriarchal, polygamous society that prized women for their ability to bear children. She ruthlessly taunts Hannah's childlessness. First Samuel 1:6 says Peninnah " kept provoking her in order to irritate her" because "the LORD had closed Hannah's womb." The emotional abuse takes its toll on Hannah. She enters a deep depression. She cries frequently. She struggles to eat. One time when Elkanah and his family visit the Temple of Shiloh, where Eli is high priest, Hannah rises at night in a distraught state and visits the temple alone. "In her deep anguish," the narrative says, "Hannah prayed to the LORD, weeping bitterly" (1:10). While praying to God, Hannah promises that if God will give her a child, she will give the child in service to them (1:11). Her emotional state was so intense and distraught that "Eli thought she was drunk and said to her, 'How long are you going to stay drunk? Put away your wine'" (1:13).

When Eli confronts her mistakenly about her presumed drunkenness, Hannah responds, "Do not take your servant for a wicked woman; I have been praying here out of my great anguish and grief" (1:16). Eli says that her prayers to God will be answered (1:17), and—in a poetic sign to the lifting of her depression—Hannah departs "and ate something, and her face was no longer downcast" (1:18). Later she becomes pregnant with Samuel. As promised, she dedicates him to God. At the age that he ceases nursing, Hannah sends him to live in Shiloh with the high priest Eli.

The narrative stresses Samuel's young age when he is sent to live with Eli: "After he was weaned, she took the boy with her, young as he was, along with a three-year-old bull, an ephah of flour, and a skin of wine, and brought him to the house of the LORD at Shiloh" (1:24). In fact, the narrative emphasizes Samuel's state of childhood not this one time, but three other times. In 1 Samuel 2:11 we read that "Elkanah went home to Ramah, but the boy ministered before the LORD under Eli the priest." Shortly thereafter is 1 Samuel 2:18, where it is written, "Samuel was ministering before the LORD—a boy wearing a linen ephod." Finally, in 1 Samuel 3:1 we are told, "The boy Samuel ministered before the LORD under Eli. In those days the word of the LORD was rare; there were not many visions." The youthfulness and earnest innocence of Samuel as an adopted, young child seem to be specifically contrasted with the evil abuses of Eli's own biological, adult children, who used their positions of authority to sexually prey on women coming to the temple.[14] In his exposition of 1 Samuel 3:1, Alexander MacLaren observes this contrast:

The opening words of this passage are substantially repeated from 1 Samuel 2:11, 1 Samuel 2:18. They come as a kind of refrain, contrasting the quiet, continuous growth and holy service of the child Samuel with the black narrative of Eli's riotous sons. While the hereditary priests were plunging into debauchery, and making men turn away from the Tabernacle services, Hannah's son was ministering unto the Lord, and, though no priest, was "girt with an ephod." . . . Samuel is the pattern of child religion and service, to which teachers should aim that their children may be conformed. . . . *When priests are faithless and people careless, God's voice will often sound from lowly childlike lips.*[15]

While 1 Samuel does not tell us Samuel's exact age, the first-century Jewish historian Josephus offers insight. Josephus says, "When Samuel was twelve years old, he began to prophesy: and once when he was asleep, God called to him by his name; and he, supposing he had been called by the high priest, came to him: but when the high priest said he did not call him, God did so thrice."[16] What is notable about Samuel's divine insight at the age of twelve is that it was a prophetic critique of a member of the ruling class—his adult male mentor, the high priest Eli himself. In 1 Samuel 3:13, God reveals to Samuel, "I told [Eli] that I would judge his family forever because of the sin he knew about; his sons blasphemed God, and he failed to restrain them." Samuel is understandably terrified at the thought of speaking this prophetic critique to his mentor. The narrative tells us in 1 Samuel 3:15 that "Samuel lay down until morning," unable to fall asleep, and "was afraid to tell Eli the vision."

It is vital that we view this moment from the perspective of Samuel. This young child was raised in a home and culture where patriarchy reigned supreme.[17] When Samuel first hears the voice of God, he thinks it is Eli calling, and Samuel rushes ("ran," according to the text) immediately to Eli's side. This repeats a second and third time, each time Samuel springing immediately to obey what he thinks is Eli's command.

Yet now with the voice of God speaking to him, young Samuel has a profound, prophetic insight into his family and his culture—an insight that requires condemning one of the highest authorities of his community, the high priest Eli. Would such a critique be interpreted as rebellion? Would Eli be upset that God chose to reveal prophecy to a young child and not the high priest himself?

In the Talmud, Samuel faces even higher stakes in confronting Eli. This is because the Talmud includes an additional story about Samuel and Eli's interactions that the Tanakh does not. In the Talmud, when Hannah first brings Samuel as a young child to Eli, Samuel makes a declaration about Jewish law: lay people can slaughter animals for sacrifice just like priests can. While Eli affirms Samuel's declaration, Eli is angered because Jewish law also forbids students from making declarations about said law in front of their teacher. The punishment for this specific offense is death. Eli makes this very point to Samuel: "Anyone who issues a halakhic ruling in the presence of his teacher, even if the particular halakha is correct, is liable for death at the hand of Heaven for showing contempt for his teacher."[18]

While one might think Eli is joking, he is not. Hannah herself has to intervene. The Talmud says that Hannah shows up and begins shouting at Eli, reminding him that Samuel is the answer to her prayers: "I am the woman who stood here with you to pray to the Lord; do not punish the child who was born of my prayers." Eli, however, still wants to punish Samuel. He replies to Hannah, "Let me punish him, and I will pray for mercy, that the Holy One, Blessed be He, will grant you a son who will be greater than this one." Hannah retorts, "For this youth I prayed and I want no other." Eli finally relents, agreeing to punish Samuel by mentoring him.[19]

In summary, then: when Samuel was a young child, he was brought in front of Eli and the public. In this public setting, Eli threatened to kill Samuel for disrespecting him. It was only Samuel's mother begging, shouting, and shaming the high priest that spared Samuel from Eli's wrath. But in the next moment, Samuel is sent to live with the very man who was threatening to kill him. That surely was not a comfortable situation for Samuel. Between Eli's assumptions about Hannah being drunk, Eli's threats against Samuel, and Eli's irresponsible approach to his own children's evil abuses, it seems safe to describe home life at the high priest's home as troubled. To make matters more awkward, God reveals their prophecy against Eli and his family not to the high priest himself, not even to another adult, but to the one child with whom Eli was already angry. That is a direct threat to the high priest's power. As Rabbi Elli Rischer writes, "Once Samuel is dedicated to a life of service in the sanctuary, he becomes a threat that may catalyze change from within and sidestep Eli's regulation of access to the Almighty. Eli indeed claims sovereignty over God's house, and it is precisely that claim that Samuel's presence undermines."[20]

Samuel's presence in the temple indicates that adults do not have exclusive rights to God. Children access God, too. And Samuel's courage indicates that even a twelve-year-old child has the courage to speak out against his family and culture's sickness.

This holds significance for children in similar situations today. Black children raised by white adoptive parents who attempt to whitewash history and teach their children that racism is dead. LGBTQIA children raised by cisgender, heterosexual parents who attempt to erase their children's gender and sexual identities. Like Samuel, these children face the terrifying, seemingly insurmountable task of offering prophetic critique against their families and cultures.

The response of Eli to his young apprentice's prophecies is noteworthy for several reasons. First, Eli encouraged Samuel to receive the message of God, rather than belittling him due to his young age or believing God would not use someone so young. According to Josephus, Eli told Samuel, "It is God that calls you; do you therefore signify it to him, and say, I am here ready."[21] Second, when Samuel's message ends up being a prophetic critique of Eli himself, Eli does not lash out at Samuel, become defensive, or ignore Samuel's critique. Eli is receptive of Samuel's prophecy. As documented in 1 Samuel 3:18, Eli accepts Samuel's critique, saying, "He is the LORD; let him do what is good in his eyes." This openness to the possibility of a child bearing God's message and the willingness to listen to a younger generation's prophetic critique are important reminders for our own lives today.

The Enslaved Servant Girl, Child Savior of a Mighty Man

Children can do even more than prophesy. We see this in 2 Kings 5, where we are introduced to a nameless young girl kidnapped and enslaved by the Syrians during an attack on Israel. The young girl became a servant of yet another nameless woman—the wife of Naaman, the very important captain of the Syrian army. Naaman is clearly a hero of the Syrian empire. The English Standard Version of the Bible describes him as "a mighty man of valor" (2 Kings 5:1). As a mighty man, Naaman was everything the little girl was not: adult, male, powerful, and free. In contrast, the little girl—a mere child, and a female, powerless, marginalized, and enslaved child at that—"is multiply disempowered."[22] Yet it was the little girl who saved the mighty man.

Naaman was not only a mighty man; he was beautiful. Or, he once was beautiful. His name in the narrative comes from the Hebrew verb *naem*, which means "to be pleasant, delightful, or lovely." Biblical commentator J. Hampton Keathley III says, "His name suggests he had undoubtedly been a handsome man, at least before the leprosy."[23] While his physical appearance once lived up to his name, when we are introduced to Naaman that is no longer the case. In a tragic irony, this mighty, attractive man was now inflicted with—of all diseases—leprosy. Leprosy destroys one's physical beauty. It involves spongy tumors, the deterioration of tissue between bones, physical deformities, and—in a gruesome finale—the loss of fingers and toes. It was incurable in Naaman's day and lasted until the victim died.

The nameless Israelite girl is introduced in verses 2 and 3 of 2 Kings 5. All we are told about her is that she wants to help cure Naaman. Though both she and her mistress lived in a patriarchal, adultist world where children and women remain nameless and faceless—even when they are the heroines of the story—the little girl was proactive. I think Alice L. Laffey makes an important observation in her book *An Introduction to the Old Testament: A Feminist Perspective*: "The Israelite maid is the first to speak."[24] That is a bold move for a child, let alone an enslaved child. She risked everything by speaking up and putting her faith on the line.

Make no mistake, it is *faith* that drove the young child to stick her neck out and suggest that Naaman consult with Elisha, "the prophet who is in Samaria" (2 Kings 5:3). The girl believed Elisha "would cure him of his leprosy" (5:3), but the text omits an important and relevant fact: Elisha had never healed anyone of leprosy up to that point. Jesus revealed this centuries later in Luke 4:27: "There were many in Israel with leprosy in the time of Elisha the prophet, yet not one of them was cleansed—only Naaman the Syrian."

In other words, the little girl had so much faith in Elisha's God that she believed God could empower Elisha to do something he had never done before: heal someone with leprosy. She had so much faith that she risked her own life in suggesting healing was a possibility. One can only imagine the horrors the little girl would face if Elisha failed to heal Naaman.

Naaman was not only powerful and skilled at violence as a military leader; he also was an angry, rageful person. We observe this later in the narrative when Elisha instructed Naaman to wash seven times in the Jordan River to cure his leprosy. Naaman was insulted by both the simplicity of the solution as well as by the fact that the Jordan River was much dirtier than Syrian rivers like Abana and Pharpar. We are told two verses in a row that Naaman became angry: first, "Naaman became angry and left" (2 Kings 5:11) and second, "He was very angry and turned to leave" (5:12). If he became furious simply because he *disliked the proposed method of curing his leprosy*, who knows how he would have directed his rage at the powerless enslaved girl who made a fool of him by suggesting he seek treatment from a false prophet.

Yet the child bravely took that risk. She had faith that Elisha and Elisha's God would perform a miracle. She also took another risk, perhaps an even more dangerous one: in speaking confidently of her own people's God, she was inherently challenging the gods of the Syrians. The Syrian gods had failed to heal Naaman.

The young girl, therefore, was speaking prophetically against those gods. She was declaring that she believed her people's God was more powerful. Protestant Tanakh scholar Walter Brueggemann refers to the child's prophetic critique as theological resistance. He writes, "Her rootage that evoked resistance is theological. This is evident in her use of Israel's traditional vocabulary, 'the prophet.' The term is deeply freighted in her utterance." By assertively naming Elisha as *the* prophet, the child is boldly witnessing to her faith. Brueggemann says she is "an explicit, determined witness to YHWH who offers, in this ostensibly Syrian narrative, her bold testimony to YHWH." He also notes what I mentioned previously: that her confidence in Elisha "is astonishing, because we have no available data that YHWH's prophet can counteract leprosy."[25]

Additionally, and also astonishingly, the child embodies a spirit of compassion and kindness. I appreciate how Heather Farrell, Mormon theologian and writer at Women in the Scriptures, describes this spirit:

This little girl's faith humbles me. I don't know if I would personally have had the faith to open my mouth and bear testimony in a strange country, among people who didn't believe like I did, and especially not to the people who had torn me away from my home and taken me captive. She is an example to me of forgiveness, of compassion, of faith and great courage. Think about the great risk she took in opening her mouth and bearing testimony of the prophet. What if no one listened to her? What if they laughed at her? What if the prophet hadn't been able to heal Naaman? But she did open her mouth, she didn't let her fear keep her silent, and God took her little seed of faith and worked mighty miracles with it.[26]

What Farrell says is illuminative. Having the courage and compassion to not only take the risk by speaking up, but to also put your life on the line for the very people who ripped you away from those you love the most is astonishing. This child displayed empathy with Naaman's pain, even though Naaman's people are the ones who kidnapped her, and was willing to try to help him. This child is a model for us of courage and a model of kindness. She may have hated Naaman. But she was willing to put aside that hate and acknowledge their shared humanity. Regardless of what she felt about him, even if she felt he was her enemy, she wanted her enemy to not be in pain. That is a powerful testimony for anyone, let alone a female child living in an extraordinarily scary situation.

Personally, the saddest part of this story to me is that the little girl vanishes from the narrative after the first paragraph. We are never told what happened to her and are left wondering: What was her name? Was she rewarded? Was she set free? Was she allowed to return home to her Israelite family? We do not know.

The writer(s) of this may not have been interested in answering such questions. The narrative's structure at first glance suggests Elisha as the hero and Naaman as the noble protagonist (despite his temper). The king of Israel and the servant Gehazi appear to be the bad guys: the king because he (in diametric opposition to the enslaved little girl) had no faith in Elisha and Elisha's God, and Gehazi because he wanted to leverage Elisha and Elisha's God to benefit himself materially. But the nameless little girl—the person most responsible for setting the events in motion—vanishes.

It is noteworthy, however, that in a world where children had the same sociopolitical status as enslaved people (and enslaved people had no rights), the writer(s) of this narrative chose to highlight the role an enslaved girl played. As Lois Wilson points out, "A nameless Israelite slave girl made the story happen."[27] The role of the girl is the anchor for the entire narrative.

What might not be obvious in the English translation is that the story contains a number of *inclusios*.[28] An inclusio is a literary device in which similar thematic materials are used at the beginning and end of a story to frame the events. Second Kings 5 has several inclusios that revolve around the contrast between the small and the mighty as well as the young and the old. Laurel Koepf highlights these.[29] She describes how Naaman is first introduced as an *ish gadol*, a "mighty man." The child is contrasted immediately with him as a *na'arah qetannah*, a "small girl." When Elisha instructs Naaman to bathe in the Jordan River, Naaman is offended. As a mighty man, he expected to receive a mighty task as his healing assignment. He also expected to bathe in a mightier river like the Syrian rivers he knew at home. When Naaman does bathe in the lowly Jordan River, his leprosy is healed to the point that his skin is like that of a *na'ar qaton*, a "small boy."

One sees the reccurring theme already. A small child sets into motion a chain of events where a mighty man is figuratively transformed into a small boy. Another example of small and mighty in play occurs in the narrative's closing image of Gehazi. Gehazi is Elisha's servant boy who is cursed by Elisha with Naaman's leprosy after Gehazi deceitfully solicits silver and clothing from Naaman (2 Kings 5:20–27). Robin Cohn, feminist theologian at Women in the Bible for Thinkers, notes, "The same word to describe the 'little captive girl' (as most commentators label her) is also used to describe Elisha's servant Gehazi."[30] The enslaved girl is a *na'arah*; Gehazi is a *na'ar*, the male version of *na'arah*. We not only see the intentional contrast between the enslaved girl's faithfulness to her God and the prophet Elisha and Gehazi's unfaithfulness to them. We also see that, in contrast to Naaman, who is figuratively transformed from a person with leprous, decaying flesh into a small boy, Gehazi is literally transformed from a small boy into a person with leprous, decaying flesh. Yet again, Elisha's treatment of children is considered inappropriate in Judaic tradition. As mentioned in chapter 4 regarding Elisha's role with the bears and forty-two children, the Talmud states, "Elisha fell ill three times." Two were punishment: once for "inciting the bears to attack the children" and another for his treatment of Gehazi.[31]

The writer(s) of the narrative frame the entire story with the themes of mighty and small, young and old. With a small enslaved girl and her boldness as the instigator of that process and a small boy another victim of Elisha's anger, we can see the narrative framing itself as a subversive act. It is subversive because it parallels and accentuates the girl's courage and bravado while highlighting the fallibility of the adult patriarchs who surround her. In terms of sociopolitical power, the little Israelite girl held the least of all the story's characters. But ultimately it was her bravery and faith that changed everything for many people who had that power, especially a mighty man of valor like Naaman.

Themes

There are several themes that I believe stand out from the stories about Miriam, Samuel, and Naaman's enslaved servant girl. The first theme is looking for liberation in the midst of oppression. There is a reason we began in chapter 4 with stories about violence against children *before* we looked to stories about extraordinary children in the Bible. It is against the backdrop of oppression that we see children being lifted up and becoming mighty.

Children can be extraordinary in ordinary circumstances, but oftentimes it is within conflict where their strengths and skills become most known. This is perhaps one of the most significant takeaways from these stories: children are capable of meeting oppression face to face. Even though they are limited by their level of emotional, mental, and physical development, children have amazing capabilities—capabilities that enable and empower them to speak about and impact our times in ways that are graced by God. Sometimes children are even braver than the adults around them, such as Miriam standing up for what is right when her father lacked the courage to do so, Samuel having the courage to call out Eli, or Naaman's enslaved servant girl speaking up about the healing available from her God.

The fact that children can be braver than the adults around them forms the second theme I see in these stories: the theme of tables being turned. In our adultist and childist world, we think of adults as being smarter, more capable, more insightful, and wiser than children. We assume that increased age means increased contact with and knowledge of God. Yet these stories remind us that this outcome is not inevitable.

The king of Israel was older than Naaman's enslaved servant girl and yet it was the child, not the king, who had the proper faith in God and trusted that Elisha could heal Naaman. It was the child, and not the king of Israel, who took an incredible risk by suggesting that Naaman consult with Elisha. In this way we see the tables being turned, as the child leads the adults toward the kingdom of God. "A little child will lead them" (Isa. 11:6), indeed! This role reversal makes sense in the topsy-turvy kingdom that Jesus has instituted, where "the last will be first, and the first will be last" (Matt. 20:16).

The third theme I see in these stories is the importance of adults listening to children. Even with these children's best efforts, the stories' outcomes would not have happened if the children's pleas, prophecies, and actions fell on closed ears and hardened hearts. While children can be mighty, they are still children—they are less developed physically than adults. They are smaller and easier to overlook or ignore. They cannot force adults to do that for which they ask.

In other words, a key part in each of these stories is the response of the adults—Miriam's plea to her father, Samuel's prophecy to Eli, and Naaman's enslaved child's suggestion to Naaman. Specifically, the adults were *open* to the children. They had responsive hearts. They did not look down upon the children because of their youth. Instead, they saw the youth as setting examples for others, just as 1 Timothy 4:12 encourages: "Don't let anyone look down on you because you are young, but set an example for the believers in speech, in conduct, in love, in faith and in purity."

We need to have this same receptive spirit today when we interact with children. We need to listen with open hearts and minds. Who knows, maybe the child in front of you today has a message from God themselves for you!

INCLUDING CHILDREN

Have the children in your family, faith community, or religious organization each pick a story from the Bible that features a child. The story could be any of the examples we have so far discussed or any other reference to children in the Bible (positive or negative). If you need more ideas for places where children appear in the Bible, *The Child in the Bible* by Marcia J. Bunge is an excellent resource. Also, please note: it is acceptable if more than one person in the group picks the same story. Overlap allows participants to see how different people respond differently to the same stories from the Bible.

Have the children think about and answer the following questions about their stories:

1. What do you think life was like for the child or children in the story?
2. How is the child, or how are the children, treated in the story? With kindness and respect or with abuse and violence?
3. Why did you pick this story? What about it speaks to, inspires, worries, or amuses you?
4. What does this story tell us about children?
5. What does this story tell us about adults?
6. What does this story tell us about God?

Give the children a week or two to pick a story and answer the above questions. After that time has passed, assemble the children in a circle and give everyone an opportunity to share their story and their answers. Make this a casual and fun discussion and allow cross-talk and questions from one child to another.

six

Gods as Children

Unquestionably, the central Christian assertion
about the identity of Jesus Christ has been
that he is both fully human and fully divine.
This characterization is unique among
world religions.

—Kristin Johnston Largen[1]

In this chapter we will be examining different world religions and how
they depict the incarnations of their gods and saviors. We will then
compare and contrast what we learn with the incarnation we see in the
Christian Gospels through Jesus the God-Child. I believe this is an important exercise for two reasons. First, it will help us to better love our
neighbors. Our neighbors include people of other faiths, and we can only
truly love our neighbors when we make efforts to know them—to appreciate and understand their points of view, even when we disagree.

And second, I believe that looking at other religions' versions of the
incarnational act will help us better understand our own faith. As comparative theologian Kristin Johnston Largen writes, "Dialogue [with other
religions] brings new insights into the familiar old stories we thought we
knew inside and out, and it brings new life into the desiccated skeletons
of beliefs and practices we had ceased to reflect on years ago."[2] This is
particularly relevant because the stories Christians tell about Jesus's birth
and childhood are repeated, sentimentalized, and commercialized so often
during the holiday season that we can become numb to their poignancy.
We sing "Away in the Manger" blithely but forget what exactly it means

that God Almighty became that little baby "asleep on the hay" with "no crib for a bed." Looking at how other religions tell similar stories can urge us to better realize how radical and liberating the God-Child's story really is.

The incarnation of a god is one of the most common tropes in world religions. Numerous stories throughout history give evidence to the vast diversity that an incarnational act can take. Gods have become swans, like Zeus did when he wanted to impregnate Leda, the mother of Helen of Troy. Gods can become lightning bolts, which is how a god impregnated Olympias, mother of Alexander the Great. Or gods can become a burning bush, which is how Yahweh communicated with Moses in the book of Exodus. In other words, gods can take and have taken just about every imaginable form, whether animal, plant, or mineral.

Gods also can take and have taken the form of humans—many times so. The fact is that the God-become-human story that is so central to Christianity is not particularly significant or unique in the context of comparative religion. I am not saying the story is unimportant; in fact, it has extraordinary significance for the meaning and application of the Christian faith. However, the story of a god becoming a human is not *unique* to Christianity. Other religions also include stories of such incarnational acts, such as the sun gods Horus and Ra becoming incarnate as pharaohs in ancient Egypt; enlightened spiritual teachers (known as "lamas") becoming *re*-incarnate in Tibetan Buddhism; or the repeated and diverse incarnations of the Hindu deity Ganesha.

More unique than the God-as-human story is the God-Child story. In Christianity, Jesus did not merely incarnate as a human. He chose to incarnate as a human *child*. Jesus became a fully human child, bound by the limitations of every stage of child development. That is something particularly special, as we shall discuss later. However, even the incarnation of a god as a child is not unique. What makes Jesus stand out from religions that feature gods as children, then, is not the fact that he is a child, per se, but rather the *form* and the *significance* that his childhood plays within Christianity. We will explore the form and significance in both this chapter and the next.

Child Deities in World Religions

Many world religions feature deities who are depicted as or become incarnate as children. The meaning of this incarnation varies from religion to religion. In some religions, that a god is a child is merely incidental. In other religions, the child aspect of the god holds special significance. Let us look at a few examples.

Egyptian mythology features the sun god Horus in multiple forms, one of which is a child. As a child, Horus represents the newborn sun rising (or being born) each new day. Horus is the son of two deities: his mother Isis and his father Osiris. Typical imagery of Horus features him with his mother, Isis, in a pose that would later inspire the traditional pictures of Mary with Jesus.[3] This imagery of Horus as child and Isis as mother calls to mind the mutual relationships between spiritual forces in the polytheistic Egyptian culture. Thus that Horus is a child is particularly important to understanding his significance. (Egyptian mythology also features other child deities, including Khonsu, the child god who represents the moon.) The image of Horus as a child was later incorporated into Greek mythology as the deity Harpocrates.[4]

In Japanese mythology, the two main deities in the Shinto creation story, Izanagi and Izanami, procreate in a way that violates a sacred rule. As a result, the child they give birth to is deformed. He is called Hiruko, or "Leech Child." The gods abandon him, sending him off all alone in a boat. He later becomes identified as Ebisu, one of the seven gods of luck. Ebisu specifically blesses fishermen and commercial deals and is depicted as a fat, smiling fisherman. Hiruko's story is one of overcoming odds as a child and growing up to be a content, successful adult. However, apart from his childhood nickname of Leech Child, that Hiruko is a child is merely incidental to his story.[5]

A more contemporary example can be found in Nepal today, where there are "living goddesses," young girls who are chosen to be Kumaris. "Kumari" literally means "young, unmarried girl." More specifically, Kumaris are selected from among young girls who have had no sexual experiences and have yet to menstruate. Those selected are believed to be, and worshipped as, reincarnations of the Hindu goddess Durga. In Nepal, both Hindus and Buddhists worship the Kumaris. The Kumaris, in turn, are said to bestow blessings upon the people.[6] Upon menstruation, losing a tooth, or bleeding in any way (even bleeding from something as small as a paper cut), the Kumaris are believed to be vacated by the goddess Durga. Then they return to being normal people, and a new, replacement Kumari is appointed. The explanation is that "a young girl is chosen over a mature woman because of their inherent purity and chastity."[7]

The Kumaris, then, are child deities who are not worshipped for being children per se as much as they are worshipped for one incidental aspect: "purity" (a lack of sexual experience). Upon any form of "corruption" by blood—whether sexual or otherwise—they cease to be worthy of worship and lose their divine spark. Theirs is a temporary, unreliable divinity, one that can easily be lost through all sorts of mundane accidents.

Four of the five major world religions today (Buddhism, Christianity, Hinduism, and Islam) feature a primary god or savior who entered life as a newborn child. The only major world religion that does not is Judaism, because the Jewish belief is that their messiah has yet to appear. Since these are the religions that are most influential on world events, we will look at each of them and how they describe or envision their child god or savior. We will also compare each set of stories with Jesus's childhood to tease out the similarities and differences. Questions to consider include: Is being a child essential to who the individual is, or is it merely incidental? Is there a connection between the child aspect of the individual and how that individual later treats other children? What sort of childhood did the individual have—one of privilege or poverty? Are the individuals growing according to normal stages of child development? The answers we give to these questions will sharpen the image of what exactly it does and does not mean when we proclaim Jesus as the God-Child.

Krishna as Child

Hinduism is the world's oldest living major religion.[8] It is not a single religion; it is, rather, a medley of various religious traditions that began in India. The numerous religions that make up what we call Hinduism today feature a number of unique attributes. First, they have no official "founder," contrary to Judaism's Abraham or Islam's prophet Muhammad. It is hard to determine when the Hindu religions began. Second, Hindu religions have no official hierarchy or council that determines official Hindu thought and practice. Third, there is no equivalent to the Bible in Hinduism—an official text that is considered the ultimate sacred authority on Hindu thought and practice. Instead, there are numerous, distinct texts that each have authority. These include the Vedas, the Upanishads, the *Mahabharata* and the *Ramayana*, and the Puranas.

Probably the most well-known Hindu text in the United States is the *Bhagavad Gita*, which is a tiny section from the *Mahabharata*, the world's longest epic poem. The *Bhagavad Gita* is particularly important because in it Krishna, the human avatar of the Hindu god Vishnu, reveals himself as the savior of all reality to the great warrior Arjuna. Also important is one of the Puranas, the *Bhagavata Purana*, for that text contains descriptions of the ten avatars of Vishnu, one of which is Krishna. The text describes the childhood of Krishna, which is relevant to this chapter's purpose.

In Hinduism, there is a primary trinity of divine persons. These divine persons manage the continual cycle of reincarnation, wherein the universe moves in and out of existence. The trinity of gods are Brahma, the creator who wills each new universe into being; Shiva, the destroyer of each universe; and Vishnu, the sustainer of each universe. Vishnu protects each universe from evil. He is traditionally depicted as a blue god with four arms. Vishnu is important to our current purposes because he is the one god who repeatedly incarnates here on earth. One can see parallels between Hinduism's primary trinity and the Trinity (the Father, Son, and Holy Spirit) in Christianity. However, unlike Christian incarnation (wherein Jesus is both fully divine and fully human), Vishnu's reincarnations are avatars—that is, they are fully divine and only appear to be earthly.

Vishnu has ten primary avatars in world history: a fish named Matsya; a turtle named Kurma; a boar named Varaha; a man-lion named Narasimha; a dwarf named Vamana; a human hero named Parashurama; another human hero named Ramachandra; the human Krishna, who is considered the highest incarnation of Vishnu; the human Buddha; and the final and yet-to-be-seen avatar Kalki, whose arrival will signal the end of the current universe.

Krishna as a child is given great importance within many Hindu traditions. Indeed, Hindu mythology has a specific name for baby Krishna: Bala Krishna. Bala Krishna is often depicted in Hindu art as a child crawling or dancing with a piece of butter in his hands. This is because the child had an obsession with butter, often mischievously stealing it from his mother Yashoda. Kristin Johnston Largen notes, "One of his favorite pastimes was stealing butter. In story after story, we read how his mother,

Yashoda, had to punish him for this or other misdeeds; but even while punishing him, she could not help but be delighted at her son, whom she loved so deeply."⁹

While stories about children stealing butter might seem ordinary, Krishna was anything but an ordinary child. He never was fully human and only appeared *like* a child. "The stories of Krishna's infancy and youth highlight that while he appears to be 'one of us,' he actually is not."¹⁰ His appearance as a human child is, rather, the result of Yogamaya—a goddess with the power of illusion. Sometimes Krishna would cast off Yogamaya's illusion and allow his mother and others to see him as he really was. For example, in Book Ten of the *Bhagavata Purana*, Yashoda is nursing the infant Krishna. As her son is drinking, Yashoda "began caressing his sweetly smiling mouth," causing Krishna to yawn. And as he yawned, she saw in the baby's mouth "the sky, heaven and earth, the host of stars, space, the sun, the moon, fire, air, the oceans, the continents, the mountains and their daughters [the rivers], the forests, and moving and non-moving living things."¹¹ In short, Krishna was a god merely *appearing* as a child; he always retained his divine powers and knowledge.

While the child Krishna is distinct from the child Jesus in lacking full humanness, there are a number of interesting parallels and divergences between their stories that are illuminating. For example, when Krishna is born, the evil king Kamsa tries repeatedly to kill him. Kamsa first orders Krishna's parents to turn over all their children once they are born. However, Krishna uses his powers to save his brother Balarama by whisking his brother out of his mother's womb and into another woman's womb. Next, when it is his own time to be born, Krishna swaps himself with Yogamaya's body so that, when Kamsa tries to bash the infant against the rocks, Yogamaya reveals her true form as a goddess. Kamsa then orders "all the babies who are ten days old or less in and around the area to be killed."¹² Once again, Krishna makes a miraculous escape.

The story of King Kamsa and baby Krishna has obvious parallels with the story of King Herod and baby Jesus (Matt. 2:13–18). Like Kamsa, Herod realizes that this newborn baby could potentially mean the downfall of his kingdom. Like Kamsa, Herod tries to gain possession of the baby so he can kill him but fails to do so. So also like Kamsa, Herod engages in a full-scale campaign of infanticide.

The similarities end there. Unlike Jesus, Krishna is not fully human. He is, rather, merely wearing humanity like a cloak. Thus, while appearing as a newborn infant, Krishna can engage in divine trickery in order to save some of the children Kamsa tries to kill. In contrast, Jesus is unable to outwit or stop Herod. He shows no signs of supernatural powers or heightened intelligence. Instead, he is fully dependent on his human parents, Mary and Joseph, to save him. Largen remarks about the story of Herod and Jesus, "If Jesus himself has any divine power, there certainly is no evidence of it yet."[13] Because Jesus took on the full humanity of an infant child—and that infant's stage of child development—we do not see him performing miracles.

Another interesting difference between Krishna and Jesus is that Hindu texts are overflowing with stories about Krishna as a child performing miracles, battling demons, and displaying his divine powers in all sorts of fantastical ways. In contrast, the Christian Gospels are essentially silent about Jesus's childhood apart from the birth stories in Matthew and Luke and the story of twelve-year-old Jesus in the temple in Luke. I would argue this lack of stories about Jesus's childhood supports the idea of Jesus being fully human. His divinity was shaped by the normal stages of child development like any other child. Jesus as an infant did not save the other infants killed by the order of Herod precisely because *Jesus was also an infant*. And later, as an adolescent, he actually "grew in wisdom" (Luke 2:25) because, unlike Krishna, his prefrontal cortex did not fully develop until adulthood.

Buddha as Child

Buddhism is a multifaceted religion that, like Hinduism, began in India. The Buddha, who lived sometime between the sixth and fourth centuries BC and founded Buddhism, taught his followers that one can find a happy medium between extremes. One can enjoy life while at the same time not being attached to it. This is known as the Middle Way, and by following the Middle Way, the Buddha taught that one could avoid the two extremes of asceticism and indulgence that were common in India during the Buddha's existence.

Unlike Christianity, Buddhism does not claim that its prophet is a god. "Buddha was not a God," writes Buddhist monk Thich Nhat Hanh.

"He was a human being like you and me, and he suffered just as we do."[14] Rather than being divine, the Buddha was simply enlightened. He became enlightened at the age of thirty-five. For the next forty-five years, the Buddha passed on his message of enlightenment: "I teach only suffering and the transformation of suffering."[15] What this means to Buddhists is two-fold: humans must recognize and acknowledge their own suffering, and by looking deeply at the seeds of that suffering (namely, attachment to the material world), humans can release their sense of attachment and thereby reach liberation or nirvana, "a state of coolness, peace, and joy."[16]

Christians study Jesus through the discipline of Christology, and Buddhists study the life and teachings of the Buddha through the discipline of Buddhology.[17] According to traditional Buddhology, the Buddha, otherwise known as Prince Siddhartha Gautama, was born in the city of Kapilavastu, located between India and Nepal. He was born into a life of power and privilege as the royal son of King Śuddhodana and Queen Māyā.

Just as wise men and shepherds came to honor Jesus after his birth, so too did many people come visit the Buddha both before and after his birth—though in a most curious way before his birth. Queen Māyā explained to a young man seeking enlightenment that, "When I became pregnant with Siddhartha . . . hundreds of millions of buddhas and bodhi-sattvas from every quarter of the universe came to pay their respects to my son. I could not refuse, and all of them entered my womb at the same time. And you know, there was more than enough room for all of them!"[18]

After his birth, the Buddha continued to receive visitors. Thich Nhat Hanh recounts the story of an old sage named Asita who came to see the newborn Buddha:

A few days after the Buddha was born, many people in his country of Kapilavastu came to pay their respects, including an old sage named Asita. After contemplating the baby Buddha, Asita began to cry. The king, the Buddha's father, was alarmed. "Holy man, why are you crying? Will some misfortunate overtake my child?" The holy man replied, "No, your majesty. The birth of Prince Siddhartha is a wondrous event. Your child will become an important world teacher. But I am too old and I will not be there. That is the only reason I am crying."[19]

Asita's encounter with the child Buddha parallels the elderly Simeon and Anna's encounters with the child Jesus. In the Gospel of Luke, Mary and Joseph bring the baby Jesus to the temple eight days after he is born (Luke 2:21). While he is there, two people—an old man named Simeon and a prophetess named Anna—encounter Jesus and make proclamations regarding the wondrous role he will play in the world.

Simeon, whom the Bible describes as "righteous and devout," is told "by the Holy Spirit that he would not die before he had seen the Lord's Messiah" (Luke 2:25–26). On the day that Jesus is taken to the temple for his circumcision, Simeon is moved by the Holy Spirit to go to the temple (2:27). When Simeon sees Jesus, he takes him into his arms and declares, "Sovereign Lord, as you have promised, you may now dismiss your servant in peace. For my eyes have seen your salvation, which you have prepared in the sight of all nations: a light for revelation to the Gentiles, and the glory of your people Israel" (2:28–32).

Mary and Joseph marvel at Simeon's proclamation: Jesus means salvation! Simeon blesses Jesus's parents and turns to Mary in particular, telling her that, "This child is destined to cause the falling and rising of many in Israel, and to be a sign that will be spoken against, so that the thoughts of many hearts will be revealed. And a sword will pierce your own soul too" (Luke 2:33–35).

After Simeon's prophetic words about Jesus, another prophet—this time a woman named Anna—comes up to Jesus and his parents. The Gospel of Luke describes Anna as an old prophetess from the tribe of Asher who worshipped in the temple nonstop, fasting and praying both day and night. When Anna sees Jesus, she approaches him and his parents and gives thanks to God (Luke 2:36–38). She then begins to speak "about the child to all who were looking forward to the redemption of Jerusalem" (2:38).

Thich Nhat Hanh sees in these stories of Buddha's and Jesus's encounters with sages and prophets the fact that children are special. Thich Nhat Hanh writes, "Whenever I read the stories of Asita and Simeon, I have the wish that every one of us could have been visited by a sage when we were born. The birth of every child is important, not less than the birth of a Buddha. We, too, are a Buddha, a Buddha-to-be, and we continue to be born every minute. We, too, are sons and daughters of God and the children of our parents. We have to take special care of each birth."[20] Children hold great potential—the potential to change the world for the better.

While these stories of the Buddha's and Jesus's early childhoods are similar, their lives also contain significant differences. As a child, the Buddha became especially struck by the suffering in the world: "The Buddha became aware at an early age that suffering is pervasive."[21] This led him, at the age of twenty-nine, to abandon his wife and child, leaving his family to seek out a way to end suffering.[22] He taught the Four Noble Truths of Buddhism until his death at the age of eighty. These Four Noble Truths are as follows: the truth about suffering existing; the truth about the cause of suffering; the truth that suffering can end; and the truth about how one ends suffering. For the Buddha, suffering is something primarily psychological, meaning it is an inner process that everyone experiences. It is caused by people becoming attached to impermanent things.[23]

The Christian Gospels, in contrast, never tell us Jesus was fixated on inner suffering. Yes, he suffered inwardly throughout his life (even to the point that "his sweat was like drops of blood" on the Mount of Olives in Luke 22:44), but the inner suffering caused by attachment to impermanent things was not the motif of his life or teachings. Jesus wanted to see immediate, external changes to the world around him. Jesus's mission was "to proclaim good news to the poor," "to proclaim freedom for the prisoners and recovery of sight for the blind," and "to set the oppressed free" (Luke 4:18–19). Jesus "did not come to bring peace, but a sword" (Matt. 10:34). In short, Jesus did not seek to achieve the end of personal suffering through detachment. He taught the end of neighborly suffering by transforming our right-here and right-now into the kingdom of God, where neighbors care for and love neighbors.

Another important distinction is that when Asita encounters the Buddha, he claims that the Buddha will become an important world teacher. A necessary implication of this claim is that the Buddha is not *currently* one. We see this confirmed when Asita mourns that he will not live to see the day that the Buddha becomes such a grand teacher. In comparison, Simeon declares that Jesus *already* is salvation for humanity. This is an important difference between the Buddha as a child and Jesus as God-Child: whatever significance and meaning the Buddha has, he does not have that until he has grown up and become an adult who can teach his important and powerful teachings. Jesus, on the other hand, has whatever significance and meaning he has *as a child*.[24] That is, what Jesus means and represents to humanity is something he can mean and represent even while an eight-day-old infant. These two religious teachers also have very different *praxis* (ways of acting out their beliefs): the Buddha abandons his own child to seek liberation, whereas Jesus says liberation comes through welcoming children.

Muhammad as Child

Muhammad, who is repeatedly called "the first of those who bow to God in Islam" in the Qur'an, straddles the line between humanity and divinity.[25] While neither God nor the incarnation of God, he is heralded as the founder of Islam, and his birth and childhood reflect this. They are marked by omens and miracles, indicating that Muhammad is no ordinary human. He is supernaturally anointed. He is also the ideal form of humanity. Middle Eastern scholar Lesley Hazleton writes, "For Muslims worldwide, Muhammad is the ideal man, *the* prophet, the messenger of God, and though he is told again and again in the Quran to say 'I am just one of you'—just a man—reverence and love cannot resist the desire to clothe him, as it were, in gold and silver."[26]

Muhammad was born around AD 570 in the city of Mecca. He was born to Abdullah and Amina. Muhammad's grandfather, Abd al-Muttalib, was the leader of the Quraysh tribe. He was well-known as the person who rebuilt the Zamzam well, which is rumored to be the well discovered by Hagar after the birth of Ishmael (Gen. 16:7–14).

Muhammad's birth was surrounded by portents. A specter of white light graced Abdullah's forehead on the night he and Amina conceived Muhammad. During Amina's pregnancy, her belly often similarly glowed. Despite these portents, Muhammad almost did not exist. Shortly before the conception of Muhammad, in a story that recalls Abraham's sacrifice of Isaac, Abd al-Muttalib had made a vow that he would sacrifice a son of his in order to prove his right to own the Zamzam well. As the fates decided it, that son was to be Abd al-Muttalib's favorite and youngest son, Abdullah. Abdullah's brothers intervened and saved his life, convincing Abd al-Muttalib to sacrifice one hundred camels as a substitute sacrifice for Abdullah. Hours later, in celebration, Abd al-Muttalib married Abdullah to Amina.

Unfortunately, Abdullah died mere days later during a trade caravan, leaving Amina a widow and Muhammad a fatherless child even while still in the womb. In sixth-century Mecca, having no father equaled devastating circumstances. Mecca was a heavily patriarchal society, unkind to widows like Amina and fatherless children like Muhammad. Unable to care for Muhammad, Amina gave her son to a foster mother, Halima. Amina had no real choice. She was a widow with no money, so she had to entrust her son to Halima. Halima raised Muhammad with her people, the Bedouin people. The Meccans referred to the Bedouin people as *arabiya*, or Arab. They considered the Bedouins to be lowlives or common people. Meccans saw them "as unsophisticated rubes, mere goat and camel herders good enough for child care and as caravan guides, but not much more" (27). Halima's foster parenting did not go unrewarded. Muhammad's five years of childhood with Halima were flush with miracles. When Halima returns with Muhammad to her encampment in the high desert, her people's sheep and goats appear blessed, producing an abundance of milk. Her livestock is suddenly strong. The mere presence of Muhammad is reported to have wrought miracles.

After those five years, Halima returned Muhammad to Amina. Tragically, Amina died a few months later from an unknown illness. Then Muhammad's grandfather died two years after that. Triply orphaned at eight years of age, Muhammad was "shunted as a child to the margins of his own society" (8). He was an outsider for much of his life, working as a camel boy for Meccan trade caravans for the rest of his childhood.

It was not until he was middle-aged and living a comfortable life as married businessperson that Muhammad finally became the person we know today as the founder of Islam. When he was forty years old, Muhammad encountered the angel Gabriel on Mount Hira. During this encounter, Gabriel gave Muhammad his first revelation from God, or Allah, meaning the High One. Muslims refer to this moment as *laylat al-qadr*, which means the Night of Power. Unlike Jesus's official moment of anointing in his adulthood, with the Spirit of God peacefully descending like a dove from the heavens during his baptism (Mark 1:9–11), Muhammad's anointing was a terrifying moment. Muhammad believed he had become possessed by a *jinn*, an evil spirit. In fact, Muhammad's immediate impulse after the Night of Power was to contemplate suicide. It was not until three years later, in fact, that Muhammad began preaching his revelations publicly.

The stories of Muhammad and Jesus have several parallels. Both fully human, they experienced childhoods marked by supernatural events—but they themselves appeared like other children, relatively normal in being vulnerable and powerless. Both were considered insignificant, unknown, and powerless children.

At the same time, the stories of Muhammad and Jesus diverge sharply on numerous points. For example, Muhammad being born as a male child afforded him privilege. During Muhammad's time, female children were often subject to abandonment and exposure at birth: "If Muhammad had been born female, he might have been left out in the desert for the elements or predators to dispose of, or even quietly smothered at birth, since the focus on male heirs meant that female infanticide was as high in Mecca as in Constantinople, Athens, and Rome" (20). In contrast, Jesus being born as a male child put him at a disadvantage since King Herod's Massacre of the Innocents was directed toward male infants. What was a protective favor for Muhammad was a risk factor for Jesus.

Arguably the most importance difference between Muhammad and Jesus is that Muhammad did not claim to be on the same level as God, or Allah. A core part of Muhammad's message was that he is "just one of you" (7). Jesus, in contrast, does claim to be on the same level as God (John 10:30). Thus while Muhammad and Jesus both share the precariousness that is inherent to full humanity, Muhammad's experience of that precariousness is the experience of a normal human. Jesus's experience of that precariousness is the experience of God become human.

Jesus as Child

Unfortunately, we do not have many stories about Jesus's childhood in the Christian Gospels. Only Matthew and Luke mention anything about Jesus's birth. What they do mention inverts our expectations about God: Jesus the God-Child is born not to a royal family, not into a family of wealth, and not even in the luxury of a home; rather, Jesus is born into a poor, unknown family of no social status and in a stable. And from the moment of Jesus's birth, King Herod seeks to kill him, despite him being an infant with seemingly no supernatural power or mighty army.

Between Matthew and Luke, only Luke features a story of Jesus in his later childhood, when Jesus studied at the temple as a twelve-year-old. In Luke 2:41–52, we read the following:

> Every year Jesus' parents went to Jerusalem for the Festival of the Passover. When he was twelve years old, they went up to the festival, according to the custom. After the festival was over, while his parents were returning home, the boy Jesus stayed behind in Jerusalem, but they were unaware of it. Thinking he was in their company, they traveled on for a day. Then they began looking for him among their relatives and friends. When they did not find him, they went back to Jerusalem to look for him. After three days they found him in the temple courts, sitting among the teachers, listening to them and asking them questions. Everyone who heard him was amazed at his understanding and his answers. When his parents saw him, they were astonished. His mother said to him, "Son, why have you treated us like this? Your father and I have been anxiously searching for you." "Why were you searching for me?" he asked. "Didn't you know I had to be in my Father's house?" But they did not understand what he was saying to them. Then he went down to Nazareth with them and was obedient to them. But his mother treasured all these things in her heart. And Jesus grew in wisdom and stature, and in favor with God and man.

When I read this story about Jesus in the temple, I cannot help but feel that Jesus as a kid was a bit sassy. Jesus's parents are worried sick about some disaster or crime befalling Jesus, yet Jesus's first response when he sees them after being missing for three days is, "Geesh, parents, you should have known better!" That is not exactly the response that conservative Christian child-training experts would call respectful. In fact, Kristin Johnston Largen describes Jesus's response as *womanish*. Womanish is a word coined by Alice Walker in her book *In Search of Our Mothers' Gardens*. The word is an adjective used to describe African American girls who are engaged in "outrageous, audacious, courageous or *willful* behavior"[27]—which is the very sort of behavior many conservative Christian child-training experts believe is sinful. Such experts would say a child who behaves like Jesus behaved here needs to have his will broken.[28]

Largen writes, "[Womanish] seems a fitting descriptor of Jesus's behavior in this account. Although still a boy, he is confident enough to stay behind, all by himself, in the big city of Jerusalem; not only that, he has the courage and the confidence to debate with the rabbis as their equal."[29] It is remarkable indeed that Jesus has these abilities. This passage in Luke 2 hints that Jesus is not merely fully human; he also is fully God. So as he grows, as his brain and body develop, Jesus has an increasingly powerful grasp on spiritual matters. He also has the confidence to break away from his parents and strike out on his own, even though he is a child. It is clear that even though he later agrees to be obedient to his parents, he is making a *concession* to them—he is doing it to be nice, not because it is necessary.

Even more remarkable is the emphasis in this passage that Jesus "grew in wisdom." While this would be normal for the human side of Jesus, it is abnormal for the divine side. Jesus, while fully God, is described as still having to grow in wisdom. He is not born with full wisdom. Like any other child, he has to learn about the world. He has to learn right from wrong, how to self-regulate, and how to express himself using words and ideas. Largen says, "The statement that Jesus 'increased in wisdom' suggests that Jesus's infancy and boyhood are not simply God play-acting; they are not a diversion or a ruse used to disguise God's true nature until the right time. Instead, they reveal a God who is coming to know the world in a new way" (129).

The story of Jesus in the temple is fascinating. Apart from it and the two stories of Jesus's birth, we know next to nothing from the Christian Gospels about what it was like for him to be a child who was both fully human and fully God. There are apocryphal gospels, however. These are gospels that are not officially considered part of the Bible that contain stories of Jesus's early and later childhood. Two gospels in particular, the Infancy Gospel of James and the Infancy Gospel of Thomas, focus on such stories. While the Infancy Gospel of James mainly covers Mary's pregnancy with Jesus, the Infancy Gospel of Thomas features a plethora of stories about Jesus when he was between the ages of five and twelve. This gospel, written by Thomas the Israelite for the purpose of "mak[ing] known the extraordinary childhood deeds of our Lord Jesus Christ," is "one of the earliest pieces of Christian writing outside of the New Testament" (96, 94).

It is understandable that the Infancy Gospel of Thomas is not considered part of the official Christian canon because of how it portrays the child Jesus. In this gospel, "Far from being the 'obedient' son of Luke's Gospel, Jesus is defiant and haughty towards everyone with whom he comes in contact, including his parents" (94). Jesus repeatedly throws temper tantrums that result in numerous people being injured and killed (though he later heals and resurrects them all). At the same time, there are some provocative passages that hint at what it might have looked like for young Jesus to grow in wisdom and power. For example, in chapter 2 of the Infancy Gospel of Thomas, the following story is recounted:

> When this child Jesus was five years old, he was playing by the ford of a stream; and he gathered the flowing waters into pools and made them immediately pure. These things he ordered simply by speaking a word. He then made some soft mud and fashioned twelve sparrows from it. It was the Sabbath when he did this. A number of other children were also playing with him. But when a certain Jew saw what Jesus had done while playing on the Sabbath, he left right away and reported to his father, Joseph, "Look, your child at the stream has taken mud and formed twelve sparrows. He has profaned the Sabbath!" When Joseph came to the place and saw what had happened, he cried out to him, "Why are you doing what is forbidden on the Sabbath?" But Jesus clapped his hands and cried to the sparrows, "Be gone!" And the sparrows took flight and went off, chirping. When the Jews saw this they were amazed; and they went away and reported to their leaders what they had seen Jesus do.[30]

These stories, apocryphal though they may be, highlight that we cannot ignore the childhood of Jesus and questions about what his childhood looked like. These are rich and important areas of inquiry, and the answers we give to them have important ramifications for how we answer so many other questions about children and childhood in general.

Between the apocryphal stories about young Jesus and the few canonical examples we do have, I think it is fair to say that "both Joseph and Mary had their hands full as Jesus was growing up" (Largen 4). We do not have much evidence to weigh, but we do know that Jesus was fully human. This means that, as an infant and child, he nursed, he peed and pooped, he screamed, he spit up milk on Mary, and he did all the other things normal human babies and children do—"none of which are 'god-like' activities" (118). And all those things human children do during their challenging twos and threes? Yes, he did those things too, temper tantrums included! As the early church father Irenaeus wrote, "It was not enough simply that the Word should become a human being: it was necessary that he should pass through every age of life, from infancy to mature years."[31] This is, after all, part of the scandal of Christianity—we claim that God Almighty became a pooping baby. God embraced the normal stages of child development by becoming a human child.[32] God embodied and experienced each and every one of those stages.

In contrast to the divine or enlightened children we see in Hinduism, Buddhism, and Islam, therefore, the God-Child we see in the Christian Gospels takes a remarkable and rather unique incarnational form. Jesus the God-Child is not simply a human child, not simply a child deity, and certainly not born into power and privilege—but a *vulnerable, dependent, and fully human God-Child born into a violently anti-child world.* The significance of this cannot be overstated. God becoming a fully human person comes with its inherent risks—disease, the exigencies of mundane life, hunger, the inglorious normalcy of bodily functions, and so on. Moreover, God becoming a fully human child comes with an abundance of additional risks. God entered the world through a human womb; birth fatalities in the ancient Middle East ran high.[33] Luke's statement "And she gave birth" (2:7) indicates that God emerged through the grueling, exhausting process of a real, human birth.[34] Jesus entered life during a time when children were violently slaughtered by the government (Matt. 2:16). The God-Child grew as an infant in a place where "high infant and child mortality rates rocked the world of God's people, where only one in two children lived into adulthood."[35] Surviving childhood during biblical times "was a major feat."[36] The risks were great.

Furthermore, by becoming a child, God accepted the possibility of child abuse. We know from stories in the Tanakh that child abuse occurred in ancient society. The stories of Lot's daughters (Gen. 19:30–36), Dinah (Gen. 34:1–4), and Tamar (Gen. 38) indicate sexual abuse of children. The stories of Abel (Gen. 4:1–8), Joseph (Gen. 37:18–28), and Saul's campaign against the Amalekites (1 Sam. 15:3) indicate physical abuse of children. Indeed, in the Tanakh alone, there are almost two hundred texts about violence against children.[37]

This is the world into which the God of Christianity actively entered in the most vulnerable form: a defenseless, utterly dependent infant. The Gospel writers go out of their way to emphasize Jesus's vulnerability. Largen writes, "The dark specter of danger and peril hovers menacingly over the whole of his early life" (77). In the Gospel of Matthew, there are multiple stories indicating that Jesus almost did not live. Before his birth, Jesus and his mother Mary are nearly abandoned by Joseph. Intervention of an angel retains Joseph's involvement in the family. Only a few days after Jesus's birth Herod first tries to find Jesus in order to kill him specifically. A few days later, Herod decrees that all infant boys are to be slaughtered (still with the death of Jesus in mind). Once again, only the intervention of an angel saves Jesus. The angel returns to Joseph and instructs Joseph to take his family to Egypt to ensure the safety of Jesus. Then in the lone story we have of Jesus's adolescence in the Gospel of Luke, his parents accidentally abandon him for three days. All sorts of things could have gone wrong in that span of time!

Considered together, these stories demonstrate just how precarious existence can be for a marginalized young God-Child who is fully human. Unlike the Buddha, Jesus is not born into a powerful, ruling family who can defend him with royal armies. He is born into a poor family who has to resort to a borrowed manger for his birth. Unlike Krishna, young Jesus does not supernaturally wage war against human kings or shape-shifting demons. He must abide by the normal stages of child development. Unlike Muhammad, he lives human experiences fully as a god. And unlike the Kumaris, Jesus does not cast off his divinity when he scrapes his knee or enters puberty. Rather, his divine calling only intensifies as he grows—leading him ultimately to his crucifixion.

One can see that Jesus taking the form of a human child is not unique among world religions. Even so, the *form* and *significance* of Jesus's incarnational act are truly unique. In no other religion do we see God becoming a marginalized, fully human child who is also fully God. In no other religion do we see a god having to grow and learn according to the normal stages of child development. In no other religion do we see a god exposing themselves to the same potential risks other children face (infanticide, poverty, and child abuse). Additionally, in no other religion does the incarnation of God as a marginalized, fully human child *mean* so much to that religion. I would argue that the incarnation of Jesus is the most essential aspect of Christianity. For it is in the incarnation, decades before the crucifixion or resurrection, where we see clearly the salvation God has brought to us. Jesus is savior from the moment of his birth.[38]

By becoming a marginalized, fully human child, God ushered in a topsy-turvy kingdom where the last are first and the first are last and children are at the center of what it means to pursue God. I believe this is the core of Christology: we must center the fact that God became a child and we must lift up Jesus the God-Child as our path to God. In the next chapter we will examine at length what this understanding of Christology means for Christian theology, especially a child liberation theology.

INCLUDING CHILDREN

Growing up, I was always interested in other religions. I accepted Jesus into my heart as a young child, yet I was nonetheless fascinated by faiths not my own. Some of my favorite books were the D'Aulaires' books for children on Greek and Norse mythology. I loved the fantastical stories they contained. The images of gods and goddesses fighting and playing filled my imagination with wonder and inspiration.

But the conservative evangelical world I grew up in did not encourage me to pursue my interest in other religions. As I grew older, the only context in which I studied them was to learn how to attack them—allegedly for the sake of Jesus. When I attended summer worldview camps as a teenager, for example, I was taught flimsy, cardboard caricatures of Buddhism, Hinduism, and Islam. And even then, I was only taught those caricatures of other faiths in order to memorize catchphrases with which I could supposedly refute them.

Now that I am an adult, I have a greater appreciation for world religions. Part of my journey toward this appreciation was getting a master's in Eastern Classics at St. John's College, where I studied religions from China, India, and Japan. For the first time in my life, I appreciated freely religions other than my own. No one was telling me what was "wrong" with them. No one was interrupting my train of thought by insisting, "But Jesus!" I simply learned what other people and cultures think about the world.

I encourage you to give the children in your family, faith community, or religious organization the opportunity to learn about other religions. As I have argued throughout this chapter, learning about other religions is essential to teasing out both the very real differences and similarities between them. This pursuit helps us understand and embody our own faith that much more deeply.

For this chapter's "Including Children" exercise, I want you to obtain an age-appropriate book on world religions for the children in your family, faith community, or religious organization. This could be an overview of many different religions, such as *The Kids Book of World Religions* (Jennifer Glossop), *Comparative Religion: Investigate the World through Religious Tradition* (Carla Mooney), *Religion around the World: A Curious Kid's Guide to the World's Great Faiths* (Sonja Hagander, Matthew Maruggi, and Megan Borgert-Spaniol). Or it could be an age-appropriate book on one specific religion, such as *Celebrate: A Book of Jewish Holidays* (Judy Gross), *The Little Book of Hindu Deities* (Sanjay Patel), or *Ramadan* (Suhaib Hamid Ghazi).

Next, read the book to the children or allow them to take turns reading from it. If the book is long, choose one or two chapters to read, or focus on the information about one or two religions. As you read the book, ask the children to think about the following questions:

1. In what ways are Jesus and Christianity similar to the religion(s) you are learning about?
2. In what ways are Jesus and Christianity different from the religion(s) you are learning about?
3. How are children or childhood treated by Jesus and Christianity?
4. How are children or childhood treated by the religion(s) you are learning about?
5. According to Jesus and Christianity, how do we best love God and our neighbors?
6. According to the religion(s) you are learning about, how do we best love God and our neighbors?

After you have given the children time to listen to or read the book, give them time to answer the above questions. You can either do this as a group discussion or let the children think on their own and write down their answers. Either way, be sure to review their answers so everyone has a chance to hear everyone else's answers.

seven

Jesus as Child

GOD IS CHILD.

—Janet Pais[1]

Many religions feature gods who become incarnate as children. However, what that means for each respective religion is different. In the previous chapter we examined religions from around the world to better understand the imagery of God becoming a child and particularly, Jesus the God-Child. This chapter will focus on what the imagery of Jesus the God-Child means for Christianity. This chapter will thus focus on Christology. Christology is the study of both the nature and the person of Jesus as documented in the Christian Gospels. Child liberation theology offers a unique Christology because it places significant emphasis on the child aspect of Jesus. Child liberation theology puts the child aspect of Jesus in the front and center and interprets biblical passages in light of it.

For many of the ideas in this chapter I am greatly indebted to Janet Pais. In her 1991 book, *Suffer the Children: A Theology of Liberation by a Victim of Child Abuse*, Janet Pais articulates the first system of Christian child liberation theology. Much of her analysis involves responding to Alice Miller, a psychoanalyst famous in the late 1900s for her work on parental child abuse. Pais argues that Miller and others are wrong to think Christianity is inherently abusive toward children. Pais seizes on the image of "God the Child incarnate" as a centering point to illuminate messages of child liberation latent in the Bible (2). These messages lead her to believe that the Church today must "live out the theology of the Child" (146). Key to this is Pais's own Christology, which I will be explaining and expanding on here.

Identifying God as Child

What is the central identity that Jesus took upon himself? Surely it was his identity as the Son of God. That identity is what got him crucified by the Roman Empire. What exactly does "Son of God" mean? While many people have interpreted "Son" to mean a divinely chosen king of an earthly or heavenly kingdom, child liberation theology suggests we need to interpret the term literally: "Son" meaning the child and offspring of an adult. In becoming the God-Child, God decided to take on the full implications of childhood. By full implications, I mean not only the positive aspects of childhood but also the negative, including having needs, being at the mercy of adults, and feeling powerless.[2]

In addition to the negative aspects *inherent* to childhood, God also took on negative aspects *potential in* childhood, such as the possibility of child abuse. God took the risk of entering a world in which children were persecuted; and as the God-Child, Jesus ultimately suffered abuse at the hands of other humans during the crucifixion. God entered such a comprehensive experience of human childhood because being a child is central to who Jesus is.

Understanding Jesus as child should also inform our understanding of the relationship between Jesus and God. Because Jesus is the Child and God is the Parent, their relationship in terms of the Trinity is a parent-child relationship. When we see Jesus and God relate, we get a glimpse into the divine relationship between the God-Parent and the God-Child.[3]

An example for understanding the parent-child relationship of Jesus and God is how Jesus prays to God in the Garden of Gethsemane immediately prior to his trial and crucifixion. In Gethsemane, after expressing that his soul was "very sorrowful, even unto death" (Mark 14:34), Jesus addresses the God-Parent as "Abba" (Mark 14:36). "Abba" is the Aramaic word that Jesus uses in all of his prayers to address God, the first person of the Trinity. While translators usually translate "Abba" as "Father," this rendering "misses the significance of the fact that Jesus used an infant's 'babbling' sound, a 'childish cry'" (59). In other words, Jesus is not only addressing the God-Parent as his Parent; he is also establishing that he, the God-Child, relates to the God-Parent as an *infant* relates to its parent.

It is poignant that Jesus so intimately prays to God as "Abba" on the eve of his trial and crucifixion. Jesus's public declaration of being the God-Child landed him in trouble in the first place. In the Gospel of John, after Jesus justifies working on the Sabbath by saying, "My Father is always at his work to this very day, and I too am working," we are told that his identification as the Child of God is what enrages those in power: "For this reason they tried all the more to kill him; not only was he breaking the Sabbath, but he was even calling God his own Father, making himself equal with God" (John 5:16-18).

Jesus is not the only one who cries to the God-Parent as an infant cries, "Abba!" The apostle Paul twice claims that the Holy Spirit channels the God-Child in each and every Christian with the Spirit crying "Abba" to God and interceding for us (Rom. 8:15; Gal. 4:6). Christians relate to (or ought to relate to) the God-Parent in the same way that Jesus does—as children. Janet Pais writes, "To call on God as 'Dada,' as Jesus did, is to find . . . the young child in ourselves" (59).

Since God became Child in order to enter into relationship with us and into relationship with the God-Parent, this seems to suggest that the purpose or end of the incarnational act is relationship itself. Perhaps God did not become incarnate to cosmically erase sin or to use Jesus's death to guilt us. Perhaps, instead, God became incarnate so that they could experience the full significance of human-human relationships as well as give humans the experience of the divine-human relationship. Pais contends, "When God enters the human condition, walks again with us in the garden, the divine-human relationship is direct, revelatory and transforming" (60).

Note that the specific form of relationship the incarnation enabled was not the relationships seen in the Tanakh: relationships between human beings and a transcendent God. Instead, the incarnation enabled a new form of divine-human relationship by revealing Jesus specifically as *Child* and giving humans the opportunity to enter into relationship with that God-Child.

In this understanding of the incarnation, we move beyond the traditional understanding of God as Father, Dictator, Patriarch. We are enabled to see with new eyes. We are enabled to see God now as Child, Sibling,

Peer: "The Childhood of God, not the Fatherhood, is of primary importance for God's self-revelation to us" (85). Through the incarnation, the Child in the Trinity is lifted up as important; the Adult in the Trinity moves to the background. This runs counter to the patriarchy and adultism inherent in our times. Against expectations, God puts a child at the center of their gospel, their good news for humankind.

The incarnation makes salient a new form of divine-human relationship through Jesus the God-Child, yet it is important to realize that the Child person of the Trinity is still part of the Trinity. Jesus—as the Child of God—has always existed and will always exist, in the same way that God and the Holy Spirit have always existed and will always exist.[4]

All of this underscores the question: *Why* would God decide that Jesus would be "Child" and not "Father" or "Adult"? I can think of several answers to this question, the first two of which we have already examined. First, God chose to reveal Jesus as Child in order that God's nature as relational would be revealed. By distinguishing between God the Parent and God the Child and also God the Holy Spirit, God shows that relationship is an essential aspect of their nature.[5]

Second, God decided to reveal Jesus as Child because Jesus *is* Child. The child aspect of the second person of the Trinity is an inherent part of that person. One cannot separate that aspect from Jesus, because Jesus is God-Child. Thus the incarnation is not God creating a new aspect of themselves to reveal to humanity; instead, it is simply enabling humanity to be conscious of that aspect.

Third, God revealed Jesus as Child in order to provide a corrective to our tendency to view power and worth as equivalent to adulthood. When we think of God being all-powerful and worthy of our worship, we are usually thinking about God as Adult. We are projecting onto God our own adult biases regarding power and worth (i.e., adults are more powerful and thus more worthy). By revealing Jesus as God-Child, God makes clear that power and worth should be found in childhood and children as much as they are found in adulthood and adults.

Fourth, understanding Jesus as Child means that we see God not only as a Parent, but also a Peer and Sibling. Jesus is Sibling to children and adults alike.[6] One could argue this means that from a divine point of view, both children and adults are siblings, too, with reference to God.

Fifth, God becoming Child also means that the image of God is reflected as fully in a newborn human baby (with little to no capabilities with regard to discernment, language, maturity, or rationality) as that image is reflected in adults. In other words, the God-Child is a bold declaration that *all* human beings, regardless of age or ability (or any other factor), are imaged after God. One cannot partition the kingdom of God, therefore, based on such factors. One cannot exclude someone from the kingdom of God because that person has not reached what some call the "age of discernment."[7] One cannot exclude someone from the kingdom of God because that someone cannot use propositional thinking. *All* people are imaged after God and therefore *all* are welcome in God's kingdom.

Sixth, God becoming Child says something really important about how God thinks about power and how God relates to our world. God chose to identify their power with an image we humans would most identify with complete and total powerlessness: a newborn human baby. Compared to other babies in the animal kingdom, human babies are uniquely vulnerable. In a bluntly titled article for *Scientific American*, "Why Humans Give Birth to Helpless Babies," the author notes, "Human infants are especially helpless because their brains are comparatively underdeveloped." The article goes on to explain, "A human fetus would have to undergo a gestation period of 18 to 21 months instead of the usual nine to be born at a neurological and cognitive development stage comparable to that of a chimpanzee newborn."[8] Considering such vulnerability, it is strange and unexpected that God chose *this* vessel to bear their spirit during the moment of incarnation.

God choosing to identify divine power and position with a newborn human baby is more than strange and unexpected, however. It is also radical. It is actively subversive and overwhelmingly destabilizing to the way we humans think about power and position. It is part and parcel with the topsy-turvy nature of the kingdom of God, where the last become first and the first become last: the powerful are rendered powerless when a powerless infant is invested with the very power of God Almighty. We also see this in Jesus's life, where Jesus consistently valued the weak, poor, and excluded over the strong, rich, and included.

God as Child is not mere sentimentality. It is not some cute story to bring out every Christmas and then return to a cardboard box we store in our garage the rest of the year. It is a radical statement about what God values and whom God lifts up. It is the very heart of the kingdom of God, the very meaning of the salvation Jesus brings.

Seventh and finally, God decided to reveal Jesus as Child in order to subvert our understanding of God's anger. When Christians read stories from the Tanakh that describe God's righteous anger toward human abuse and oppression, we often think that God is showing the anger of a parent toward their children. However, because of the God-Child we can view God's anger in a different way.

There is continuity from the anger of God in the Tanakh and the anger of Jesus in the Christian Gospels. Just as God grows angry in the Tanakh toward human abuse and oppression, so too does Jesus condemn political and religious injustices and shout "Brood of vipers!" in condemnation of those abusing their power. As the anger of Jesus—the God-Child— parallels the anger of the God-Parent in the Tanakh, God's anger could (and should) be seen as the righteous anger of a child. Janet Pais writes, "Many adults misunderstand God's anger as being like fathers' anger at their children" (74). This is a problem because when adults believe that God's anger toward human abuse and oppression justifies their own anger toward their children's misbehavior, it can lead to child abuse. This false sense of justification can cause adults to "believe that God's anger is a model for human parents. Having projected their misunderstood and displaced anger onto 'God,' many parents, often unconsciously, claim what they have projected as justification for behaving like wrathful gods toward their children" (74).

But God's anger cannot be reduced to or compared to parental anger. God's anger also includes the anger of children. God is Child, too! And as a Triune God who rages against human abuse and oppression, God rages most against those who have the power to abuse and oppress. This would imply that God identifies more with the powerless children than with the powerful adults, which is in line with what the Jewish prophets and Christian liberation theologians teach us. We find God on the underside of history, where the powerless and the oppressed are. So too we find God with the children. Thus, we too must reject the image of God as being on the side of the powerful. God is not an angry patriarch. "The wrathful 'Father' model is an idol" (74).

Identifying the God-Child as Judge

We must not be content with merely subverting our view of God's anger and suggesting through Christology that we should view the anger of God as the anger of the God-Child. We must go a step further, seeing how it is God as Child—and not God as Parent—who will judge humanity at the end of times. After all, it is Jesus, the Divine Infant, who cries "Abba," who will "bring a sword" (Matt. 10:34). It is Jesus who "comes in his glory" and "will sit on his glorious throne," separating "the people one from another as a shepherd separates the sheep from the goats" (25:31–32).

In one of her most provocative critiques of Alice Miller, Janet Pais asserts that while Miller rightly says the Bible lacks a commandment saying, "Honor your children," Jesus himself as the God-Child subverts the commandment we do have to honor our parents (Exod. 20:12). Pais illuminates, "In John's Gospel, Jesus *does* say, 'He who does not honor the Son does not honor the Father who sent him' (Jn 5:23)" (107, emphasis added).

Jesus inspires this moment of revelation for child liberation in the Gospel of John: "The Father judges no one, but has entrusted all judgment to the Son, that all may honor the Son just as they honor the Father. *Whoever does not honor the Son does not honor the Father, who sent him*" (John 5:22–23, emphasis added). By saying this, Jesus subverts the patriarchy inherent in his social context. Jesus makes clear that if you do not honor the God-Child, you do not honor the God-Parent. This honor extends to all human children, considering Jesus's declaration in the Gospel of Mark, "Whoever does God's will is my brother and sister and mother" (3:35). If you do not honor human children, you do not honor God.

We see, therefore, how Jesus subverts a commandment commonly used to justify parental power and sometimes child abuse and transforms it into a divine warning *against* that power and abuse. Those who tower over children or abuse them are not honoring children and are therefore dishonoring God. By trying to shape children into their own desired image rather than allowing them to blossom into the image of God they already are, such parents are playing God, which is the height of sacrilege.

There is an additional level of meaning available from the aforementioned passage from the Gospel of John: "The Father judges no one, but has entrusted all judgment to the Son" (John 5:22). One can interpret this to mean that during the end times, it is not God the Parent who will judge humanity but instead God the Child. Judgment will be from the viewpoint of the God-Child. A *child*, the God-Child who became human and experienced all the wrongs, abuses, and oppressions inherent to human childhood, will scrutinize our adult sins and our adult abuses. As Pais concludes, "The Child will return to judge us all" (108).

Christology and Liberation Theology

What is the significance of a child-centric Christology for the American church today? How does Christology relate to our current task of developing a child liberation theology? The assertion that God is Child is important for establishing a connection between Christology and child liberation theology. For just as the image of the God-Child is central to Christology, so too is that image central to child liberation theology. The former extends naturally into the latter.

Christology is a key part of liberation theology. The image of Christ on the cross is an image of God being present with human suffering. Liberation theology seeks to find a contemporary event or symbol onto which one can overlay this image of Christ on the cross. Thus finding a contemporary image of suffering enables the liberation theologian to extract meaning from comparing the two images.

An example here will be helpful. Black liberation theologian James H. Cone identifies the suffering of Jesus on the cross with the suffering of the Black person hung on a lynching tree. For Cone, the lynching tree is a powerful representation of the suffering Jesus today. It is a contemporary image that can make poignant and applicable the *content* of the historical image of the suffering Jesus and how God is present with and a witness to that suffering. The contemporary image of the lynching tree can—and ought to—jar white Christians and awaken them to the immediacy of the image of Jesus and his suffering as exemplified by the murdered Black person. In turn, Cone believes, the historical image of Jesus and his suffering can bring hope to Black people when they see that "God [is] with them, even in suffering on lynching trees just as God was present with Jesus in suffering on the cross."[9]

Janet Pais identifies a contemporary image of God as suffering in abused children today. As Black liberation theology sees God through the suffering of Black people, or womanist theology sees God through the suffering of women of color, or LGBTQIA liberation theology sees God through the suffering of queer people, Pais's child liberation theology asks us to see God through the suffering of children. This is the context for Pais's all-caps declaration that "GOD IS CHILD." Pais writes, "Just as in biblical times, the power of God will move with those who are disadvantaged and cry out for God's help in their struggles for liberation in the world today. Each group has a unique way, or set of ways, of expressing the movement of God's power on its behalf. For example, a black theologian may assert that God is black; a feminist theologian may assert that God is woman. Following their example, this theology for the liberation of children asserts: GOD IS CHILD" (15).

Like Pais, I am a survivor of child abuse. Also like Pais, I consider the image of an abused child to be a powerful and symbolic representation of the suffering Jesus today. An abused child reminds us of the horrors at work in our anti-child world and just how desperately we need to create a better world. Child abuse is a visceral representation of why we need a gospel in its purest sense in the first place—*good news*. We need good news both for today's abused children and yesterday's abused-children-turned-adults. Where is the hope for those of us who suffer from the consequences of adult sin committed against children?

There is indeed hope. Jesus has shown us the way by becoming a human child, lifting up children during his years of adult ministry, and transforming how we should think about and act toward children. The image of the abused child is thus not only a reminder of the world's evil; it is a reminder that because of the God-Child who shares in our suffering, we can create a better world, a more loving tomorrow. If we dedicate ourselves to the message of child liberation, if we commit to better loving and protecting children, we can make hope for abused children not just something for the distant eternal future, but a vibrant reality in the present.

INCLUDING CHILDREN

A brief note to families: this chapter's "Including Children" focuses on child protection policies for faith communities and religious organizations. While families themselves do not need child protection policies, families do need the principle underlying those policies: a commitment from you and everyone around you to making children feel comfortable and safe. Such a commitment is absolutely something you can and should participate in as a family. If you are a family reading this, your exercise will be as follows: Gather together all the children and adults in your family and create a document as a group. The document should begin with the following: "In this family, we do the following things to keep each other comfortable and safe . . ." Then, as a group, list as many things as you can think of. This could include, for example, stopping tickling when someone says, "Please stop," not hitting someone when you are angry, giving each other privacy when privacy is requested, knocking before opening a door, and so forth. After you have finished your list, review it together and commit as a family to honor the boundaries and guidelines established in your document. Post it in a place where everyone can see it daily.

For groups other than families: If the gospel of Jesus is to be good news for children today, then the places where the gospel is shared must be safe for children. If children are not safe or do not feel safe in their faith communities and religious organizations, no amount of preaching will be good enough news to erase the reality of abuse invading a child's life. Your faith community or religious organization needs a robust child protection policy. Hopefully this book inspires you to embark on a journey to equip and empower children to become more involved in their larger communities. If so, it is vital to have safeguards in place that will ensure those children thrive from that involvement, rather than creating opportunities for an older child or adult predator to prey on them.

If your faith community or religious organization does not have a child protection policy already, please make establishing one a top priority. A child protection policy sets the tone for participants and establishes the foundation for everything that child liberation theology aims to accomplish. It provides a context and rationale for why we advocate for children, it offers a framework for understanding risky or dangerous situations for children, and it establishes the tools and procedures your faith community or organization will use and follow while advocating for and with children. The best resource I can recommend on creating a child protection policy is *The Child Safeguarding Policy Guide for Churches and Ministries* by Boz Tchividjian and Shira M. Berkovits.

If your faith community or religious organization already has a child protection policy, that is awesome. Consider this a prompt to review it for areas of improvement. Use the opportunity to solicit feedback from the very people the policy is meant to protect: children themselves. What do the children in your faith community or organization think about the child protection policy? Are they aware of its existence and what it says? Do you allow them to review it regularly and give feedback? If not, I want to encourage you to be intentional about creating time and space for children to not only understand, but also be able to claim some ownership over, the policy that directly affects them.

If you already have a child protection policy, plan a time when both adults and children from your faith community or organization can gather to listen to children's thoughts about the policy and ideas they have for improving it. To facilitate this, distribute the policy to everyone several weeks in advance. Ask the children to think about three questions while they read and review the policy:

1. What parts of the policy do you have questions about?
2. What parts make you feel safest?
3. What are other things your faith community or organization can do to make you feel even safer?

Older children should read the policy themselves. Help younger children understand the policy by providing a paraphrased version and explaining the more difficult concepts in age-appropriate ways.

On the planned day and time, have your faith community leader, pastor, or religious organization's director first give an overview of your child protection policy to those in attendance. Next, explain why it is important to your faith community or organization to have the policy. Explain to the children that, since this policy is about protecting *them*, you want them to know about it and buy into it and its importance, too. Tell the children you are ready to hear their answers to the first question (i.e., what questions they have). Then answer any questions brought forward by the children about the policy. Once their questions have been answered, allow the children to answer the second two questions: What parts make the children feel safest? And what are things your faith community or religious organization can do to make children feel even safer?

Finally, make this review and discussion of your child protection policy an annual event for your entire community. Pick a day and time during the year that makes sense—perhaps right before all the summer activities and camps begin or right before children go back to school in the autumn—and set aside time to repeat this activity. Child protection policies are not meant to be passive documents; they are principles, guidelines, and best practices that everyone in the community needs to understand, endorse, and live out on a daily basis.

eight

Children as God-to-Us

God entrusted Godself to human adults
as a human child in the incarnation,
and in some sense God continues to entrust Godself to us in every human child
created in the image of God.

—Janet Pais[1]

Jesus is not simply God incarnate; Jesus is specifically the incarnation of the *child* aspect of God. It was not God the Parent or God the Spirit that became incarnate; it was God the *Child*. As we discussed in the previous chapter, this understanding of the God-Child should have a big impact on how we think about Jesus (what theologians call Christology, or the study of Jesus).

In this chapter, we will look at what theologians call *eschatology*. This is the study of the future, the study of how the kingdom of God breaks into our right-here and right-now and creates profound changes to our lives. In liberation theology, eschatology is the focus on how powers around us—our churches, our government, our economic order—need to be redeemed. They need to be redeemed because they are set up in a way that makes it harder for us to love our neighbors as ourselves. They need to be redeemed because they do not place the first last and the last first. Liberation theologians want us to think about how the kingdom of God should disrupt these powers around us. "Hope in the future seeks roots in the present."[2]

Child liberation theology raises the same issues, but with regard to children. Child liberation theology also engages eschatology by asking how we can better realize the kingdom of God in the right-here and right-now for children. The path to doing this involves taking Jesus seriously when he said in Mark 9:37, "Whoever welcomes one of these little children in my name welcomes me; and whoever welcomes me does not welcome me but the one who sent me." What I am going to argue might seem too audacious or maybe even sacrilegious. Part of realizing the kingdom of God in the right-here and right-now is seeing children as *God-to-us*. Children are not simply representatives or servants or mouthpieces of God. They are, in a profound and real sense, God's chosen and royal substitutes. They serve as God-to-us in our right-here and right-now.

Now before you discard this book, let me tell you what I am *not* saying: I am not saying that children are gods. I am not saying that we should worship children. And I am not saying that children are substitutes for God in the sense that we no longer need God. What I am saying is that Jesus called us to see children as God-to-us in our right-here and right-now. They are the neighbors who we are supposed to love as ourselves. And just as the commandment to love our neighbors is rooted in the greatest commandment to love God (Matt. 22:36–40), loving children is similarly rooted in loving God. This makes loving children an act of worship.[3]

How We Should Not See Children

Because the idea of children being God-to-us is a bit difficult to explain, it will help to first look at several different ways that our world thinks about children mistakenly. These are specific ways that are *not* how God calls us to think about children. By a process of eliminating the ways we could think about children that would be unhelpful or even hurtful, we can more easily understand the helpful, healing way to think about children that I propose—and that Jesus asked us to embrace.

Vipers

I will start with an idea that is very common in the world in which I grew up. In the conservative Christian homeschooling world, there is a popular idea that children are little murderers-in-the-making, or *vipers*. A child is a "viper in a diaper"—that is a direct quotation from a well-known leader in evangelical homeschooling.[4] Many Christian homeschooling leaders and parents take a traditional theological idea—original sin—and pump it full of steroids. Instead of seeing children as human (imperfect and needing guidance), children are seen as the lowest of the low (evil and needing policing). Basic human needs (such as sleep and eating) are labeled sinful desires in children.[5] Children are devils, beasts—animals like dogs[6] or mules[7] that need to be corralled and beaten into submission.

This idea of children as deeply, inherently evil is usually used to justify and promote spanking children. Sadly, the Bible has become the most powerful source for the promotion of physical punishment.[8] There is a vast conservative Christian "child training" industry, including companies that sell spanking instruments ("Bible-approved rods") and books outlining the spiritual necessity of physical punishment.[9] Christian advocates of physical punishment encourage inflicting pain on children by a variety of means, including belts,[10] branches,[11] cold water,[12] dowel rods,[13] hands,[14] sitting on children,[15] and wooden paddles.[16] If children are not physically punished, the argument goes, they will grow up to become parents' worst nightmares—murderers, rapists, and so forth.[17] Even now those evil seeds exist; one homeschool leader has suggested that if newborn infants were larger, they would kill their parents.[18]

To justify this harsh, punitive approach to raising children, many people point to King Solomon's parenting advice in Proverbs 13:24: "Whoever spares the rod hates their children, but the one who loves their children is careful to discipline them." They point to King Solomon as an authority even though 1 Kings 12 shows us the fruits of Solomon's parenting were anything but enviable. Solomon's child Rehoboam grew up to imitate the exact same harsh, punitive style of his father in how he governed Israel. "My father made your yoke heavy," Rehoboam tells Israel, "I will make it even heavier. My father scourged you with whips; I will scourge you with scorpions" (1 Kings 12:14). Instead of seeing Solomon's advice as the wisdom about children and childhood, we should see it as a cautionary tale and look to Jesus for parenting wisdom instead.

Jesus did not view children as vipers. In fact, the only times Jesus referred to humans as vipers was in the context of abusive religious leaders

(Matt. 3:7; 12:34; and 23:33).[19] Instead, Jesus viewed children as people who deserve to be not only respected, but also prioritized. From placing a child in the center of his disciples' midst (Mark 9:33–37) to rebuking his disciples for keeping children away from him (Mark 10:13–15) to defending the loudness of the children running through the temple courts (Matt. 21:14–16), Jesus was constantly reminding the adults around him to think about children.

Jesus demanded more from adults than simply thinking *about* children. He called adults to think about children *differently*. While Jesus did not live in a time and place where children were considered vipers, he did live in a time and place where children were considered property akin to enslaved people. This context is important to understand the impact of Jesus's actions and words. When Jesus centers, prioritizes, or defends children to other adults, he is not merely suggesting that we care a bit more about children or put a bit more effort into our child advocacy. He is making a radical claim: whoever loves a child—loves this lowly piece of property with no legal standing—is loving someone who bears the very image of God Almighty.[20]

That is a far cry from portraying children as vipers.

Subordinates

Another way adults think about children in our world is as *subordinates*, and this is especially true in evangelical homeschooling. Children are viewed as links in a chain of authority, and they are at the very, very bottom of that chain. They have no claim to authority and they have no right to challenge the authority that bears down on them. The father reigns supreme in the family, godlike.[21]

An image that is popularly used is that of an "umbrella of authority"[22] or an "umbrella of protection."[23] In this idea, there are levels of command starting from God and extending to the husband, then to the wife, and finally to the children. Each authority above the children holds an umbrella. When children step outside from under one of those umbrellas, they are "rained on," meaning that Satan and evil forces can attack them.[24] Adults warn that all sorts of unpleasant things can happen to children who step outside from under the God-appointed umbrellas, including child molestation.[25] This is a particularly damaging idea for survivors of child abuse, because survivors are partially blamed for their own abuse.[26] "Well, if they hadn't stepped outside of that umbrella of protection . . ." becomes a phrase spoken against abused children. One of the many problems here is the mistaken idea that children who obey God and their parents and remain under the umbrellas would never be abused.

But advocates of this children-as-subordinates belief system do think that children who obey God and their parents have some magical protection against the bad things in life. They also think that, even if some children who remain under umbrellas are abused, it is better to be abused than to go against what God has commanded. In the minds of authoritarian parents, God *has* commanded children to respond to adults with unquestioning and immediate obedience.[27] Anything less than that is sin. Voddie Baucham, a popular conservative Christian speaker on parenting, has said, "If I tell [my children] to do something and they don't do it when I tell them to do it? That's delayed obedience and the technical Greek word for delayed obedience is disobedience. . . . And according to Scripture, I cannot tolerate that. If I tolerate that, I'm tolerating sin."[28]

To avoid such sin, parents aim to have "a controlled child,"[29] even a silent child. Some parents believe they have succeeded only when their children sit still and say nothing during church.[30] If this sounds to modern ears like bullying, it is. Some parents embrace the idea of being a bully to their children because they think it will make their children better people: "Meeting a bigger bully cures most little bullies."[31] This is a far cry from how Jesus responded to children. Jesus loved when the children ran through the temple court, singing and making a scene in Matthew 21. Jesus embraced the rowdiness of children. He embraced their loud noises in sacred spaces, and he rebuked the adults for becoming angry at the children by saying, "Have you never read, 'From the lips of children and infants you, Lord, have called forth your praise?'" (Matt. 21:16).

One particularly damaging part of seeing children as subordinates is that an authoritarian structure engenders the belief that children do not have direct access to God.[32] Rather, children can only access God through their parents.[33] The parents are God's representatives to their children.[34] But "serving God does not make one God."[35] And the Bible never says parents are God's representatives to children. Jesus *does* say that when we welcome children, we welcome God. Thus, there is a sense in which *children* are God's representatives (though I will later discuss why this imagery is insufficient). This understanding is quite the opposite of the message given by those who see children as subordinates.

Tools

Children can also be seen as *tools*: instruments for their parents to employ to accomplish their own adult goals. Parents from all political and religious leanings can take this approach. I have seen both conservative and progressive parents force their children to be the faces of various ideological battles.

In evangelical homeschooling, this idea of children as tools is most observable in those who believe in *dominionism*. Dominionism is a worldview in which the United States is seen as God's chosen nation—much like Christian nationalism argues. American Christians are supposed to "take back" the United States for God's glory.[36] For example, George Grant, the former executive director of Coral Ridge Ministries, wrote, "Christians have an obligation, a mandate, a commission, a holy responsibility to reclaim the land for Jesus Christ. . . . It is dominion we are after. World conquest. That's what Christ has commissioned us to accomplish."[37] Elsewhere, Grant writes, "The army of God is to conquer the earth, to subdue it, to rule over it, to exercise dominion. Christians are called to war."[38]

While "world conquest" and "called to war" sound militaristic, dominionists usually mean them on a spiritual level, and the "army of God" refers to one's children. Parents are to train up their children to be God's *cultural* warriors, warriors who can infiltrate all areas of social and governmental power for the sake of Jesus. These children—many of whom were born in the 1980s, 1990s, and 2000s, but some in the 2010s as well—are often described by their parents as the Joshua Generation: those to whom the Promised Land of the United States will eventually belong after being trained by the Moses Generation (the parents). Homeschooling advocate Michael Farris writes that "the homeschooling movement will succeed when our children, the Joshua Generation, engage wholeheartedly in the battle to take the land."[39]

The problem with this worldview is that children are reduced to tools instead of being lifted up as image bearers of God. This worldview values children for *what they do* instead of *who they are*. This worldview encourages parents to make their children carbon copies of themselves instead of allowing children to chart their own paths.[40] It also places a huge amount of pressure and responsibility on children's shoulders. If children have been told their lives need to have a national impact but they do not grow up and become the president of the United States or some other public figure, they can feel like failures. There is intense pressure for children to strive to be exceptional, even though who they are is already beautiful and good. Jesus said to welcome the children, not to change them or shape them into tools for adults' culture wars.

Blessings

Another questionable way to think about children is as *blessings*. I know what you are thinking already: blessings are good things! The Bible directly states that children are blessings in Psalm 127:3–5a: "Children are a heritage from the Lord, offspring a reward from him. Like arrows in the hands of a warrior are children born in one's youth. Blessed is the man whose quiver is full of them." Yes, I know, but here is a tricky thing with blessings: you want as many as possible, so you end up with a blessings competition where the people with fewer blessings feel inferior and the people with more blessings feel superior. When the number of children you have supposedly reflects your level of blessedness, you are operating with a truly unhealthy approach to families.

I have witnessed this destructive belief firsthand in the Christian home-schooling movement. There is a line of thought based on Psalm 127:3–5 that is called Quiverfull because the psalm describes the man who "fills his quiver" as being very blessed. In this literal application of the verse, children are explicitly identified as blessings. But Quiverfull proponents are not content with mere identification. They exhort parents to have as many "blessings" (in other words, children) as possible. If parents do not embrace the pursuit of a large family size, they are judged as having less faith than other parents.[41] Some Quiverfull movement leaders even suggest that such parents are directly sinning against God.[42]

This is an example of how different sins intersect: when you sin against children by thinking of them primarily as blessings to collect, you sin against women by forcing them to feel they are most valuable as babymaking machines. You encourage women to think, "My body is *not* my own."[43] You also communicate to infertile women that something is wrong with them—or even worse, that their infertility is a divine curse.[44]

Property

Another unhelpful way of thinking about children is as *property* or belongings. This is one of the oldest ways of seeing children. It dates back to the Roman Empire, where the idea that the father is the supreme ruler of the family was popular. This concept of *patria potestas* "embraced the broad range of the father's commanding authority over children and slaves, estates and retainers. With respect specifically to children, this power additionally embraced the 'right and power of life and death.'"[45] *Patria potestas* was prevalent during Jesus's time and remains a popular idea today.

Adults who see children as property now include those in today's "parental rights" movement.[46] Parental rights advocates believe that children belong to their parents, not themselves or their broader community.[47] They want parents to have supreme power over children because they do not want the government interfering with how parents decide to raise and educate their children.[48] In other words, parental rights advocates are not content with simply affirming the rights of parents as one set of rights—a set alongside the rights of the government to protect children and the constitutional rights of their children to life, liberty, and the pursuit of happiness. Parental rights advocates want to deny children their own rights.[49] They do not believe children should have the right to receive medical help without parental approval; they do not believe children have the right to decide what they believe about God; they do not believe children have the right to offer input on their own education.[50]

This is not the message or example of Jesus. We see Jesus striking out as his own person with his own rights when he was a child. When Jesus leaves his family to pursue his own religious studies in the temple (Luke 2:41–52), we see that Jesus had a right to choose his own beliefs. While the household codes in the Christian epistles clearly state that children are to respect their parents (Eph. 6:1–3, Col. 3:20), they are similarly clear that parents are to respect their children. Denying your children their own rights surely falls under the command to fathers to "not exasperate your children" (Eph. 6:4) and "not embitter your children" (Col. 3:21). When children are not allowed to individuate (develop their own identity or sense of self) from the adults in their lives, great psychological and relational damage can occur.[51] In fact, research demonstrates that children who have a strong sense of self have better relationships with their families than children who feel controlled.[52]

Consumers

People in the United States are obsessed with money. Capitalism is a primary value, and that is a me-first economic system.[53] The "me" is always adults. Those who are prioritized least are children, which is already a sign of social structures contrary to what Jesus wants. In the United States, children are seen as *consumers*—economic means and opportunities. Children become the targets of mass media and marketing experts with the express purpose of using children to motivate their parents to spend money and become the next generation of adult consumers.

In her book *Welcoming Children: A Practical Theology of Childhood*, practical theologian Joyce Ann Mercer argues that the United States is built around consumerism, which she defines as "a way of life structured by and around various practices of consumption and accumulation."[54] One result of consumerism is that children are primarily viewed and targeted as money-making opportunities: "For the most part in the U.S. context, children occupy a key place in the market, that of consumers" (79). In fact, Mercer refers to children as "consumers *par excellence*," because they are particularly vulnerable to the manipulative effects of marketers (84). Children today are one of the most profitable market niches; they spend $35.6 billion of their own money annually as well as both directly and indirectly influencing their parents to spend almost $500 billion annually (95–96).

The pursuit of children by advertisers and marketers is not limited to obvious lures such as toys and candy. Rather, every aspect of children's lives is becoming commercialized. Mercer points out, for example, "Public education is thoroughly enmeshed with these market interests as various corporations provide monetary and in-kind support that places their names and products (from soft drinks to computers) prominently in school settings around the nation" (89). Product placement is everywhere, even family mealtime: "Toys become characters in animated feature movies. Then toys also decorate cereal boxes and appear on playground equipment in public parks. Children's play spaces and breakfast tables are as infused by market forces as is their Saturday morning entertainment" (90). Even some church services on Sunday are not immune to this kind of influence due to many aspects of those services becoming increasingly commercialized, including the worship music![55] Everywhere children look, marketers are there, ready to urge them to consume more and more.

The end result of this is that children are encouraged to transform from being God-to-us and the beautiful, unique image bearers of God that they are into ever-needy consumers. Make no mistake: this kind of pressure and change impacts children's psyches. Between preschool and second grade, children start to "make inferences about people based on the products they use," and parents also begin to believe that, if they do not buy their children the latest products or toys, they will fail at parenting (96). Both parent and child thus "misrecognize the interests of market forces," confusing what the market wants them to consume with what they actually need to thrive (98–99).

In reality, children's worth is not dependent on what they own, what clothes they wear, or how much money they have. This is why Christianity declares that children's worth is immutable. Children are worthy of love no matter what! Children are worthy of not only love, but also everlasting life! Children are valuable because children are made in the image of God. God created each and every child with the utmost care, attention, and love: "For you created my inmost being; you knit me together in my mother's womb" (Ps. 139:13). This is the radical claim that Christianity makes in a consumerist world: children require *nothing* that the world offers in order to be valuable.

Addenda

Often we see children as *addenda* in our everyday lives or in relationship to our theologies—as one more thing to deal with in addition to the more important, adult stuff. This false belief can occur in all sorts of communities, regardless of how conservative or progressive. In fact, I am *most* struck by how low of a priority children are in liberal or progressive theologies. For example, while rightly calling our attention to poor people or Black people or LGBTQIA people, many liberation theologians neglect to place any emphasis on thinking about poor *children* or Black *children* or LGBTQIA *children* specifically.[56] If and when children are talked about, it is usually briefly or in passing. And children are still considered in the context of *adult* issues—for example, how the sin of white adults' racism against Black adults *also* impacts Black children. No additional thought is given to the unique challenges Black children *as children* face. In this way, children are seen as addenda to the "real" work of adult theology.

Innocents

Viewing children as *innocents* is a perspective I usually only see in progressive Christian circles. According to some progressive theologians, children are born as innocent, pure creatures.[57] This can mean one or both of two things: that children are born unaware of or unshaped by human imperfection, or that children are born unaffected by the human experience. Basically, children are born "whole" and with "unaltered human nature"[58]—and it is life, sin, or other humans that "break" their wholeness. Without such interventions, children would remain perfect, exactly who God intended them to be.[59]

The problem is children are *not* born "whole." No matter what environments they are born into, children still inherit experiences and traits from their parents. Obviously, this kind of inheritance is not equivalent to original sin, but it is sort of the scientific version of it. Science demonstrates that trauma, for example, can be passed on generationally. One study found that the grandchildren of Holocaust survivors have the same altered stress hormones as their grandparents who were actually in the Holocaust. These grandchildren are born more vulnerable to stress and even post-traumatic stress disorder (PTSD).[60] So some of those so-called broken aspects of adults are actually a part of children from the moment they exist.

This is because unborn children's environments—their parents, what their parents eat and drink, the support systems their parents have—can greatly impact children. For example, if an unborn child is in the womb of a person experiencing a lot of stress, that child feels the effects of the stress, too. That child can be born with a propensity toward anger issues, even if the child's later environment does not encourage the child to have a surplus of anger.[61]

Another problem with viewing children as innocents is that it causes adults to be overprotective of children. If we think children need to be shielded from every potentially negative aspect of life in order to preserve their innocence, they end up not knowing how to deal with reality. Over-protected children become ill-equipped to interact with the world on healthy terms. US poet laureate Billy Collins penned a darkly humorous poem about this entitled "The History Teacher." In the poem, Collins writes about a history teacher who tries to protect his students' innocence by telling them that various tragedies and injustices throughout history were actually benign. The discussion of the Spanish Inquisition, for example, becomes reduced to nothing more than "an outbreak of questions such as 'How far is it from here to Madrid?'" The result of keeping these children ignorant is bigotry and violence, as the history teacher's students "would leave his classroom for the playground to torment the weak and the smart, mussing up their hair and breaking their glasses."[62]

Depriving children of experiencing reality simply to preserve some idealistic adult notion about innocence or perfection is thus another way we treat children as less than adults.[63] We value romantic notions of what the "essence" of childhood is—some generalized idea of "openness" or "wonder"—and then we apply it to all children even though every child is unique. In this way we actually are *erasing* children, even though our intention was to better care for and respect them.[64]

When we argue that children are innocents, therefore, we are not simply idealizing children and not paying attention to the real children around us or their real issues. We are also overlooking each child's unique issues and struggles from the moment of birth. These struggles can very well be the same struggles adults have—stress, anger, deceitfulness, stubbornness, and so forth. Children are by no means innocent or angelic because children are every bit as real and human as adults are. As real humans, they are imperfect, they make mistakes, they can be selfish, and they become grumpy when they are hungry or tired. This does not mean children are vessels of wrath, but it does mean we cannot lose sight of their humanity and its messiness. Yes, "children promise delight, bewilderment, and enlightenment, certainly," writes feminist theologian Bonnie J. Miller-McLemore. At the same time, "undiscriminating assertions run the risk of romanticizing and idolizing children, stigmatizing those unable to bear or care for them, and overlooking the possibly harsh realities of child care and the many times in which children do not promote revelatory insight."[65] Humanity is messy; children are too.

Representatives of God

Another unhelpful and potentially damaging way we think about children is as *representatives of God*. This view argues that we should love and protect children because it is through interacting with children that adults fully access and experience God. God has appointed children to be a divine portal of sorts. Children are God's messengers, representing God to the adults in the right-here and right-now. Of all the views discussed so far, this one comes closest to the vision of child liberation theology. I think it is *far* healthier and more helpful than the other ways, but there are still some shortcomings. The view of children as representatives of God still dehumanizes children—even while appearing to lift them up.

I do not think we should view children as representatives of God for two reasons. First, we treat representatives differently from the people they represent. Think about US ambassadors who represent the president of the United States to other nations; we and the leaders of other nations know there is a difference between the ambassador and the president. We *do* treat them differently. We respect representatives less than those they represent. We are willing to "settle" for interaction with representatives. We do not become as excited, joyful, and honored by their presence. This is why we are not supposed to view children as God's representatives. Doing so limits our encounters with children and with God. We are supposed to accept children *as if they are Jesus, just like we would accept Jesus*.

Second, representatives are sometimes viewed as a means to an end and not ends in themselves. However, we are not supposed to love children because they bring us one step closer to God. We are supposed to love children *because they deserve love*. For our right-here and right-now, children are the destination, not the stepping stones to it. The kingdom of God has "come near" (Matt. 3:2, 4:17; Mark 1:15) and it not only prioritizes "the least of these" (Matt. 25:40, 45) but also "belongs" to "little children" (Matt. 19:14, Luke 18:16). Note that Jesus does not say children are just holding the kingdom temporarily until he returns. Jesus says the kingdom is upon us and it is theirs. Children deserve liberation because of who they are, not because of whom they represent.

How We Should See Children

Who are children and how should we see them, then? I believe that children are image bearers of God, or *God-to-us*. I draw this conclusion from Jesus when he says in Mark 9:37, "Whoever welcomes one of these little children in my name welcomes me; and whoever welcomes me does not welcome me but the one who sent me." We should see children as Jesus sees them: as substitutes for him in the right-here and right-now.[66] How we treat children is the barometer of how we would treat Jesus. Since Jesus is not with us in the flesh but children are, it is in relationship with children that we are in relationship with God.

Part of that relationship, as Jesus says, involves *accepting* children. Seeing children as God-to-us means that we see children as God made them—*the people they are*—and not the people we want them to be. It means that we see children as image bearers of God, not as vipers to dominate, subordinates to direct, tools to use, blessings to collect, property to own, consumers to reach, mere addenda to our theologies, innocents untouched by reality, or representatives to gain favor with God. No, children should be none of those things. They should be themselves and we should be content and overjoyed to be in their lives.

Ironically, this also means that we should not think about children as God-to-us—even though I am saying that we need to for the purposes of this chapter. When we think of children as God-to-us, it is too easy to start seeing them as representatives of God, and I have already explained why that is problematic. Seeing children as valuable for their utility means we miss their inherent value as people. In a sense, the God-to-us designation needs to fade into the background. We need to love children because they deserve love, not because loving children means we are loving God.

This is a really important distinction. Here is a similar example. When I love and respect my spouse, I do not do so because God said to. I do not do so because it will help me get into heaven. I do not do so because not doing so is a sin. I love my spouse because I really *do* love and respect my spouse. If I only love and respect my spouse because God says so, that is a cheapened version of love and respect. When love and respect become means to an end instead of the end in themselves, they become something else entirely. Love and respect are not generated from commands. They come from the heart, mind, soul, and will—all of who you are. All of who you are is what motivates us to see children as God-to-us.

Seeing anyone, including children, as God-to-us is a weird thing because it requires, in a sense, that we do *not* see a person as God-to-us. Instead, we see the person *as they are* and we embrace them unconditionally. By seeing them as they are and embracing them unconditionally, that is when they *are* God-to-us. But if we do that *for the purpose of making them God-to-us*, they no longer are. We would be *using* them to get to God instead of loving and respecting them as human beings. As comparative theologian Kristin Johnston Largen explains, "Salvation is fundamentally relational. It is always experienced in the larger context of one's relationships with family and friends, rather than in some exclusive, isolated connection between God and an individual."[67] In other words, we find and work out our salvation in relationship with other people, by seeing them and treating them as God-to-us.[68]

You can see how this works in Matthew 25:31–46, where Jesus talks about those who love and serve him without having an idea they are doing so. When we love and feed the poor and needy, Jesus says, we are responding to people as God-to-us, as image bearers of God. Jesus explains why this is in verse 45: "Truly I tell you, whatever you did for one of the least of these brothers and sisters of mine, you did for me." In selflessly, spontaneously loving and serving our neighbors (especially children) as we would ourselves, we are loving and serving Jesus.

We live in the right-here and right-now, and Jesus is no longer a human here. But there are humans all around us who are. The way we show our love for God must involve the people in the right-here and right-now. "Acknowledging God and loving God [is] expressed in loving neighbor."[69] We are not of this world, but we are fully in this world (see John 17:13–18).

We must embrace it with love and abandon. We must love the people in it. Children are not only included as people; they are also *prioritized* by Jesus for our right-here and right-now lives.

How do we see children as they are and embrace them unconditionally? I think a fruitful exercise is to imagine every child as the child Jesus.

Imagine Every Child as the God-Child Jesus

The entry point here is to think about how Mary and Joseph interacted with and treated Jesus as a child. Jesus was a fully human child. He experienced everything every other child experiences. He went through every stage of child development and his parents had to deal with each of those stages. The difference between Jesus and other children is that in addition to being fully human, Jesus is God and other children are not. But I would argue that difference in terms of childcare and child development is less significant than we might think. If we understand Jesus as God-Child and children as God-to-us, then we can see how Jesus and children reflect one another. Accordingly, I believe that how we parent and care for children should take into account how Mary and Joseph might have parented and cared for Jesus.[70]

Kristin Johnston Largen writes, "This relationship Jesus had with his parents was, at least in some ways, like most relationships between children and their parents: there are guidelines to be followed—'house rules,' if you will, certain freedoms that are first prohibited and then permitted as the child grows. Like any child, Jesus received a certain amount of nurturing, education, and discipline, all of which are necessary for any child to grow into a responsible, knowledgeable adult, one who is able to function in the world at large."[71] We know that Mary and Joseph *did* parent Jesus because all human children—which includes Jesus—require parenting in order to flourish. Sometimes we believe mistakenly that Jesus being God means Jesus did not need parenting. But I would argue that such a belief is flawed. If Mary and Joseph did not parent Jesus, that would be parental neglect, and neglect would have hurt Jesus. Neglectful parenting leads to "poor impulse control, social withdrawal, problems with coping and regulating emotions, low self-esteem, pathological behaviors such as tics, tantrums, stealing and self-punishment, poor intellectual functioning and low academic achievement."[72] Since Jesus was fully human, parental neglect of him could have yielded similar results.

As a fully human child, Jesus needed boundaries and rules and love and guidance. He needed to learn and grow and stumble and fall. He likely stubbed his toe and scraped his knee. He became hungry and cried. He threw tantrums and said no to his parents. He went through puberty. How do we know this? Because he was fully human.

Consider the topic of tantrums in light of Jesus's full humanity. I would argue that Jesus threw tantrums when he was a toddler. Tantrums are a normal part of child development.[73] I think most people who picture Jesus as the sinless God-Child are actually picturing Jesus as a child with perfect self-regulation. But a lack of self-regulation is not sin. *Every* child is born with a lack of self-regulation. *Every* child is born with a prefrontal cortex in need of development. Learning how to control one's actions, emotions, and thoughts is simply a part of growing up. If Jesus was born with perfect self-regulation, that would not mean Jesus was born sinless; that would mean Jesus was born *not fully human*. Since Jesus was fully human, he would have needed to throw tantrums and say no to his parents—*in order to develop as a child*. A lot of the behaviors that fundamentalist child training experts cast as sinful are behaviors Jesus likely exhibited simply because of his full humanity.

When we interact with children, we need to keep these truths in mind. When a child throws a tantrum, we should ask ourselves what Mary would do, knowing that her tantrum-throwing child is God Almighty. Do we think she punished Jesus harshly for demonstrating temporary emotional dysregulation? What then should *we* do, knowing that children are image bearers of that same God-Child? How do we respond to the tantrum lovingly and respect the child's reflection of the divine at the same time?

Child liberation theologian Janet Pais says,

> As a child I can say to those who would rear me: "Treat me as Mary and Joseph must have treated Jesus. Enter into relationship with me and be guided by the divine Father-Child relationship revealed in the gospel. Take care of my needs. Give me structures and limits that let me know you care. Protect me from harm. Love me. Hold me. Value

me. Let me know that I am your beloved daughter, that you are well pleased with me, and that you know I am worth listening to. Respect me and my feelings and my perceptions of reality. Do not have contempt for me. . . . Do not use or abuse me. Do not exercise power over me just to show me that you are the boss. Do not try to break my will or my spirit. . . . If you are in doubt about the way you are treating me in any situation, ask yourself if you would behave the same way toward the Child Jesus. Ask yourself if you would behave the same way if I were your age."[74]

Pais points the way to how we can begin to realize the eschatology of child liberation theology for our right-here and right-now—that is, how we can welcome a brighter future for the children around us into our present.

By seeing, valuing, and interacting with children as the image bearers of God that they are, we are entering into true fellowship with them. We are loving them for who they are—and in doing so, we are loving God, too. We are challenging and transforming systemic powers in our world that hurt and control children. We are saying a resounding no to people and powers who want to reduce children to vipers to dominate, subordinates to direct, tools to use, blessings to collect, property to own, consumers to reach, mere addenda to our theologies, innocents untouched by reality, or representatives to gain favor with God. Instead, children are God-to-us. Every child is a unique reflection of Jesus.[75]

Loving and embracing Jesus means loving children for who they are, not who or what we want them to be. As God's image bearers—God-to-us—children already have eternal and inherent worth.

INCLUDING CHILDREN

Appoint either an adult or an older child in your family, faith community, or religious organization to assemble a list of everywhere children are participants in your group. If you are a family, have the list-maker think about the activities your children are involved with and the places they go throughout the week: home, church, school, extracurricular activities (like band practice and Boy or Girl Scouts), therapy, the internet, and so on. If you are a faith community or religious organization, have the list-maker think about the activities and programs that you offer to children: Sunday school, mission trips, food pantry ministry, musicals, sport clubs, Bible quizzing, and so on. Encourage the list-maker to ask the other adults and children in your group to add any activities or other opportunities they may have missed during compilation.

Next, have the leaders in your group (parents if you are a family, elders or pastors if you are a faith community, or directors if you are a religious organization) plan a time to meet with all the children and discuss the items on the list together. Ask the children how each activity, place, and program makes them feel or treats them. To guide this discussion, use the following questions for each of the listed items:

1. How does this activity, place, or program treat you? Do they treat you with love and respect or something else?
2. How does this activity, place, or program make you feel? Happy? Sad? Bored? Tired? (It is okay if children express more than one emotion.)
3. If you could change any one thing about this activity, place, or program to help children feel more welcome, safe, and included, what would it be?

As you go through the list, appoint a scribe to record the children's answers. (This could be on paper or a computer screen, but it would be even better to use a whiteboard or projector so that everyone can see the answers as well as hear them.) If you would find it helpful, pay attention to where the children's answers line up with the categories outlined in this chapter (vipers, subordinates, tools, blessings, property, consumers, addenda, innocents, representatives of God, and God-to-us). Be sure to focus on listening and learning, even when the children have critical or negative things to say. Do not interrupt and do not try to justify or explain. Simply be present and open to hearing the children's feedback.

Once you have gone through the entire list and given all the children an opportunity to share their feelings and thoughts, review the answers given to the third question (If you could change any one thing about this activity, place, or program to help children feel more welcome, safe, and included, what would it be?). Ask the children to prioritize their desired changes. Finally, where feasible, commit as a family, faith community, or religious organization to implement at least two of these desired changes over the next couple of months.

nine

Children as Agents of Liberation

We will have an authentic theology
of liberation only when the oppressed
themselves can freely raise their voice and
express themselves directly and creatively
in society and in the heart of the People of
God, when they themselves "account for the
hope" which they bear, when they are the
protagonists of their own liberation.

—Gustavo Gutiérrez[1]

We cannot give liberation to children as if it were a gift. We cannot purchase it at a store or wrap it in paper and ribbons. Ada María Isasi-Díaz explains, "Liberation is not something one person can give another." Instead, it is "a process in which the oppressed are protagonists."[2] To be authentic, the people creating the theology should be the ones seeking liberation. A liberation theology for the poor, for example, will be inauthentic if it is dictated and controlled by the rich. A liberation theology for Black people will be inauthentic if it is dictated and controlled by white people. The whole point of liberation theology is to empower the marginalized to rise up and claim their voices, their destiny, and their God-given right to speak about God from their own unique perspective.

Liberation theology is a theology of *self-determination*, in other words.

Liberation theology is a word of welcome to the marginalized like Jesus welcomed the children, saying, "Let the little children come to me, and do not hinder them, for the kingdom of God belongs to such as these" (Mark 10:14). The kingdom of God is not just for the white person, for the male person, for the able-bodied person. The kingdom of God is for everyone, for every person of every age and gender and sexuality and race and ability and financial status.

The kingdom of God is the kingdom that liberation theology proclaims. It is a prophetic critique against the privileged and the oppressors, those whom—like the disciples around Jesus—want to keep away the children, the misfits, the pariahs. The whole point of liberation theology for the privileged and the oppressors, then, is to enlighten them: they have no monopoly on the right to speak about God. The right is universal. And no one—especially not the privileged and the oppressor—speaks about God from an objective, neutral point. Our fingerprints are all over our own ideas, yet it is the privileged and the oppressor who—accustomed to having and keeping to themselves the power to speak about God—most want to deny that.

If liberation theology needs to be developed from the ground up and needs to allow the marginalized to self-determine theology (and restore their right to do so), then child liberation theology will only be fully authentic when it is created by children themselves. If a liberation theology for the poor will be inauthentic if it is developed by the rich, then a liberation theology for children will similarly be inauthentic if it is controlled and dictated by adults.

This creates a problem for adults like me who believe in the importance and significance of establishing a child liberation theology. The very reason child liberation theology is so important, so significant, and especially necessary is because much of the American church today (and much of the church in the past) is held captive by the sins of adultism and childism. Many Christian faith communities have allowed ideological strongholds about the inadequacy of children to take root. There is no space in many faith communities for children to participate in theological work. In fact, many faith communities would think this is an outright impossibility, even a blasphemous proposal. Theology is for adults, not children. Children are meant to sit quietly and absorb what the adults teach; they are to say, "Yes, sir" and "As you wish." Children are not to stand up and speak out and proclaim their theology loudly and joyfully alongside their adult brethren.

If there is no space in our faith communities where children can participate in theological work, how can children create a theology that will liberate them? And if our faith communities do not acknowledge that children can be theologians, how will we ever get to the point where a space for children's own theological work exists in the first place?

This is the most significant challenge, then, with which we adults who believe in child liberation theology must wrestle. We must develop a child liberation theology such that children will be liberated to the point they can rise up and establish that theology themselves. As adults, we are inherently those in power in relation to children. Yet we must use our power not to increase our privilege and opportunities to oppress but rather to systematically redistribute that power and share it with children. This is a process that Ada María Isasi-Díaz speaks of in *Mujerista Theology*:

> In a liberative use of power a dominant agent exercises power over a subordinate agent for the latter's benefit. However, the dominant agent's aim is not simply to act for the benefit of the subordinate agent; rather the dominant agent attempts to exercise his power in such a way that the subordinate agent learns certain skills that undercut the power differential between her and the dominant agent. The liberative use of power is a use of power that seeks to bring about its own obsolescence by means of the empowerment of the subordinate. . . . In a liberative use of power, the learning of skills by the subordinate agent is a matter of taking power, of becoming self-defining and self-actualizing. It is precisely because of this that the power of the dominant agent becomes obsolescent, non-operative.[3]

One can say the same about the parenting journey in relationship to child liberation theology. Parents interested in liberating their children from adultist and childist forces in this world should be using the power they have over their children for the purpose of *empowerment*, not *domination*.[4] Parents should be working to redistribute the power differences that exist between themselves and their children. As feminist theologian

Bonnie J. Miller-McLemore writes, "Children need . . . a gradual transfer of power that involves receiving responsibility for progressively greater choices within a range appropriate to their age and situation. . . . People . . . mistake shaping children into socially acceptable adults as the chief task of parenting. Instead, at the center should stand the gradual transfer of appropriate responsibility."[5] As their children grow, parents should aim to make their power over their children obsolete, moving toward a relationship of *guided partnership* where they walk arm in arm as spiritual siblings toward God.

This is the model for child liberation theology to follow in its preliminary stages. In these preliminary stages, adults must never lose sight of the end goal: to equip children to develop this theology on their own. As such, it is inherently a theology of *praxis* (action): every ideological nook and cranny should be practical, should be aimed toward liberating children in the right-here and right-now, and should be aimed toward liberating children so they can seize their God-given right to speak about God from their own unique perspective. Only then will child liberation theology flourish. And only then will the work of child liberation theology have truly begun.

Child liberation theology has much to say to and teach us adults. It exhorts us to recognize and counter childism and adultism. It challenges adults to treat children better and also think about children in a very different way. It can illuminate the importance of doing inner-child work— the work of adults getting in touch with their own childhoods and healing their own wounds from those days.[6] Ultimately, though, child liberation theology belongs to children. And it belongs to children not because we give it to them, but because—like the kingdom of God—it is theirs in the first place. As adults, our job is to deconstruct the many obstacles we have already set up to keep children away from their holy tasks.

INCLUDING CHILDREN

By reading this book, you are already taking the first step necessary for child liberation theology to occur: being interested in how you can empower the children in your family, faith community, or religious organization. Now it is time to take the next step: actually empowering children.

One of the best ways to accomplish this is to increase child involvement in your family, faith community, or religious organization. The website youth.gov has an excellent self-assessment tool that the leaders of your group (parents, elders and pastors, and directors) can take to ascertain how involved children are currently. You can take that assessment and find additional suggestions for improving child involvement here: https://tinyurl.com/2wezt7zu.

After taking the self-assessment, consider the following ten ways you can empower children right now to become more involved. Pick three of them and start implementing them as soon as you can in your family, faith community, or religious organization.

1. Start asking children about their feelings and thoughts about decisions your group needs to make. You do not need to start off big. Start with small decisions ("Where should we eat tonight?" "What songs should we sing next week at church?") and work your way up to more important matters gradually ("Do you want to be homeschooled or go to public school?" "What topics would you like to hear preached on during the church service?"). Include children in the decision-making processes of your group, beginning with letting children express their opinions and moving all the way up to letting them make decisions themselves.

2. Create a library of resources for children to learn more about getting involved in their surrounding communities. This could include everything from picture books for young children, like Cindy Wang Brandt's *You Are Revolutionary* and Keilly Swift's *How to Make a Better World*, to how-to books for teenage activists, like Amnesty International's *Know Your Rights and Claim Them* and Jamie Margolin's *Youth to Power*.

3. Start an intergenerational book club that focuses on the agency and power of children throughout history. Read general books, like Penguin Random House's *Kid Legends* series, which includes books like *Kid Activists* and *Kid Trailblazers*. Or pick a specific moment in the history of children's advocacy and focus on that. For example, you could read books about the 1963 Children's March during the Civil Rights Movement, such as Monica Clark-Robinson's *Let the Children March* or Cynthia Levinson's *We've Got a Job*.

4. Make sure children have both peer friendships as well as intergenerational friendships. Give children ample time to socialize both with peers and with trusted, safe adults. Socializing with peers will increase the fun that children have, and socializing with trusted, safe adults will increase a sense of partnership between adults and children.

5. Give children the opportunity to create and lead their own projects within your family, faith community, or religious organization. Give them a sense of ownership over these projects to increase their level of commitment.

6. Recruit older children who are experienced leaders and pair them with younger children who need assistance or guidance on their projects. For example, if your church sponsors a Boy Scout or Girl Scout troop, AWANA group, or another program that teaches leadership skills, recruit junior high or high school students from that program to work with children a few grades younger than them.

7. Make sure there are adults available to help children with their projects as well. Even though children might want their independence, they still might need help from adults.

8. Allow children to invite guest speakers from your larger community to come speak regarding issues the children care about.

9. Be sure to acknowledge and praise children for their efforts as regularly as you acknowledge and praise adults for their efforts.

10. Don't force children to become more involved who are not ready. Make sure there are resources available to children who feel like they want or need to develop a specific skill set before becoming involved. For example, some children may need to develop communication, leadership, or other social skills before attempting certain projects. Think about how you can help children master those skills in your specific context.

ten

Seeing Children as Prophets

If "Wives, submit to your husbands" and
"Slaves, submit to your masters" have been
contextualized, analyzed, and ultimately seen
as harmful, perhaps "Children, submit to your
parents" might similarly be examined for the
ways it promotes unhealthy relationships and
family structures.

—Kathleen Gallagher Elkins
and Julie Faith Parker[1]

Christians have not written a lot about the prophetic power given to children in the Tanakh. I find this strange because Jesus reintroduces and affirms that power in the Gospels. On more than one occasion and documented in more than one of the Gospels, Jesus declares that children receive divine insight and speech (Matt. 11:20–27 and 21:12–16; Luke 10:13–24). To aid his message, Jesus points to passages from the Psalms and highlights a well-known tradition of his time that children have prophetic power.

This tradition is important because it is the context in which Jesus speaks and is the context that Jesus's contemporary audience knows. That context acknowledges a respect and healthy fear that should be afforded to children as people who have the potential to speak truth into our time—and even speak truth to power, challenging authorities and bringing them before the judgment throne.

This idea of prophets speaking truth to power is expressed by liberation theology's concept of "prophetic critique." Prophetic critique is one way that religion relates to society. When religion serves as prophetic critique, it rightly calls out the ways that society hurts people. Feminist theologian Rosemary Radford Ruether describes the prophetic critique model as "[locating] God and the spokespersons for God on the side of those victimized or despised by the social and political elites."[2] To critique prophetically is to challenge the seemingly "ordained" way society is ordered. It is to speak out against the false idols of our society and to melt the golden calves of our world powers.

But religion can also be wrongly used to justify the way that society hurts people. When religion is used as an excuse for sin, it ceases to serve as prophetic critique and instead becomes what is called "the sacred canopy."[3] This is because it protects like a canopy and sacralizes the current hurtful way of doing things. Ruether describes the difference between the sacred canopy and prophetic critique as "two types of understanding of religious faith, one that sacralizes the social status quo and another that challenges it."[4] Child liberation theology encourages us to see children as prophets who offer prophetic critique. To better understand how such acts of prophecy and prophetic critique work, and how children can engage in them, we will look at three passages from the Gospels: Matthew 11:20–27 and its parallel in Luke 10:13–24, and Matthew 21:12–16.

"From the Lips of Children and Infants"

The first passage to consider is Matthew 11:20–27. In this part of Matthew's Gospel, Jesus's reputation is reaching increasingly larger numbers of people and cities. John the Baptist, while imprisoned by King Herod, hears of Jesus's growing reputation. John sends messengers to Jesus and instructs them to ask Jesus, "Are you the one who is to come, or shall we look for another?" Jesus tells the messengers to simply report to John what they see: people are being healed. Jesus intends for his actions to speak for themselves. Relevant to our understanding of the importance of praxis, it is to his own actions that Jesus appeals, not to his teachings.

While John the Baptist's messengers understand Jesus's message, unfortunately many of Jesus's audience members have failed to do so. Thus

Jesus begins denouncing all the cities that remained unmoved after they saw with their own eyes the miracles he performed. They *saw* his actions and yet did not allow that to change and transform their beliefs about God and God's kingdom. In this condemnatory context, Jesus contrasts those who saw yet did not believe with children. Jesus speaks of children as those who *do* believe, who receive the truth about God's reign: "I praise you, Father, Lord of heaven and earth, because *you have hidden these things from the wise and learned, and revealed them to little children.* Yes, Father, for this is what you were pleased to do" (Matt. 11:25–26, emphasis added).

Jesus declares that the "wise and learned" adults, the ones who witnessed his miracles, did not repent of their injustices. Instead, it is "little children" who understand the message about who Jesus is and what his purpose is. This event was of such significance that Luke recounts it in his Gospel as well. From Luke 10:21: "I praise you, Father, Lord of heaven and earth, because *you have hidden these things from the wise and learned, and revealed them to little children.* Yes, Father, for this is what you were pleased to do" (emphasis added).

A while after declaring that God has revealed divine insight to little children, Jesus reinforces this message. After marching through Jerusalem in a parade of men, women, and children shouting praises to Jesus in light of the miracles he has performed, Jesus enters a temple court. In the temple court we witness the arresting moment in which Jesus overturns the tables of money changers and dove sellers he argues are welding together religion and profit (Matt. 21:12). We hear Jesus denounce them for making the temple court "a den of robbers" (21:13). And then Jesus begins once again to heal people, this time in the temple court. The image here is intended to be stark, with Jesus transforming a place where power holders preyed upon the underprivileged and oppressed into a place where the underprivileged and oppressed can be healed.[5]

As the conflict escalates, a group of loud, raucous, unruly children are running through the temple. They are excited about Jesus. They are excited about the things he is doing. They are excited by his praxis. And so, they shout. They shout, "Hosanna to the Son of David!" This angers those in power, even though they themselves also "saw the wonderful things" Jesus did. Unlike the children, though, they are "indignant" by Jesus's protests and acts of healing (21:15). This then sets the stage for Jesus's declaration in Matthew 21:16 about children and their prophetic power: "Have you never read, 'From the lips of children and infants you, Lord, have called forth your praise'?"

In order to make his point. Jesus cites from one of the psalms written by King David centuries prior concerning the majesty of God. It begins and ends with the same repeated phrase: "LORD, our Lord, how majestic is your name in all the earth!" And in between those phrases King David details how various aspects of the earth point to God's majesty and how God chose to give special meaning and honor to humanity. This includes giving special meaning and honor to human children, as seen in Psalm 8:1–2 (emphasis added):

> LORD, our Lord,
> how majestic is your name in all the earth!
> You have set your glory
> in the heavens.
> *Through the praise of children and infants*
> *you have established a stronghold* against your enemies,
> to silence the foe and the avenger.

From the lips of children and infants God has ordained *praise*. From the lips of children and infants God has established a *stronghold*. This is a declaration that has continuity all the way through King David's lineage and into his descendant Jesus of Nazareth, the one who ushers in the kingdom of God. This continuity points to the honored prophetic power of children and the role they play in God's kingdom. They are the speakers of praise to God; they are the witnesses to God's strength. They have courage to run through a temple court and shout a message that scandalizes and offends those in power.

This is the prophetic power of children: their ability to speak truth to power.

Figurative, Metaphorical, or Literal?

One might wonder, Do these texts refer to actual young people or are they metaphors for adults who exhibit "childlike" or "childish" natures? This is a matter for significant debate. Many scholars interpret "children" in the phrase "revealed them to little children" from the parallel texts of

Matthew 11:20–27 and Luke 10:13–24 metaphorically. There is more of a divide between literal or metaphorical interpretations among readings of Matthew 21:12–16. The problem is that even the slightest bit of figurative or metaphorical interpretation requires *essentializing childhood*. In other words, we have to determine (basically guess) what "being a child" is "like" in order to figure out how adults (who are no longer children) can be "like" children. This means we have to reduce childhood to some essence that adults can access. Theologians across the spectrum of theological conviction have reduced childhood to attributes like "receptivity to God's revelation,"[6] "simple-heartedness,"[7] "teachability" and "independence from human rationality,"[8] "social lowliness,"[9] "humble reliance,"[10] "vulnerable, threatened, and dependent on others and God,"[11] and "faithful discipleship."[12]

These descriptions may sound helpful, but childhood cannot be essentialized any more than adulthood can. There is no "essence" to childhood. Childhood looks different from context to context. Practical theologian Joyce Ann Mercer explains, "Childhood and children take shape in relation to particular cultural, historical, and social contexts. To speak of children in general risks imposing an uninterrogated norm of childhood drawn from one social location onto all children."[13] To impose what Mercer calls "an uninterrogated norm of childhood" onto all children is a form of violence. It is to force one culture's understanding of children onto all others. More to the point, arguing for an essentialized idea of childhood is a distinctly Western endeavor. As such, it can become a "hegemonic force,"[14] a form of and vehicle for colonialism and imperialism—two oppressive forces we as Christians who believe in liberation ought to resist.

Even though so few scholars have interpreted these passages literally as referring to actual children,[15] we nonetheless need to resist the figurative, metaphorical tendency. We must resist this tendency to force an Americanized, twenty-first-century vision of childhood on other people groups and cultures. We also need to resist because a plain, straightforward reading of the text opens up new possibilities of interpretation and liberation.

Child Prophets Elsewhere

There is a rich tradition of children possessing divine insight and speaking prophetically within Judaism. As we saw in chapter 5, two of the most significant prophets in the Tanakh—Miriam and Samuel—began their prophetic careers as children. According to Jewish tradition, Miriam was but five years old when she began issuing prophetic critiques and Samuel was only twelve years old. Thus they are both prime examples of how children are *literally* those to whom God gives divine insight and speech.

The possession and use of prophetic power by children is also seen outside the Judaic tradition. Throughout Greco-Roman antiquity, children would sometimes be viewed as mediums for the divine and supernatural. (This was true even while children were considered to be on the lowest rung of social standing and possessing no rights.) Sometimes children would become mediums by means of a formal process, such as when a young girl was chosen to be the Pythia, a prophetess at the Oracle of Delphi.[16] But other times children would become mediums rather spontaneously, simply by means of speaking or shouting during play.

For people living in Jesus's time, then, there would be natural associations they could make to familiar stories when Jesus talks of God revealing divine secrets to children. Judith M. Gundry-Volf makes this very point: "The notion of children who uttered divinely inspired speech is not unparalleled in Greco-Roman antiquity. In fact, W. D. Davies and Dale L. Allison . . . note that Greeks and Romans viewed the shouts of children at play—especially in the vicinity of pagan temples, where revelation was likely to take place—as omens."[17]

One can find a first-century allusion to Greeks and Romans viewing the shouts of children at play as omens in Plutarch's *Moralia*. In his section "On the Worship of Isis and Osiris," which has become a vital source of information on Egyptian religious ceremonies, Plutarch describes the story of the goddess Isis wandering around in search of a coffin that holds the body of her husband Osiris, the primeval Egyptian king and god. A group of little children aid Isis in her search for the coffin. This story led Egyptians to believe not only that little children can "possess the power of prophecy," but also that adults can "divine the future" by means of "children's words, especially when children are playing about in holy places."[18]

Another instance wherein children's words can become prophetic can be seen in Dio Chrysostom's first-century work, *Discourses*. Dio Chrysostom makes reference to the Alexandrian people's belief that the sounds of children at play can be used as a source of divination: "You are acquainted no doubt with the prophetic utterances of Apis here, in neighboring Memphis, and you know that lads at play announce the purpose of the god, and that this form of divination has proved to be free from falsehood."[19] To a modern American Christian, these Greco-Roman references to children's play as prophecy may seem alien, especially considering they are from polytheistic cultures unlike our own. However, it is worth pointing out that these beliefs permeated the early Christian church as well. For example, the great Christian saint Augustine believed in the prophetic power of children's play. In his seminal *Confessions*, Augustine credits a critical moment in his conversion story to a child chanting, "Pick it up, read it," which inspires Augustine to pick up and read the Bible.[20]

There is a rich history of child prophets both within and outside of Judaism. This history clearly informed the way that Jewish people thought of verses in their religious texts about children's ability to speak prophetically. Such verses would indicate concrete examples of real children rather than suggesting some "essentialized" ideal of childhood.

Reading the Gospels with Actual Children in Mind

The rich history of child prophets within Judaism and Jesus's wider Greco-Roman historical context should inform and become the backdrop for understanding Jesus's claims about children in the Gospels. Since his audiences would undoubtedly understand the role children can play as divine messengers, it seems the natural interpretation of passages like the three discussed above (Matt. 11:20–27; 21:12–16; Luke 10:13–24) should be that Jesus is speaking *literally* of children. Children have been given a special role by God to speak prophetically, a role that places them at the center of God's vast, unfolding, cosmic plans for the universe.

We see this phenomenon play out in Matthew 21:14–16. After the crowd of adults boisterously proclaims Jesus as Son of God, Jesus enters the temple and starts acting in ways that made the same "respectable" adults feel uncomfortable. They wanted to believe Jesus was the Son of God, but not *that* sort of Son of God. The sort of Son of God that would cause property damage in a protest and condemn world power structures made them feel uneasy. The adults want an easy *shalom* (peace, wholeness), not the messy, chaotic *shalom* that includes struggling for justice. The crowds' cheers, therefore, grow silent.

But the children are not afraid.[21] The children are not silent. The children are unembarrassed by and unashamed of Jesus's antics, and also *excited* by them. They believe Jesus to be the Son of God, and thus if the Son of God protests something as wrong, so be it. They continue their praise of Jesus regardless of consequences or reputation. The children "recognized not just who Jesus was, but what Jesus was," and they also "were led by God to speak out what they knew." This highlights that "children are spiritual beings, they are open to God."[22] The children, as opposed to the adults, are not ashamed of the Gospel of Christ; the children, as opposed to the adults, see the power of God that brings salvation at work (alluding to Rom. 1:16).

This passage in Matthew 21 also highlights children's capability to understand the insights they are given. Even young children can grasp religious truths and speak about them. They have a capacity to understand God, a capacity that comes naturally as they are made in the image of God.[23]

While there are many provocative implications of seeing children figuratively or metaphorically in these passages, I think they are ultimately temptations that need to be resisted. Children are a marginalized group; they already are erased or ignored in both society at large as well as by Christian theologians.[24] We need to be sure that we elevate the role of actual children in these passages, rather than push them to the side just to make some spiritualistic point about essentialized childhood.

Even though children were on the bottom rung of Jesus's sociopolitical context, he chose to highlight their worthiness to bear the truth of God Almighty: "Though secondary socially," Craig S. Keener argues, "children could be conduits of divine wisdom."[25] As conduits for the divine, children are lifted up from being last to first.

This theme of making the last first is common in the Bible. In the Tanakh, for example, Jacob overturns social hierarchy when he blesses Joseph's younger son Ephraim before his older son Manasseh (Gen. 48). Jesus similarly destabilized his culture's way of doing things by prioritizing rights-less children before rights-full adults. This theme of power inversion and destabilization is seen no more clearly than in to whom God entrusted their divine revelations: infants and children, and literally so. As Yahweh revealed themselves and their messages to a five-year-old girl and twelve-year-old boy in the Tanakh, so too does Jesus reveal his true identity to unruly children running through a temple. Children are thus lifted up to become both revolutionaries who speak out against world power structures like patriarchy (Miriam speaking against her father) as well as prophets who declare the reign of God (children in the temple).

Implications for Child Liberation Theology

These realities should be a starting place to inform how we construct a child liberation theology. We must not only change how we see and understand children, such that we see and understand them as God sees and understands them (vessels worthy of divine prophecies and prophetic critiques). We must also change practices in our world that prevent children from filling these roles. And we must decenter ourselves as adults and create space for children to teach us. How can we create room for children within our faith communities, for example, to fill prophetic roles instead of reducing them to weekly sermon disturbances or participants once a year in a holiday choir?

A few ideas:

First, we need to listen to children and youth—and change how we think about what they are saying.

What prophetic critiques are children on the margins of society saying to the American church? What prophetic critiques are children on the margins of your church saying to your church specifically? Think about what the apostle Paul wrote to Timothy: "Don't let anyone look down on you because you are young, but set an example for the believers in speech, in conduct, in love, in faith and in purity" (1 Tim. 4:12). Think about the children and youth around you. What examples are they showing your church for how the adults in your church should live? What are they saying?

Black youth are saying that Black Lives Matter.[26]

Transgender kids are saying they are dying because they are not being treated like human beings.[27]

LGBTQIA youth are saying they are being kicked out of their homes.[28]

The next generation of autistic activists is saying the obsession with "curing" them is harmful and offensive.[29]

Girls are saying the modesty and purity culture has done great damage.[30]

Homeschooled children are saying they need better protection.[31]

Youth around the world are begging adults to take climate change seriously.[32]

Instead of dismissing these prophetic cries as immature and instead of saying, "Oh, they'll think differently when they are our age or when they have their own children," we need to take children seriously now. We need to understand they might have unique vantage points or life experiences that we do not have. And we need to listen.

Second, we need to empower children to be prophetic within their own families.

One place where seeing children as prophets is particularly important is evangelical homeschooling. In that world, there is an increasingly popular movement revolving around "parental rights," which I touched on in chapter 8.[33] This movement has become the idol of the Christian Right, turning parents into gods. The problem with the movement is not that it values the role caregivers play in children's lives—caregivers play vital, irreplaceable roles. The problem is that the movement so elevates parents that it erases or neglects children's God-given right to challenge their caregivers. Children are not parental property. They do not "belong" to their parents.[34]

Furthermore, children are not to submit to authorities without question, whether those authorities are parental or governmental. Children are made in the image of God, not the image of their parents. As a result, children have a right to decide what they believe, to determine who they want to be, and to speak up about those things if they are different from their caregivers' opinions—the very things that parental rights advocates find horrifying.[35] Children in the Bible demonstrate this kind of resistance, as we see in the stories of Joseph, Miriam, Samuel, and many other important biblical characters. These children were considered rebels and troublemakers in response to their prophetic acts. They refused to remain under their caregivers' "umbrellas of authority."[36] They preferred to run wildly into the rain instead, and God blessed them for their rebellion. Like young Jesus striking out on his own to learn in the temple (Luke 2:41–52), they engaged adults whether or not they were welcome and they made independent choices, all guided by their own consciences and relationships with God.

The Bible speaks to the divinely established right of children to disobey parents in certain contexts in Ezekiel 20:18–19. There we read God's declaration, "I said to their children in the wilderness, 'Do not follow the statutes of your parents or keep their laws or defile yourselves with their idols. I am the LORD your God; follow my decrees and be careful to keep my laws.'" In these verses, God specifically commands children to push back against their parents when they do wrong. Yet how often do we hear pastors or Sunday school teachers teach this passage? Hardly ever. Or in my case, *never*—and my experience is not unique.[37] I never heard a sermon or lesson on this passage, although I heard countless sermons and lessons on the idea from Ephesians 6:1: "Children, obey your parents in the Lord, for this is right." Ezekiel 20:18–19 clearly indicates that there are situations where the more appropriate message title would be: "Children, *Disobey* Your Parents in the Lord, For This Is Right."[38]

Throughout history, diverse theologians have affirmed the right of children to rebel against their parents in certain contexts. The Catholic saint Thomas Aquinas, for example, strongly believed that children could go against their parents' wishes for numerous reasons: if their parents wanted them to marry someone they did not want to, if their parents were not letting them pursue a career, or if their parents wanted them to do something sinful.[39] "If our parents incite us to sin," Aquinas wrote, "and withdraw us from the service of God, we must, as regards this point, abandon and hate them."[40] Additionally, "Thomas approved of conscientious disobedience. For older children as for all people of mature reason, the conscience . . . trumps other ostensible obligations."[41] Aquinas had faith that children could trust their consciences—like adults do.

The Protestant reformer Martin Luther also believed in the right of children to self-determine over and against their parents' wishes. Indeed, a "concern for self-determination and the respect accorded one's decisions appears in Luther's writings concerning the obligations of the parent-child relationship."[42] Luther grounded a child's right to self-determine in the idea of Christian freedom. "His concept of Christian freedom, by which the believer is lord of all and servant of all, allowed children some means to counter their parents' demands based on the Fourth Commandment."[43] Luther believed that Christian freedom, in fact, greatly limited what parents could demand from their children. "Parental authority is strictly limited," Luther wrote. "It does not extend to the point where it can wreak damage and destruction to the child, especially to its soul."[44]

Another, more contemporary theologian who believed in the right of children to not mindlessly obey their parents is Karl Barth. Barth argues in his influential work *Church Dogmatics*, "It is an error to suppose . . . that the youngster is to behave merely as the object of parental wishes." Rather, "parents must appeal to the child's budding freedom and responsibility by way of the 'higher court' of divine jurisdiction." In other words, parents are to appeal to children because of children's already-existing relationship with God. Children should continually learn that they "must already render [their] own account to this higher court, engaging in personal reflection on the meaning and purpose of what [their] parents expect of [them], treading in [their] own ways and making [their] own judgments."[45]

Children's ultimate allegiance is to God, and parents must not intervene in God's relationship with their children. While children are to honor and respect their parents, parents must also honor and respect their children. Part of that mutual honor and respect requires parents to create space for children to speak prophetically within the context of their families when children believe their parents are straying from God's path. Families need to foster an environment, therefore, where children feel comfortable being the sort of "conscientious objectors" that Aquinas envisioned.

> *Third, we need to rethink what the term "Christian worldview" means so that children of all ages can promote such a worldview in prophetic ways.*

If our idea of a "Christian worldview"[46] can be reduced to propositional truths about politics and philosophy, that necessarily means that younger children—who have not yet developed the ability to reason and rationalize propositional truths—cannot develop, share in, and shape said Christian worldview. Reimagining the meaning of a Christian worldview as something more than propositional truths—something like the apostle James's definition of "pure and faultless" religion, which is "to look after orphans and widows in their distress and to keep oneself from being polluted by the world" (James 1:27)—thus enables more children to participate.

Chinese feminist theologian Kwok Pui-lan has a beautiful essay in the book *Inheriting Our Mothers' Gardens* that touches on this idea. She writes about her experiences as a high school child volunteering through her church to take care of the sick and the elderly. She describes how her volunteer work became a form of worship that brought her into deeper relationship with God. Kwok writes, "As a high school girl, I used to accompany [women from church] in visiting the sick and calling on those old people who were too weak to come to church. Some of these women volunteers were widows; a few were rich; others came from poor and middle-class backgrounds. Their dedication to others in ministering to the needy helped me to see glimpses of the divine and sustained me through many doubts and uncertainties."[47]

Opportunities where children learn or inherit the practices of treating their neighbors justly, compassionately, and lovingly are at the heart of liberation. And they are lessons and practices that children can digest and participate in regardless of age. Children of all ages can participate in a Christian worldview when it is defined as pure and faultless religion. Children of all ages can "take care of orphans and widows in their suffering" and thereby work against injustice. When we reorient ourselves to Christlike actions and align with Jesus's praxis, we create room for people of all ages—not just adults—to live and realize the meaning of God's kingdom on earth. And we empower children to breathe new, prophetic life into the community.

INCLUDING CHILDREN

Find a moment in history when American Christians failed to love, protect, or liberate children. For example, during the nineteenth and twentieth centuries, tens of thousands of Native American children were kidnapped from their homes in order to "civilize" and "Christianize" them in assimilation boarding schools.[48] They endured a ban on their native languages, harsh beatings, and even forced sterilization.[49] "Kill the Indian in him, and save the man" was the expressed purpose of these schools, according to their founder Richard Pratt.[50] The long-lasting impacts of colonialism and imperialism on Native American children can still be seen today: they experience death by suicide at a rate more than three times the national average, a full quarter of Native American children live in poverty, they graduate from high school at a rate 17 percent lower than the national average, they face two times the rate of abuse and neglect compared to other children, and "their experience with post-traumatic stress disorder rivals the rates of returning veterans from Afghanistan."[51] These effects are heartbreaking.

As a family, faith community, or religious organization, devote a month to learning about a topic like this. If you're a family, use your daily or weekly devotional or family meeting time.[52] If you're a faith community, consider devoting teaching time on Sundays for a month (such as during the sermon, Sunday school, or Christian education hour). If you're a faith organization, weave this project into your regular programming.

During the first week, focus on learning together with humility. If you're a family, check out a book from your local library about the issue you're studying. Read it aloud or listen to it together. If you're a faith community or religious organization, invite a guest speaker who has personal childhood experience with the Christian abuse or cruelty on which you are focusing.

During the second week, focus on confession. Confess the sins of American Christians who hurt and fail similar children—and lament. In the context of a family, confession could involve creating a report together about the subject of the book you read the previous week (perhaps with words and pictures, or even YouTube and TikTok videos if you want to get creative). In the context of a faith community or religious organization, confession could be using Sunday's service time or your regular programming time to educate your group members about how widespread the selected abuse or cruelty is or was within the United States and pointing out the specific ways in which Christianity was used to endorse it. In all contexts, remember to create time for lament in addition to confession. For example, incorporate a time of silent reflection or encourage public prayers of lament after your act(s) of confession.

For the third week, focus on transformation and justice. Dedicate your week or Sunday to serving a related, underserved people group in your wider community. Reach out to a local organization that advocates for or is made up of people directly impacted by the injustice and ask how you can partner with and help them as a family, faith community, or faith organization. Then use that week or time on Sunday to take direct action and do what was recommended.

For the fourth and final week, focus on commitment. Commit as a family, faith community, or faith organization to do better in your local community by serving children who are most in need of love and protection. To make your commitment real and concrete, work together to list three other moments in history when American Christians failed children in particular. Commit to learning about and addressing one of these moments in the above fashion every four months for the next year.

eleven

Seeing Children as Priests

Children speak to questions of faith and
doubt, vengeance and power, and justice
and love—these same elemental pairings
that we adults seem to rally our God
representations around. In their simplest
phrases and play actions, their lives sometimes
offer educational and religious lessons more
profound than the prepared curricula and
sermons of the adult world. We need to
provide a forum for the children to express
themselves, and we need to listen to their
words with an open, religious heart.

—David Heller[1]

In the previous chapter we discussed how we need to *listen* to children—how we need to see children as prophets and hear their prophetic critiques. In this chapter we examine how we can see children as priests. Children can *teach* and *lead*, and we as adults can create spaces in our faith communities to enable and empower them to do so. The theme of this chapter comes from Isaiah chapter 11, verse 6 in particular: "Then wolves will live at peace with lambs, and leopards will lie down in peace with young goats. Calves, lions, and bulls will all live together in peace. A little child will lead them" (ERV). Just as a little child will lead even the most ferocious beasts in the kingdom of God, so, too, can children teach and lead even the wisest adults among us. This is, after all, what it means to be a priest: to be a teacher and leader in one's faith community.

One good starting place for seeing children as priests is the topic of children's spirituality. Before we can believe that children are capable of instructing us in spiritual matters, we need to believe that children have deeply meaningful, spiritual lives. This claim may be a nonissue to some people, but to others it is contentious. Some people do not believe that children wrestle with existential or spiritual questions. In fact, some people do not even believe children are *capable* of such wrestling. Moving to a place where we can see and appreciate that children are existential and spiritual explorers is key to moving the church one step closer to child liberation.

Note that what I have said applies to even very young children. Children of *all* ages explore the innermost depths of their selves. Children of *all* ages explore their existential and spiritual questions, fears, longings, and hopes. It is important to acknowledge that those explorations take place within different developmental stages depending on a child's age; we will be looking at the importance of child development in chapter 13. But the purpose of this chapter is to realize that within each stage of child development, children are fully reflective of the image of God and are thus fully human. They share adults' needs to figure out the world. As children attempt to figure out the world, they have insights into existence and spirituality that adults should heed.

"A Little Child Will Lead Them"

Isaiah 11:6–9 contains some of the most beautiful verses of poetry in the Bible, so I want to begin with those verses (ERV):

> Wolves will live at peace with lambs,
> and leopards will lie down in peace with young goats.
> Calves, lions, and bulls will all live together in peace.
> A little child will lead them.
> Bears and cattle will eat together in peace,
> and all their young will lie down together and will not hurt
>   each other.

Lions will eat hay like cattle.
Even snakes will not hurt people.
Babies will be able to play near a cobra's hole
and put their hands into the nest of a poisonous snake.
People will stop hurting each other.
People on my holy mountain will not want to destroy things
because they will know the LORD.
The world will be full of knowledge about him,
like the sea is full of water.

In this passage, the prophet Isaiah speaks to a future that reflects the kingdom of God. In this future, a just and merciful king will rule. The poor will be treated with kindness and fairness. Even more importantly for our purposes, that kingdom will fully reflect a world in which children are respected, valued, and protected. There will be an end to child endangerment; babies can play near previously dangerous entities without being hurt. There will be an end to child abuse because "people will stop hurting each other" (11:9 ERV). And a child will be given a position of authority and leadership, leading a large procession of parading animals. Later in Isaiah 65:20 and 23 (ERV), we learn there will also be an end to infant mortality: "In that city there will never be a baby who lives only a few days" and "Never again will a woman suffer childbirth and have her baby die."

It is remarkable that in the prophet Isaiah's imagining of the future kingdom of God, the future features such prominent images of children. Perhaps the most significant takeaway is that children receive the same amount of focus in this poetic future as the just and merciful king. Those who would be considered the lowliest in social status at the time this text was written—children—receive the same attention as the highest. The last have become first. Children are indeed first, *leading* the parade of animals.

This future is also something we can work toward during our present. It is the future that we see in the kingdom of God, yet Jesus proclaims that the kingdom of God has "come near" (Matt. 3:2, 4:17; Mark 1:15). This returns us to *eschatology*, which we explored in depth in chapter 8. We can begin to make the future described in Isaiah 11 our present when we begin to see children as God-to-us. And one key part of that effort is seeing children as priests, teachers, and leaders who can lead a parade of not only animals but also adults toward a better, brighter future. This vision of the kingdom will remain the future and not emerge in the present if we cling to the anti-child notions of previous generations. If we allow anti-child notions to control our present, then our future will continue to be similarly anti-child. But if we allow Isaiah's eschatological vision to influence our present, we can change our future accordingly.

Understanding Children's Existential Struggles

Robert Coles, a Harvard professor and student of children's lives, describes "children as seekers, as young pilgrims well aware that life is a finite journey and as anxious to make sense of it as those of us who are farther along in the time allotted to us."[2] Just as adults want to know the whats and whys and hows about life because they are humans, so too do children want to know. Children want to know because they are equally human. They have the same burning curiosity that adults do, though they sometimes express it in different ways because of their various developmental stages.[3]

Existential questions are big questions about life: Who am I? What is the meaning of life? What is my purpose here on earth? Is there a God? We often think about these questions as ones that only the "professionals" answer—professionals such as adult philosophers and theologians with PhDs and impressive research grants. However, all humans wrestle with these questions, whether highly educated or not, whether adult or child. Yes, even children wrestle with them and try to discover answers. In fact, researchers have found that people begin to "construct systematic belief and disbelief systems about the universe in which they live, including the natures of physical and social reality and God, by about four to six years of age."[4]

Bad experiences often provoke people to ponder these big questions.[5] Having to face the death of a close relative or a beloved pet, for example, can prompt a child of even a young age to think about the edges of life; that is, the edges where one goes from living to not living, being to not being.[6] An experience of pain can inspire a child to wonder, What is the point of *my* suffering? Godly Play founder Jerome Berryman says such moments or experiences bring about for children "an awareness of the existential limits to their being and their knowing."[7]

Coles writes about his experience in Boston in the 1950s as a pediatrician helping children who contracted polio. The disease paralyzed these children and made them unable to breathe. They were consequently placed in giant respirators called iron lungs. Faced with the prospect of their conditions never improving, these children turned inward, reflecting deeply on their lives and earnestly asking existential questions. "These are young people," Coles says, "who suddenly have become quite a bit older; they are facing possible death, or serious limitation of their lives; and they will naturally stop and think about life, rather than just live it from day to day."[8]

Coles gives the example of Tony, an eleven-year-old boy who grew up Catholic. The boy was previously an athlete who played football and basketball in his school. Now confined to an iron lung, Tony asks Coles, "Why me? How did this happen? What did I do? That's all I do, ask these questions." These larger questions about life quickly became spiritual for Tony, "I ask: OK, God, I must have done something to deserve this! Tell me!"[9] Though only eleven, Tony is adept at asking questions about the purpose of existence and the meaning of suffering. He is probing issues of *theodicy*—the "answer to the question of why God permits evil"[10]—that adult theologians have wrestled with for centuries. And he reaches to his spiritual tradition to find answers: "I remember in Sunday school, we read of Job. . . . He didn't know what to make of it all, and I don't either."[11]

Coles notes that Tony's "spirituality was, I think, evoked by the distinct possibility of death," and that Tony's brush with death led to him "giving himself over to questions our philosophers and theologians and novelists have asked over the centuries." To put this observation another way: eleven-year-old children are capable of profound existential contemplation! As Coles reflects, "The discourse of children rivals that of Christian saints, such as Augustine and Teresa of Avila and St. John of the Cross."[12] Children may not be as articulate or systematic as a saint, but that makes them no less human and no less prone to asking deep questions about life.

Understanding Children's Spirituality

Existential questions inevitably become spiritual questions. Just as children are existential beings, they are also spiritual beings. They find meaning in religion, in pursuing God, and in challenging God. While their notions about God may be less developed and formally structured than adults, they are meaningful notions just the same. I think sometimes we consider children's ideas about God to just be "cute" because they appear to us "half-baked." However, thinking that an adult's elaborate, systematic theology is superior to a child's simple ideas about God is a form of adultism.[13] And who knows? Sometimes a child's ideas about God are anything but simple. Sometimes they are just as complicated and cavernous as adults' speculations. Other times they might be more profound.

Take the example of Stephanie. Stephanie is a sixteen-year-old Black girl described by Brett Webb-Mitchell in his book *God Plays Piano, Too: The Spiritual Lives of Disabled Children*. Stephanie likes to tap dance and loves to write poetry. When she is home, she attends a Baptist church. This does not often happen because she has been institutionalized due to her disabilities. Even though she is only sixteen, she has experienced great tragedy in her life: Stephanie was sexually abused and forced to have an abortion as a young teen. While she finds hope in God and her church, she also lashes out against God, asking why they have allowed bad things to happen to her: "Let's talk about why I think God has said, 'Fuck me,'" she challenges Webb-Mitchell.[14]

Stephanie also sees right through the hypocrisy present in many religious communities. In a poem she shared during a group therapy session, this is evident. She wrote, "Mr. God, help me if you are so mighty and powerful! Or is it that you only help people who give money to the churches, with fake preachers who has a cold beer after services?"[15]

Webb-Mitchell describes Stephanie as "a theologian in search of God."[16] For despite her on-and-off hostility toward God and the hypocrisies of religious people, she finds immense meaning and hope in Jesus. She says, "I believe that his love and mercy for us is real. Because if it's not, then I would have been dead by now."[17] Her belief in Jesus gives her a reason to keep living, despite all the bad things life has thrown her way. This hope is reflected in some of her favorite Bible verses, Psalm 124:2–3a: "If the LORD had not been on our side when people attacked us, they would have swallowed us alive."

Stephanie does not only find hope in religion. She also has profound, poignant insights into that religion. For example, Stephanie recounts the creation story from the book of Genesis with her own, unique perspective on it and the origin of sin:

In the beginning God . . . creates the first man, and the man would teach other animals how not to hurt each other and stuff. Then he created a woman, and she take care of all the flowers and stuff. . . . The man was black and the woman was Indian. And then, then they'd have children. . . . (How did sin come in to this world?) One of the children hurt somebody else . . . willingly. Through hatred and jealously, and then that's how they discovered that feeling of hating, or wanting to hurt someone or wanting to kill someone or something.[18]

She is only sixteen and confined to a hospital due to disabilities, yet Stephanie has a striking vision of Eden that is much like the prophet Isaiah's vision of the kingdom of God: one in which people treat each other kindly and humans teach each other how not to hurt one another. The above vision is as vivid and full of colors and details as any creation story I have heard from adults. And Stephanie has an uncanny grasp on the reality of sin: sin is the dissolution of community. Sin is when one person hurts another person, which Stephanie can speak to because of the many people who have hurt her. She is only sixteen and she is disabled, but she is wise and more than able to identify religious hypocrisy, understand Jesus's gospel, grasp cosmology (the study of the universe's origin), and pinpoint the nature of sin.

When I read Stephanie's words, I learn more about life than I do from most sermons I have heard delivered by professionally trained pastors. Her words are refreshingly candid and honest despite her childish phrasing. Her thoughts on theology and ethics are brash and bold (even if she would not use those terms). And her willingness to speak out against the role of money in religion reminds me of Jesus condemning the money changers and dove sellers in the temple court. She is, in every sense of the word, a priest—albeit without a church to instruct. Thus we arrive at the point of this chapter: not only are children capable of amazing insights into life, but they are also capable of really, truly teaching us adults about life.

Intersectionality and Children's Spirituality

When we think about children's deeply spiritual lives, it is important to place them into the larger context of liberation theology: the context of intersectionality. The idea of intersectionality in liberation theology is that no sin happens in a vacuum. The sin of childism hurts children, for example, and the sin of racism hurts Black people—but *Black children*, standing at the intersection of childism and racism, are hurt in more ways than one. They are *multiply oppressed*, because so many Black children are hurt by more than one evil power within our world.

I want to give special attention to the spirituality of these children who are multiply oppressed for two reasons. First and foremost, as we engage with liberation theology, we ought to look to the margins of society—to those groups of people who are most alienated from society because of discrimination and oppression. Jesus has come to make the last first and the first last. It is in the margins of society that we find the last, and it is to the margins where we must go if we are to empower the last to become first.

Second, multiply oppressed children deserve special attention because those children have profound testimonies. They have particularly liberating insights into how spirituality can empower children. This is because multiply oppressed children have the experience of daily digging deep into their faith in order to find the courage to keep going despite the obstacles life throws their way. Through their lives, they demonstrate to us that children—even young children—are more than capable of not only *understanding* religion, but also *using* that religion to better their own and others' lives.

Let us look at a few examples. In 1962, during school desegregation in Georgia and North Carolina, Robert Coles interviewed several Black children about their experiences of spirituality and racism in public schools. These children experienced overwhelming amounts of discrimination and hatred from white people. Their faith in God, however, promoted resilience—"the ability to adapt effectively in the face of threats to development."[19] Their faith also equipped them to stand strong despite all the forces working against them.

One young man looked to the suffering of Jesus on the cross. In the image of the suffering God-Child, he found an anchor to which he could secure his own sufferings. Fifty years before Black liberation theologian James H. Cone wrote *The Cross and the Lynching Tree*, this boy was already employing Cone's imagery in his own life for the sake of personal liberation. The boy told Coles, "You've been asking me about how it feels, how it feels to be a Negro in that school, but a lot of the time I just don't think about it, and the only time I really do is on Sunday, when I talk to God, and He reminds me of what He went through, and so I've got company for the week, thinking of Him."[20] This young man essentially created his own liberation theology, even though he had yet to graduate from high school.

Coles found that even young children are profoundly impacted by religion and can reach to their spiritual tradition to protect themselves. An eight-year-old girl from North Carolina spoke to Coles about how her faith protected her against a white adult who flung racial epithets at her. This young girl trusted God to work miracles in her life to defend her. Speaking of her experience entering a recently desegregated school, the young girl said, "I was all alone, and those [segregationist] people were screaming and suddenly I saw God smiling, and I smiled. A woman was standing there [near the school door], and she shouted at me, 'Hey, you little n****r, what are you smiling at?' I looked right at her face, and I said, 'At God.' Then she looked up at the sky, and then she looked at me, and she didn't call me any more names."[21]

In her book *African-American Children at Church*, Wendy L. Haight also explores how spirituality encourages resilience in Black children who experience racism in the United States. She notes that "in many African-American communities the church is the only institution that is owned, managed, and supported by African-Americans." As a result, the church plays a central role in many Black children's lives by helping them learn about their heritage, offering them messages of hope for the future, and giving them "a healthy way of coping with racial hatred." Haight shares the following example of how this can occur. "Mrs. Edith Hudley, a 73-year-old African-American, recounted to me her experiences as a 7-year-old child walking to a segregated school. 'The whites would be walking one way, and we'd be walking the other. They'd yell at us, "You dirty, black n*****s! We hate you! We hate you!" I'd go to Mama and ask her, 'Why do they hate us?' She'd always take me to the Bible. She taught me that God loves us all. God is the judge. She taught me not to take hate inside of myself."[22]

These examples from Coles and Haight show how children can use religion to find comfort in spite of abuse. They use religion to protect themselves both internally and externally: internally, by using their religious beliefs to devalue racist insults and cling to the religiously grounded value they place on themselves; externally, by using shared religious beliefs, such as the belief in the existence of God, to rebuke their oppressors and possibly create empowering communities. Religion can also encourage children, as in the case of Edith Hudley, "not to take hate inside."

Like Black children, children with disabilities are also multiply oppressed, meaning that Black children with disabilities even more so. Black children with disabilities not only face racism and childism; they also have to live in a world that is deeply ableist and intolerant of people with disabilities. Despite these many forces working against them, Black children with disabilities can understand God and can use that understanding to anchor them in the midst of life's storms.

Brett Webb-Mitchell gives the example of Kenzie, a fifteen-year-old Black girl with disabilities. Kenzie grew up in an African American Baptist congregation. Her favorite part of church is "learning something that I need to know about God."[23] One part of church that she particularly enjoys is hearing the choir, though Kenzie is very aware of the fact that the choir in her faith community is an adults-only arena. "Us young kids aren't allowed in the choir," she observes. "I don't think that's fair, you know what I mean?"[24] (This is unfortunately true about many aspects of American churches today.) What should be a place of comfort and joy for Kenzie (a young girl who desperately needs a safe space for creative expression) is unfortunately closed off to her.

This limited access does not, however, stop Kenzie from being empowered by her faith in God. Webb-Mitchell recounts how Kenzie—a fierce advocate for the right of her fellow institutionalized peers—brings her Bible to him to read passages aloud. "Find me a verse from the Bible to calm myself down," she asks Webb-Mitchell in the midst of a meeting where institutional staff are unmoved by her pleas to help her peers. "I'm just mad and need something to put this in perspective," she tells him. Webb-Mitchell says, "It was as if I were a medical doctor trying to unwrap the syringe to quickly give her a shot to calm down," though in this case, he was reading her Bible verses to help her self-regulate. Kenzie requests Matthew 11:28, where Jesus says, "I will give you rest," which she finds particularly soothing. In fact, hearing the verse helps her enough that she is able to calm down and continue her peer advocacy.[25]

Children as Teachers

Kenzie's case is unique. Despite her being Black, disabled, and institutionalized, some of the adults around her are willing to listen to her. She is specifically given opportunities to better herself and others by teaching. In her unit, she is allowed to run Bible studies for other young girls. Given this new role of teacher, Kenzie "was eager to talk about the Almighty."[26]

Much of the time, however, we do not respond to children by allowing them to lead. We deny children the chance to be advocates or teachers. When children try to speak up, we often reject their teachings in a patronizing manner. Robert Coles gives an example of this rejection in the context of an American public school. There, a ten-year-old Hopi girl feels discouraged from sharing her religious beliefs with her teacher. The girl tells Coles, "The sky is where the God of the Anglos lives, a teacher told us. She asked where our God lives. I said, 'I don't know.' I was telling the truth. Our God is the sky, and lives wherever the sky lives. Our God is the sun and the moon, too; and our God is our [the Hopi] people." Coles asks the girl if she explained that to her teacher. She says, "No . . . because—she thinks God is a person. If I'd told her, she'd give us that smile." Coles asks, "What smile?" The girl responds, "The smile that says to us, 'You kids are cute, but you're dumb.'"[27]

This particular story is about a child following a religion other than Christianity. However, the point made is universal: This sort of patronizing attitude toward children's religious beliefs is more than inappropriate. As Coles's story shows, such dismissiveness is actively damaging by discouraging children from sharing their thoughts. The young Hopi girl that Coles talked to had no interest in speaking up about her spiritual experiences because of her firsthand experiences with adult contempt. But if the teacher in the story had expressed willingness to listen, she could have been taught an immense amount about the Hopi girl's faith, which could have fostered better interfaith understanding.

If children are to teach and lead, we need to create the space for them to do so. And if there is any doubt that children can actually instruct adults, consider the words of Jerome Berryman in *Godly Play*. Berryman talks about his experiences with children on the verge of death due to terminal sickness. In the Texas Medical Center where he worked, Berryman saw young children face the possibility of death and help one another cope with the resulting fear and pain. These children also helped their own parents. Berryman writes, "I watched as children helped one another prepare for death when parents and other significant adults were not able to help them. . . . It was as if the little ones became wise beyond their size and years. At times, the children even parented their parents as the end came near."[28]

While I appreciate Berryman's story, I think that the descriptive words he uses are unfair to both the adults and the children. The children did not become "wise beyond their years": the children *already* had that wisdom; they *already* had the potential to teach their parents many things. And the adults were not "reduced" to the status of being parented—in other words, reduced to the level of being children. For one thing, that description is demeaning toward children. For another, adults do not have to be "reduced" in any way to learn from children. Adults have much to learn from children, if they will only open their hearts and minds.

Coles's mentor, Anna Freud, told him the following about working with children: "You'll be asking them to be your teachers, to help you learn. You will no doubt discover that they have many psychological matters to discuss. . . . You'll be having talks about philosophy and theology—and children can hold up rather well, sometimes, in those kinds of discussions, provided the adult doesn't assume too little of the child being interviewed."[29] If we humble ourselves and approach children as people with truth and wisdom to share, I believe they will continually surprise and challenge us with their vital perspectives.

Children as Leaders

Children are not only capable to teaching adults about life and God. They are also capable of taking adults by the hand and leading them toward their own liberation. The question is, Are adults willing to follow children? Berryman gives the perfect example of this:

Somewhere between the ages of five and nine a little boy grew more and more outraged by the pictures at church that made Christ look like a weak person. He also rejected the "miserable sinner" language of his Church of England worship experience. He wrote, "I hated it, and felt more and more strongly that it somehow blasphemed against the beauty, light and all-embracing fusion of God, man and matter which I thought I saw all around me."

When the boy was nine he "leapt up in the Church service, unable to bear the 'for there is no health is us' intoning any longer, and shouted that God wasn't like that at all; that he was nearer than one's own hand. And I was hustled out in floods of tears." He wrote that he was shaken by this event and begged not to be sent to church again. "My mother, while not comprehending my distress, allowed regular churchgoing to end at this point." Despite being silenced by misunderstanding and a lack of respect more surely and more deeply than adults have been silenced by official declarations of heresy, the child "knew what he knew."[30]

Some people might read this story and interpret the child's actions as rebellious and troublesome. Others might even see a sinful, hellbent child because the child refuses to walk the established path laid out for him by his elders. But I see a child who *leads*. I see a child who has the courage to not only say, "This is wrong," but also the courage to leap up and declare, "This is wrong and I know a better path! Who is with me?" It is that second component—calling those around one's self to a brighter, better future—that distinguishes a leader. And as Berryman's story shows, children are more than capable of being leaders. The child was right: God "wasn't like that at all"; God is "nearer than one's own hand." And it was the child who noticed the misinformation, spoke up, and led.

We need to let go of the idea that children who try to lead are only rebellious, troublesome, sinful, or whatever other negative adjectives come to mind. If we intend to see children as leaders, we need to make distinctions between children who are simply acting out because they have not yet learned to self-regulate and children who have been inspired by God with a divine message. Perhaps we even need to rethink the lack of self-regulation in children. Perhaps that inability to silence oneself—the inability to sit quietly in the midst of injustice or unfairness—can be a *good* thing. Perhaps dysregulation is a way in which children are uniquely gifted by God. The resulting candor and urgency can breathe new life into our faith communities.

Implications for Child Liberation Theology

We can apply several points from this chapter to further our understanding of child liberation theology. Children can be priests, teaching and leading in their faith communities, and here are three charges to help us welcome the priests in our midst.

> *First, we need to eliminate barriers in our faith communities that prevent children from fully exploring and expressing their own spirituality.*

Unfortunately, there are many aspects of the majority of churches that are closed off to children. As the aforementioned story of Kenzie revealed, even something as innocuous as a choir can be declared a child-free zone. Imagine how Jesus would react to that! Imagine how many fig trees he would curse (Mark 11:12–14)! If we are truly committed to the idea that children lead deeply spiritual lives, we need to commit to allowing children to participate in our religious rites and sacraments. Yes, I believe this includes communion. We need to see such rites and sacraments less as confirmations of one's spiritual status and more as ongoing developmental processes—like children themselves.

Methodist pastor Robb McCoy makes an important observation: at God's banquet feast, *there is no children's table.* There is only God's table, where *all* people are invited to partake. McCoy asks, "If we consider kids to be a part of the family of God, why would we exclude them from the family meal?" When we start to section off different parts of God's kingdom and God's house and when we restrict access to sacraments or sacred practices, we start chopping up God's table. We rebuild the very barriers that God broke down when they invited *everyone* to their feast. And we communicate that God's kingdom is not here for children in the right-here and right-now. Rather, children must wait until they are adults to fully experience God. But as McCoy says, "Children are the right now of the church. They are the church just as much as anyone else."[31]

Additionally, when we exclude children from the Lord's table, we are making the implicit argument that children cannot be a part of the kingdom of God until they reach a certain level of rationality or mastery of propositional thinking. Yet the very fact that Jesus became an *infant* means that even infants—who are the least skilled among humans when it comes to rationality or propositional thinking—are full image bearers of God, and thus fully welcome in God's kingdom. If we lift up rationality or propositional thinking as litmus tests for who can or cannot enter that kingdom, not only are we contradicting how God established their kingdom, but we will also exclude many people, not simply children. As comparative theologian Kristin Johnston Largen writes,

> Many church bodies do not offer communion to and/or baptize infants and young children, instead waiting until they have a certain level of reason or understanding of the sacrament. Such a conclusion may seem quite sensible and fully benign, until its ramifications are followed through to their logical ends. If rationality and intellect are the mark of what it means to be human, what does that say about the full humanity of children, for example, or the mentally ill, or those with diminished mental capabilities? Surely, then, a theological justification has been laid for seeing them as somehow "less."[32]

But even those whom society has deemed as "less" are fully welcome at God's table. This is the point of Jesus's parable about the Great Banquet, where those who are marginalized from society—"the poor, the crippled, the blind, and the lame" (Luke 14:21) are given priority by the banquet host.

> *Second, we need to question practices in our faith communities that deny children their own agency with regard to spiritual matters.*

Consent is a foundational principle in the world of child protection. Teaching children that their bodies are their own, that their bodies are good, that their bodies deserve to be safe and secure, and that they have a right to say no to touch that makes them feel unsafe and uncomfortable are all important aspects of teaching consent to children. But the principle of consent is important beyond simply protecting children from physical and sexual abuse. Yes, we want to protect children from physical and sexual abuse. We also want children to feel confident in saying, "My body is my body. It belongs to me."[33]

I want to take this idea of consent a step further, however. This is because consent is important not simply for a child's physical safety. Consent is also important for a child's emotional and mental safety. A child's mind is a part of their body. This means a child's feelings and thoughts also belong to them, not to adults. Consequently, we need to extend our ideas about child protection beyond physical safety to include emotional and mental safety.[34] Children have a right to their own feelings and thoughts—even when they conflict with the adults in their lives—just as they have a right to say no to a hug. That would include spiritual feelings and thoughts, indicating spiritual autonomy is as essential to child protection as bodily autonomy.

If this is the case, if "spiritual autonomy is a human right,"[35] then we need to start questioning a lot of religious practices. For example, if a child is not old enough to consent to something (whether that is infant dedication, infant baptism, or infant circumcision) that binds that child to a given church or tradition, we should start asking whether it is appropriate or not to force that something onto the child. If children have a right to their own spirituality, that right has to be exercised on their own terms and in their own time. Otherwise, the right is meaningless.

This does not mean that infant dedication, infant baptism, and infant circumcision are categorically wrong. One can dedicate or baptize one's children in ways that do not violate the children's autonomy. Sometimes infant circumcision is necessary for medical purposes. The principle here is simply that children have a right to follow their own faith paths and should not be forced to follow the exact same paths of the adults in their lives. Author C. Madeleine Dixon writes, "We forget that the probing of strange phenomenon, creation, God, death, magic, has made our scientists, our artists, our religious leaders, throughout the ages. Why should we shorten this probing or cover it up for children?"[36] As much as Christian parents might want to pressure their children into becoming Christians, they must not treat their children like objects. Parents should respect their children's agency in the same way that they would respect the agency of an adult. Children deserve to make their own decisions when it comes to something as intensely personal as faith.

> *Third, we need to allow children to fill leadership roles within churches.*

Many Black churches already do this to some extent. That is, they give children opportunities to participate in their communities by being "junior" leaders. Wendy L. Haight writes:

> Active participation in the communal worship of God is an important socialization goal [for Black churches]. Over time, children increasingly participate in, and even shape, worship services. As toddlers, they may sit through worship services with adults for up to 2½ hours with encouragement to clap their hands, sing, or pray when appropriate. As preschoolers, they also may participate in special events, such as Christmas programs, and in groups, such as the children's choir. During middle childhood and adolescence, children are given increasing responsibilities as ushers and through leading devotions as junior deacons and deaconesses.[37]

It is rare to find a predominantly white church in the United States that gives children such a diversity of similar opportunities to both participate in and shape worship. While many white churches have similar *entertainment* programs for children, most do not give children the opportunity to lead worship as junior deacons and deaconesses. Even the most progressive white churches tend to segregate children from the adults right after the "children's message" is delivered (or from the adult worship service entirely).

I would argue that churches also need to offer children more opportunities to serve not only in behind-the-scenes or "junior" roles, but also in prominent leadership roles. Children's participation should not be limited to "special events"—it should be actively encouraged for all main community events. Children should be able to participate in not just the children's choir, but also the main choir. Children should be able to lead devotions not simply as *junior* deacons and deaconesses, but as deacons and deaconesses without qualification. This does not mean you cannot offer specific ministries to specific groups of people (a children's ministry or a single adults' ministry or a new parents' ministry, for example); it just means children should be generally welcome to participate in all aspects of the community.

This kind of change to service assignments and opportunities will take significant work and require a lot of scaffolding to begin, but I know it will be well worth the effort.

INCLUDING CHILDREN

Many faith communities and the religious organizations that serve them recognize they have a true problem: they do not engage children and youth. As a result, churches and ministries have come up with all sorts of solutions to better engage. For example, children are put in children's church settings or youth groups or other religious programs where they are bombarded with entertainment (loud music, silly games, video content). This is unhelpful. Entertaining children has its place in the larger scheme of church life, but reducing the participation of children in church to entertainment alone is dehumanizing. It is a soul-sucking extension of capitalism: the transformation of children from agents into consumers.

Children deserve better. They *know* they deserve better, which is part of why many are disengaged from and disillusioned with their faith communities, despite the skate parks and Christian dubstep and gross-out games youth groups and other religious programs pitch to participants.[38] Children know they are more than objects to babysit. They are living, growing human beings who can contribute to the world. Instead of distracting them with mindless entertainment, we need to engage them in spiritual practices. We need to honor their thoughts and we need to intentionally and methodically welcome their participation.

Consider the following question as a faith community or religious organization: When you think about the board or group of leaders that makes the most important decisions, is there at least one child or youth on that board—and is that child's inclusion more than simple tokenism? (By tokenism, I mean including a child so that your community or organization *appears* inclusive but in actuality the child is not allowed to actively contribute ideas or participate in making decisions.[39])

If you want to truly welcome children and treat them as equals, I would argue that you need to include children in the decision-making processes for your faith community or religious organization. Consider allowing children to participate in and vote on the same matters as adults. Intentionally seek out their input on church government matters. Secure ideas from them about how to better involve other children and youth in the church.

If allowing input from children on official church matters is too drastic a step for your faith community, start small. For example, allow the children to vote on who is their Sunday school teacher or youth group leader. Involve them thoroughly in the selection process. Let them interview potential applicants, let them conduct an election among their peers on the candidates, and then let them have the final yes or no vote in the matter.

If you think this is impossible or impractical, know this: I have seen the practice work in a public charter school. In that school, children take turns interviewing and vetting potential teachers. While there are also adults in charge who make decisions about hiring and firing, the children are fully vested with approval or veto power. No teacher is hired without the children's stamp of approval; no teacher is hired that the children veto. To some readers, this may seem to open up the possibility of children making frivolous or rash hiring decisions, but it actually has the opposite effect. Children take their responsibilities seriously in this arrangement because they are ultimately responsible for the strengths and qualities of their teachers. If they do not like teachers they vetted and hired, they only have themselves to blame. Empowering children to determine their own educational destinies inspires them to engage more in their learning environment.[40]

Keep in mind that involving children is not simply a matter of training children to be the adult leaders of tomorrow. It is a matter of empowering children to be *the child leaders of today*.[41] By welcoming children today as leaders, you are combatting the childism and adultism that is so common in our contemporary faith communities. You are demonstrating how those principalities and powers can be overcome by your community in the right-here and right-now.

Partnering with children in leadership also helps to protect children. This is for a number of reasons. First, gradually bringing children into important decision-making processes gives children the opportunities and support they need to succeed in other areas of their lives.[42] Second, the skills that children learn when taking on leadership roles are the same skills that serve as protective factors against abuse, neglect, and other adverse childhood experiences and traumas.[43] Third, giving children the ability to have a significant impact on their own community and environment gives them an internal sense of control, which is a key factor in child resilience.[44] And fourth, involving children in important decision-making processes means increasing children's connection to their own community and environment.[45] Having those sorts of connections are vital to the health and well-being of children because "opportunities to participate in community life help older children and adolescents overcome adversity."[46] Thus by bringing children into leadership roles in your faith community, you are not only empowering children and opening up your community to be blessed by them; you are also contributing to better child protection.

A final note since one can never be too careful: In any interactions between children and adults, your faith community or church needs to follow best practices for child protection.[47] For example, you should always employ a buddy system: no one adult should be alone with one child at any time. All interactions between adults and children—even ones that need to be private—should be conducted where others can at least *see* the interaction. These concerns are equally relevant to children serving in leadership roles. The need for best child protection practices is even more important in these cases because potential predators in leadership roles might try to take advantage of the children who are feeling more "adult" due to their participation in the "adult" world. For this reason, I would encourage you to include more than just one or two children in leadership roles so that the world of leadership is *not* an "adult" world but rather a world representative of your entire community.

twelve

Seeing Children as Theologians

Although childhood is surely a period of
development, already children play with God.

—Patrick McKinley Brennan[1]

W e often think of theology as something intellectual, something
that is done by thinking really, really hard while sitting in a leather
armchair. But theology is not just about the human intellect. Theology
is the study of God. We study God through all sorts of means: reading
the Bible, praying, helping in a soup kitchen, assisting a single parent,
donating to disaster relief, struggling for social justice, and so on. Each
of these acts gives us a better picture of who God is and what God loves.
These acts are theological by nature.

When I say that children can be and are theologians, I am not saying
we should force children to read Thomas Aquinas's *Summa Theologica*, nor
am I saying children can write their own *Summa Theologica*. I am arguing
a much larger point: we need to rethink our assumptions about what
theology is and who theologians are such that children and child-centered
activities are included.

The theme of this chapter is *play*. Play is the perfect example of a child
activity that should be considered theology. Not only is play inherently
theological; it is also through play that we can see children engaging theology and it is through play that children can become more theological.
When we start to expand our definition of theology and when we include
child's play, we will see children with a new perspective: as capable theo-

logians with profound theological insights. We also will better empower children in their theological play. This, in turn, can inspire us as adults to play ourselves, to join children as they joyfully engage our Creator, walking hand in hand with children as our partners toward the kingdom of God.

Taking Play Seriously

Before we can fully explore how play is theology and how children are theologians, we need to address the elephant in the room: most Christians do not take play seriously. In fact, some of you reading might be bristling at the idea of "playing" being categorized with theology, perhaps even offended at the idea that engaging God is "child's play." Should we not approach God with the utmost seriousness and maturity? This is an important question.

In many American churches, we assume that knowing God is *work*. It is *work* to study the Bible. It is *work* to create theology. And we assume this belief is right and good: work is serious and it is something mature adults do and it is therefore all business. And since we assume God is serious and all business, too, work is the best way to know God and do theology. To know God any other way than seriously would be sacrilegious.

As a result of these beliefs, we often denigrate anything appearing to be the opposite of work; that is, anything appearing like play. It is not that we think play is *wrong*, per se, but we consider play to be less important when compared to work, especially when it comes to knowing God.[2] Consider one way this often plays out: many Christians would consider children playing with toy Bible characters to be less important than adults interpreting a Bible passage in a group setting. What the adults are doing, many Christians would argue, is *work*, while the children are merely *playing*. The adults are contemplating theology; the children are not.

We apply this idea to adult play, too. For example, an adult painting a picture of Jesus is often considered recreation or leisure, whereas an adult preaching a sermon on Jesus is considered work. Thus, we consider the sermon to be more important or valuable than the painting. This is because preaching a sermon (what we consider work) is seen as serious, whereas painting (what we often consider play) is seen as less serious, perhaps sometimes even frivolous (especially if the painter is younger in age).

We must ask ourselves: *Is* God serious and all business? Because if they are not, then our value system might be askew. Personally, I believe God is not serious and all business. In fact, I believe that if we only know God seriously, we fail to know God completely. Additionally, play can be as important and equally as serious as work. Something like painting can have as much value in the eyes of God and give us as much information about God as preaching. This is because God is a God of play.

The Playfulness of God

Playfulness is inherent in God's nature. We see this when the Bible begins with a divine act of play in Genesis 1:1: "In the beginning God created the heavens and the earth." Theology professor Robert K. Johnston says that, "In creation God 'played' meaningfully and freely with his own possibilities, not needing to be productive but demonstrating the wealth of his riches joyfully, according to his own good pleasure." Johnston extends this notion of God's play from God's act of creation all the way through to God's act of incarnation: "Similarly, there was no compelling reason for God to become man in Jesus other than that it was according to his good pleasure."[3]

We also see God's playfulness—and the importance they place on it—in God's commands to the Israelites to rest, dance, and be festive in their worship. Calvinist theologian David Naugle points to these facts in his "Serious Theology of Play." Naugle highlights the Sabbath as an example of God placing limits on work and thereby creating space for play. "As the Sabbath limits labor, and opens up a window for rest," Naugle says, "this biblical theme creates space in our lives for play and leisure in which we eucharistically enjoy the works of God and the life He has given us." Furthermore, God established numerous festivals for the Israelites, implying that "human beings, by divine design, are also homo festivus!" Inherent to these festivals are song and dance, by which God is worshipped. Finally, Naugle claims that Jesus's very life—and his actions, like turning water into wine—indicates that Jesus possesses a "festive nature and delightful personality."[4]

All of these facts add up to a serious conclusion for Naugle: that part of being a disciple of Jesus is to "cultivate a spirit of playfulness." Naugle writes, "If God is a God of play, and if human play is, indeed, rooted in divine play, then we, as humans, ought to develop our abilities at play and cultivate a spirit of playfulness. This is both our gift and our responsibility in an often-serious world."[5]

The biblical narrative abounds with stories of God's playfulness. In the story of Balaam and his donkey (Num. 22:22–35), the donkey sees an angel of the Lord but Balaam does not. God causes Balaam to hear his donkey speak in order to warn him about the angel. While God could have simply allowed Balaam to see the angel, they chose a more humorous mode of communication.

Or consider the story of Jonah and the whale. Jonah rebels against God's command to speak prophetically against the city of Nineveh. God could have brought about Jonah's repentance in all sorts of mundane ways. Instead, "the Lord appointed a great fish to swallow up Jonah. And Jonah was in the belly of the fish three days and three nights" (Jon. 1:17). The whale's role is entirely unnecessary. Nonetheless, a giant sea creature makes its way into Jonah's story of redemption, demonstrating the child-like, fantastical charm of God.

We also see the playfulness of God reflected in the *grace* that God has gifted to humanity. Pentecostal theologian Nimi Wariboko explores this idea in *The Pentecostal Principle*. Wariboko argues since grace is a spontaneous gift, it has no purpose or instrumentality. Grace is thus not the "work" of God but rather the "play" of God: "Grace is characterized by play; no purpose at all."[6] So not only are we saved by God's grace (instead of by our own works), but grace itself is divine play (instead of divine work). God's redemption of humanity is play, play, play, all the way down. Wariboko writes, "Grace . . . by definition is a genuine gift and not a secretly instrumentalized one. . . . It has no purpose. No self-addressed envelope from the giver to send something in return. . . . It is play, not because it is trivial and worthless, but because it has no end, an unended action."[7]

Wariboko relates God's playful redemption of humanity to the playful nature of children. When Jesus says to become like children, Wariboko interprets that phrase to mean *embrace play*. He says, "Play is the essential character of spirituality governed by the grace-principle rather than the work-principle. It is the state of religion that is deprived of the spur of necessity, want, and purpose—human-divine relationship reorganized in the spirit of play. Jesus said, 'unless you change and become like children, you will never enter the kingdom of heaven' (Matt. 18:3)."

Wariboko is not the only Christian theologian to consider embracing play to be an explicitly Christian duty. While imprisoned in Nazi Germany, Lutheran theologian Dietrich Bonhoeffer wrote the following: "I wonder whether it is possible (it almost seems so today) to regain the idea of *the Church* as providing an understanding of the area of freedom (art, education, friendship, play)."[8] To Bonhoeffer, play means freedom. Play means that we are free to enjoy life without utility and without guilt. When children play, they are engaging—knowingly or not—in an act of theological resistance. They are resisting those forces in our world that say everything needs to be focused on the financial bottom line and efficiency. When we give children the freedom to play or we ourselves cast off the burdens of work, we enter into the life of grace.[9] We "become like children," as Wariboko suggests.

God's creation, love of dance and festivals, penchant for humor, obsession with sea creatures, and grace indicate that God is indeed a God of play. This supports my earlier statement: if we only try to know God seriously, we will fail to know God completely. There is much in God's nature that is not dry and serious. Approaching God and theology playfully, in a childlike manner, and *with actual children* might very well reveal insufficiencies in our current understanding of God.

Play as Theology

If God is a God of play, then the act of play is, to some extent, theological by its very nature. When children play, theology happens. When we play, we are reflecting something about who God is and what God values. The act of play reflects God's nature. Yet play is also theological for practical reasons. Beyond the abstract point that children playing mirrors the essence of God, there are practical reasons for seeing play as theology and encouraging play among children for theological purposes. Play is a veritable playground for children's theological explorations. Through play, children become budding theologians in a twofold way: play helps children process their spirituality and play helps children enter religious language.

In his book *The Children's God,* David Heller speaks to the first point. Heller's book reveals the findings of a study he conducted on children's spirituality. The core of Heller's study involved children showing him what they think about God and their own spirituality through play (by using dolls to act out various spiritual scenarios). Heller came to realize that play is not only a powerful medium for children to explore their own spirituality; it also empowers children to communicate that spirituality to adults. Additionally, play gives them the freedom to doubt, and in doubting, gives them the opportunity encounter God on their own terms. Heller concluded from his study that children are in fact "fledgling theologians."[10]

Why is this the case? One possibility is that children explore their spirituality through play because doing so is part of what being made in the image of God means. Since God is a playful God, it makes sense that play would be the arena God created for humans to plumb the depths of their own selves. "Play," Heller suggests, "provide[s] a vehicle into the inner sanctum of the child."[11] It is a safe space—sometimes literally so, as children explore all sorts of serious matters through play. For example, children who have experienced trauma often use play to process the aftereffects of that trauma.[12] Play also helps children recover from other life stressors.[13] There is something powerful about play that makes it have great utility when it is undertaken for no utility whatsoever.

Another potential reason comes from the second point about seeing children as budding theologians: play helps children enter religious language. This is an idea explored in depth by Godly Play founder Jerome Berryman. Berryman argues that play opens a child up to *wonder,* and that it is through wonder that a person approaches the throne of God. This forms the basis of Berryman's religious education system, Godly Play. As the title indicates, playfulness is key to Berryman's worldview. He sees play "as a life-giving act."[14] Because of this, he believes that associating religion with play will also be life-giving: "If the language of religion can be associated with the creative process, it can help with one's life pilgrimage."[15]

Berryman's education system revolves around adults helping children to think about religion and spirituality with the phrase "I wonder. . . ." He explains, "Children need to learn how to wonder in religious education so they 'enter' religious language rather than merely repeat it or talk about it."[16] By beginning with wonder, Berryman believes children can better access religious language and thus will be empowered to name and understand their own spiritual experiences.

In Godly Play, children come together in a circle with the teachers and take turns using concrete objects to wonder aloud about biblical parables. The use of concrete objects enables children not only to play with the stories but to feel a sense of ownership over them. As Berryman writes about each parable and its object, "It's theirs as well as mine. We all come equally to the parable to discover what it means for our lives. That's really all I have to teach."[17]

Berryman was greatly influenced in his ideas by the Catholic children's educator Sofia Cavalletti. Like Berryman, a key part of Cavalletti's religious education system involves using concrete objects to symbolize to children the messages of the Bible. As children play with these concrete objects, the objects become a portal for children to *personally* interact with and enter into the meanings of biblical stories. Explaining the ideas of Cavalletti, Vivian L. Houk writes, "As children begin to encounter symbols of faith, they enter into the mystery and wonder of what faith might mean and will gradually come to know in fuller ways what the group they belong to believes it means."[18]

Both Cavalletti and Berryman believe that as children play, wonder happens. Children are particularly skilled in this area, because children naturally love to play. According to Presbyterian minister Marjorie Thompson, "Cavalletti reports that children love to play . . . and can spend remarkable periods of time contemplating biblical stories with the aid of concrete objects. Over time, and through play, they will gradually assimilate biblical meanings."[19] By allowing children to process their own spirituality and enter religious language with play, play itself becomes a theological act. It enables children to explore who God is and what God values. Play makes all children theologians.

Play as Recontextualization

Let us consider an example of how play can create theological insights for both children and adults. One fruitful example of play is *recontextualization*. We see children do this when they take characters or parts from one toy set (My Little Pony characters, for example) and place them in the context of another toy set (say, a Lego Star Wars scene). When we take something from one context and place it within a new, strange, and foreign context, we create *juxtaposition*. As Jerome Berryman explains, "The logic of juxtaposition, used naturally by the preschool child, is the logic of play. It is also the logic of scanning. Piaget noticed that preschool children do not have internalized structures of classification by which to sort out things in the way most adults and children do. Preschool children juxtapose bits and pieces of the world and language in novel ways."[20]

Juxtaposition through recontextualization is seen beyond childhood as well, such as when a DJ mashes up two styles of music: syncing Beethoven's Ninth Symphony with dubstep beats. Recontextualizing the old (a romantic symphony) with the new (electronic dance music) can help us appreciate the old in a new and unique way. It can even provoke revelations about the original meaning. Having dubstep beats elucidate the melody of Beethoven's Ninth Symphony might help us relate to certain emotions or meaning Beethoven hoped to communicate to his original audience that might not be obvious to contemporary listeners.

How could this form of play be applied to theology? Children already do recontextualization with theology, though many adults simply consider it "cute" and not provocative in a serious manner. Just as children take characters or parts from one toy set and place them in the context of another toy set, they also take characters or parts from the Bible and place them in non-Bible contexts (and vice versa). They may reimagine Jonah as a cave person in the belly of a dinosaur, or they may reimagine Jesus as a savior in a futuristic Lego land. They may send their dolls back into Jesus's time in a time machine to have their dolls engage Jesus. These moments of play are "cute," yes, but they are also moments where children are imagining relationships with, within, and without the Bible in new, unique, and creative ways.

How can such child's play be considered to be significant theologically? It lays groundwork for us to allow members of our faith communities the freedom to ask questions. Especially among Millennials who grew up in the modern, evangelical, American Christian world, many people feel they were not allowed to ask questions. They were not allowed to approach the Bible or their struggles with faith in a creative way. They were not given the opportunity to reimagine or push back on Bible stories. They simply had to passively accept the information presented to them.[21]

Blithe acceptance is not the only option. We should have the freedom to reimagine or push back without having our faith communities respond as if we are heretics.[22] As children's educator Vivian L. Houk writes, we should "teach children to ask 'what if?' questions. Considering alternatives will stimulate inventive or imaginative thinking."[23] Children (and adults!) should be able to ask questions like, "But what *if* Jesus was just a human and not God?" "What if the stories of creation in Genesis (Gen. 1:1–2:3, Gen. 2:4–25) are poetry, not history?" "What if God makes mistakes?" "What does this or that biblical passage look like if it was a different context—if, say, God's response at the end of Job was put in the context of child abuse?"[24] To some Christians, asking questions like these is simply encouraging sacrilege, heresy, or disbelief. I would argue that such fears and hesitations indicate a lack of confidence, empathy, and imagination. Take the Job and child abuse example (that is, the idea that God's treatment of Job would constitute abuse in a different context). Instead of taking the fearful stance that such an interpretation means God really is abusive, we can use the reimagined discourse to help us empathize with those who *do* think of God as abusive. This can help us think about how we talk about God and, by extension, how we can talk about God better and more precisely. Such exploration can help us imagine how child abuse survivors in our faith communities might hear biblical passages differently than non-survivors.[25] This in turn can help the church better serve child abuse survivors.

Such a simple act of play—recontextualizing a popular biblical passage—can yield immense fruit.

For reasons like this, we should be able to ask playful questions. We should be able to explore them fully with the blessings of our faith communities precisely because we should possess the sort of faith that can withstand such explorations. We should be able to relate to those questions and nagging doubts. In fact, we should encourage their public expression without fear. Responding with fear or threats only implies that we are not confident in the foundations of our faith traditions—that we think the playfulness inherent to our being made in the image of God can destroy the very God who made us playful.

Play as Adult Discipleship

Juxtaposition is a great example of how play can develop theologians out of children; it is also a great example of how play can enrich adult discipleship. By engaging in a life of play, by juxtaposing biblical passages with current events, adults can learn new ways of understanding God and interpreting the Bible—new ways that better reflect God's diverse and liberative nature. By reimagining and questioning and talking back to and wrestling with God and the Bible, just like how Jacob once wrestled with Yahweh and was blessed for it (Gen. 32:22–32), we become better disciples. In short, both children and adults serve and honor God with our recreation—which, as Kristin Johnston Largen points out, is *re-creation*, mirroring God's own act of creation: "It is not coincidental that one synonym for play is 'recreation'— that is, 're-creation': the activity of creating anew, celebrating both God's creative activity and the creative gifts of others in our own unplanned and spontaneous inventive behavior. Play, as well as work, honors God."[26]

Play honors God because it reflects God's own creativity and imagination. Largen explains that, "Our own creative play—painting, singing, playing music, writing—all without skill or purpose—could be seen as mimicking the play of God who takes delight in the created world, sometimes engaging creation just for the fun of it."[27] Largen thus asks, "Who would argue, for example, that a parent is not honoring God when he whiles away the afternoon playing Legos with his son, or that two girls are not honoring God when they play with their dolls, or spend the morning swinging on swings in the playground?"[28] When we start to see children playing as an act of theology, we open ourselves up to the possibility of *adults* playing *also* being an act of theology. The act of play is transformed into "a means of becoming attuned to the divine presence in life and learning to respond with reverence and joy."[29] In this way, play becomes a holy act for disciples of all ages.

Play as Divine Transformation

The Bible repeatedly testifies that children at play are images of divine favor and wisdom. The prophet Zechariah, for example, presents the image of children at play in his vision of a restored Zion. Zechariah prophesies that in the future, when Jerusalem is restored, one of the signs of such restoration will be evidence of play: "The city streets will be filled with boys and girls playing there" (Zech. 8:5). And in the book of Proverbs, the personified character of Wisdom speaks about her childhood playing in the presence of God in Proverbs 8:30–31 (ERV): "I grew up as a child by [God's] side, laughing and playing all the time. I played in the world he made and enjoyed the people he put there."

Child theology founder Marcia J. Bunge relates these ideas of child's play leading to restoration and wisdom to the idea that children refresh or awaken adults' perspectives. When children are given permission to play with the way their elders think about and do things, real transformation for the whole community can occur. Bunge writes, "Children are also gifts in the sense that they offer us fresh and open perspectives. They often ask fundamental questions about life that open our eyes to new possibilities in our thinking. They are like the new employees in a company who can ask, 'Why do you do things like this?' Their questions force us to reevaluate our priorities and to reexamine 'business as usual.' The biblical texts go further to suggest that play, too, is an aspect of true wisdom."[30] When children are free to approach God and theology with playfulness, they can breathe new life into our own approaches to God and theology.

Implications for Child Liberation Theology

How does reimagining theology as play relate to child liberation? I can think of at least three answers.

First, reimagining theology as play invites children to be active participants in their faith experiences.

When we invite children to play theologically alongside us, we invite them to be active participants in God's kingdom. They are no longer relegated to being passive recipients of adult knowledge. This enables us to move beyond the "information dump" or "banking" model that we see in so many religious education systems.

Feminist educator bell hooks describes the banking model of education as "based on the assumption that memorizing information and regurgitating it represent[s] gaining knowledge that [can] be deposited, stored and used at a later date."[31] In this model, hooks says that "students are regarded merely as passive consumers."[32] Children consume whatever information adults feed to them and have no say in the process. A great example of this model in Christian children's education is AWANA, the immensely popular Bible verse memorization program for children.

Evangelicals Lance Latham and Art Rorheim founded the AWANA program in 1950. AWANA stands for "Approved Workmen Are Not Ashamed" (an acronym taken from 2 Tim. 2:15). The program emphasizes the memorization of Bible verses by children ranging from preschool to high school. Nearly one million children participate in AWANA in the US.[33] AWANA employs the banking model of education. Using the promise of rewards like plastic jewelry and candy to entice children, Bible verses are "deposited" into children's memories with the hope and belief that the memorized verses will "become the means that the Spirit uses to activate faith."[34] The curriculum is set and rigid. Children are not given the freedom to participate in its creation or implementation; adults have already made the plan. Children are simply to follow the rules.

Former AWANA directors Greg Carlson and John K. Crupper explain that Scripture is "the foundation of what an individual needs to know and trust in order to develop a relationship with God."[35] As a result, they believe the best way to instill faith in children is through the accumulation of knowledge—specifically, the knowledge of Bible verses. "Salvation is known from Scripture," they write. They appear to elevate cognition (particularly a cognitive skill like memorization) over and above other ways of experiencing God. Carlson and Crupper say, "Knowing, memorizing, studying, obeying, and proclaiming the Scripture takes priority over any other study, discipline, endeavor, or experience."[36] Their assertion runs counter to James 1:27, however, which underscores caring for widows and orphans as evidence of "pure and faultless" religion.

Memorization has its place and scripture can be a source of comfort. I used to repeat Bible verses I had memorized in my head in the middle of the night to calm myself after childhood nightmares. Even so, I fear we put too much emphasis on memorization. Doing so makes children *passive* learners. The banking model treats children as empty vessels for adults to fill instead of respecting them as active participants and agents in their spiritual education. As practical theologian Joyce Ann Mercer explains,

With children, learning too often gets reduced to remembering, as children's responses to questions such as, "Do you remember the story of Jacob and Esau?" signal whether or not they have 'learned' that story—that is, whether or not they can recall its details. How they make sense of the story and how they engage the story to make sense of their own worlds are not taken into consideration. . . . [The banking model of education] treats learners as empty receptacles waiting to be filled with informational knowledge that could then be withdrawn at another time like a bank deposit.[37]

There is another problem with the banking model followed by religious education programs like AWANA. Such programs leave no room for children who process information differently or for children who have not yet developed—or even *cannot* develop—the necessary cognitive abilities to do so. As Christian education professor Scottie May points out, programs like AWANA suggest that "cognitive development is necessary for a child to have a *salvific* relationship with Jesus Christ." May asks Carlson and Crupper, "What does that mean for the person who is mentally or socially disabled, such as severe autism or Down syndrome? How does this model work for those children?"[38]

Not only does the banking model exclude and marginalize various groups of children; it also reduces one's relationship to God to the mere acquisition of knowledge. AWANA does not put a significant emphasis on actually putting one's faith into practice—for example, by tending to the needy and vulnerable in one's community. Joyce Ann Mercer puts it well, "Learning is much more than 'cognitive recall.' Learning is transformation."[39] We need to move beyond educational programs that assume learning is "the ability of an individual's memory to store and recall information." Learning should be seen, instead, as "the process of meaning-making, or how persons—including children—make sense of their worlds in increasingly more adequate and complex ways over time."[40]

A prime example of how play can help us in this endeavor can be found in the aforementioned example of Godly Play, which is based on the Montessori method of learning.[41] Godly Play advocate Emily A. Mullens describes the day-to-day reality of Godly Play in the following manner: "In most religious education, children are *told* who God is. In Godly Play, children *discover* who God is. Using the principles of learning in the Montessori method, we respond to the child's request to 'help me do it myself.'. . . This puts the teacher in the role of spiritual supporter or guide who fully accepts that each child has his or her own relationship with God *already*."[42]

What I most appreciate about Godly Play is this underlying belief that "each child has his or her own relationship with God *already*." This counters the evangelical belief that children must be "trained up" or "controlled" like dogs, horses, or vipers[43] in order to have a proper relationship with God. Godly Play, in contrast, assumes a child's relationship with God already exists. Children are born already bearing God's image; they do not need to be re-imaged by their parents, as someone like Michael Pearl argues, in the manner that the Amish re-image their mules.[44]

Most of the American evangelical child training industry denies, either explicitly or implicitly, that children have a direct, one-to-one relationship with God. The majority of the industry's experts—from Michael Pearl to Tedd Tripp to Bill Gothard to John MacArthur—believe children stand under an umbrella of parental authority that interrupts the child-God relationship. Until children reach adulthood, these experts believe parents serve as God's official voice to children, the children's representative to God, or even an earthly metaphor for God. The child cannot obey or serve God *as God*; rather, the child obeys or serves God *by obeying or serving the demi-God, the parents*.[45]

In these experts' minds, the child and the adult are locked into an authoritarian, top-down system. "The child's 'rightful position' and 'proper place,'" J. Richard Fugate says, is always on the bottom.[46] The father, in contrast, is always right beneath God, an indication of the patriarchy inherent to many of the evangelical child training experts' beliefs. The adults, especially the father, stand between God and the child and cause the child to follow them directly (and thus God only indirectly).

Using Godly Play as a counterexample, we can envision an alternative: the adult does not interrupt the child-God relationship, nor does the adult act as God to the child. Rather, the child has a direct, unmediated relationship to God and the child's own spirituality. We can take Jesus's assertion that the kingdom of God will belong to little children and apply it now: the kingdom of God *already* belongs to them (Luke 18:16). The adult, then, walks alongside the child as a guide.

Buddhist scholar Yoshiharu Nakagawa talks about the potentially beautiful and cooperative relationship adults and children can have. "In the Buddhist tradition," writes Nakagawa, "the relation between child and adult plays an essential role in which each of them benefits each other's spiritual development, for each one is a good friend on the path."[47] I believe this principle can be applied equally to Christianity. For in relationship to God, both the child and the adult are peers. Since they are both considered children of God, we could even call them spiritual siblings. They are both walking the same path together toward God. Yes, in relationship to each other, the child and adult are not siblings. But neither are they stuck in an authoritarian, top-down mode. Instead, the adult—who has more life experiences and is more emotionally, mentally, and physically developed—guides the child as a good friend would. But as good friends, the adult should always be open to being guided by the child in turn, always open to learning from the child and seeing the child as a source of wisdom and revelation. Authority symbolizes the evangelical models; as Tedd Tripp says, "Authority best describes the parent's relationship to the child."[48] *Guided partnership* symbolizes the alternative model.

The guided partnership nature of Godly Play is admirable. By being an extension of the Montessori method, however, Godly Play has some weaknesses. Mullens admits to one of these; namely, that the materials needed to implement Godly Play "can be time-consuming to make and extremely expensive to buy."[49] This reduces accessibility for under-resourced families or faith communities. Berryman admits to another weakness: Godly Play is a small group method that assumes a classroom of fifteen children or fewer, and "you need two people [adults] in each room."[50] With high costs, small classrooms, and significant adult involvement required, Godly Play can be difficult to implement in many underprivileged faith communities. If an educational method is only liberative to privileged communities and children, that method fails to be adequately liberative.

It is important, therefore, to focus not on the method of Godly Play itself (though it certainly has strengths), but rather on the foundational belief. The belief is beautifully expressed by Berryman: "Godly Play does not teach conclusions—it has the confidence that the children will find those conclusions. . . . [Children] can become the theologians and they can make their own conclusions. We don't stunt their growth by giving them conclusions, *we give them the ability and the means to make their own theology.*"[51]

The belief that children already have a relationship with God and the confidence that children can be theologians can be separated from Godly Play as a specific educational method and serve as a foundation for other methods and ideas. We can use this as a starting point from which we explore ways children can play alongside adults theologically. By embracing this idea that theology truly can be child's play, we can better dismantle those aspects of our faith communities that oppress, rather than liberate, children. In turn, we can encourage play as a way for children (and adults) to be active participants in their faith experiences.

> *Second, reimagining theology as play invites us to imagine new futures in which children guide their own education.*

Reimagining theology as play also relates to child liberation as it invites us to imagine new futures for children—futures in which children can help guide their own educations in novel ways. The spontaneous nature of play joyfully disrupts the instrumentality of work. This allows play to open up the potential for alternatives: spaces in which we can imagine ways of being and doing that differ from present systems.[52]

Joyce Ann Mercer speaks to how viewing play in terms of theology can create such alternatives, saying, "Play (like art) is a way to construct 'counter-environments' and 'anti-environments' to the status quo that give people the freedom to imagine new futures. Fear and worry keep human beings stuck on the ground . . . while freedom begins when people act without fear. Play draws people into freedom."[53] How exactly does play do this? I know of no better way to explain how play draws people into freedom than the following description that Robert K. Johnston gives of C. S. Lewis's interest in play:

> In his autobiography, *Surprised by Joy*, C. S. Lewis describes several play experiences of his childhood and youth in which he was pointed

to something beyond the ordinary horizons of our world, in which he was opened outward to the transcendent. The first such experience occurred when he was six, as he gazed at a toy garden that his brother made for him out of moss, decorated with twigs and flowers, and set in the lid of a biscuit tin. In the years that followed, he heard play's voice of Joy when he smelled a flowering currant bush, when he discovered the autumn of Beatrix Potter's Squirrel Nutkin, when he read Longfellow's Saga of King Olaf, and again when he later became involved in Wagnerian Romanticism.

Lewis had continuing difficulty defining or even describing these experiences of "Joy." For him, Joy was distinct from mere happiness on the one hand, and from aesthetic pleasure on the other. He thought that authentic Joy was characterized by "the stab, the pang, the inconsolable longing" that was aroused. . . . In describing this experience of Joy, Lewis was attempting to circumscribe that non-sought-after result of play which we have described as play's proclivity to open one outward to the transcendent. . . .

Lewis thought that one's play experiences offered the possibility of being transformed by Joy as one entered fully into the play event. In play, Joy's "bright shadow" might reveal to the participant that indefinite, yet real, horizon of meaning beyond his normally perceived world.[54]

Lewis identified the unique power of play to "open one outward to the transcendent." Play does this by transporting the person playing to different modes of consciousness that are not part of everyday existence. And lest you consider this the ravings of a progressive mystic, consider that even a conservative Catholic philosopher like Josef Pieper has made the same point. In his book *Leisure: The Basis of Culture*, Pieper writes, "Leisure is a receptive attitude of mind, a contemplative attitude. . . . When we really let our minds rest contemplatively on a rose in bud, on a child at play, on a divine mystery, we are rested and quickened. . . . It is in these silent receptive moments that the soul of man is sometimes visited by an awareness of what holds the world together."[55]

One important future that play can open up is one in which children give guidance in the creation of new religious education systems. So many of the current ways we educate children about God and theology are imagined, designed, and implemented with zero input from those most directly impacted by the education: the children themselves! This leads to problems, as Marcia J. Bunge argues: "The curricula of many [religious education] programs are theologically weak and uninteresting to children, and they assume that children have no questions, ideas, or spiritual experiences."[56] Religious curricula should address not only what adults want children to learn, but also what children themselves want to learn. And more specifically, *how* specific children *want* to learn. Since "people come to experience God and learn about him in unique and personal ways,"[57] it makes sense that "learning, much like developing spiritual maturity, is highly personal; and no one description fits all individuals."[58]

Should we not involve children in the process of imagining and creating the curricula that they will use? Children are the perfect sounding board for these ventures. And children have a right to weigh in on how they learn about God. It is *their* education, after all.

Third, reimagining theology as play encourages us to focus on empowering children to create their own theologies.

In David Heller's study of children's spirituality, he found a common theme. Children "desire a more direct encounter or experience with their God." But, Heller writes, there is a problem: "They seem to feel that such encounters are forbidden; they also harbor much trepidation about foregoing the intercession of adults."[59] In other words, children very much want to know and love God for themselves, on their terms, and without the intervention of adults. Children have difficulty doing this, though, because adults often make them believe they are not allowed to. Adults communicate to children that God is not directly accessible to them. Instead, children have to obey their parents in order to know and love God.

Heller says that this makes children feel they are "the small marionettes of religious theater, acting and revealing a prepared script,"[60] instead of being able to define and actualize their own relationship with spirituality. It also makes children believe that certain ways of knowing and loving God are either impossible or inappropriate. Heller interviewed one five-year-old boy named Harold, who said, "I wish my Sunday school teacher would let us draw." Harold found drawing to be a way to commune with God, but his teacher forced Harold to follow the preapproved models for knowing God. This "tendency of formal religious teachers and parents to block noninstitutional or unconventional views," observed Heller, "discourage[s] original belief and discovery."[61]

As adults, we need to give children the freedom to be their own theologians—to discover and love who God is and what God values *on their own terms*. Children are desperate to do so. Heller remarks that child after child was eager and enthusiastic to share with him their *own* thoughts and their *own* questions and their *own* ideas, but were scared to do so with other adults. When they finally felt safe doing so in the context of play, they were overflowing in their desire to be theologians. "Now, can I tell one of my own [biblical stories]?" asked seven-year-old Hallie. "Can I say some things about God I thought up myself?" asked seven-year-old Jeri. "These are the voices of children," Heller implores, "who search for a certain spiritual and expressive freedom. . . . They seem to be asking for a free atmosphere to discover what the nature of God might be."[62]

If we want children to personally know and love God, we need to give them the freedom to do it on their own. We need to let them create their own theologies and to figure out for themselves who God is and what God values. "Participation is the active agent in empowerment."[63]

INCLUDING CHILDREN

To begin this project, put together a list of the various curricula that your family, faith community, or religious organization use to educate or engage children. For example, if you are a homeschooling family or a private religious school, this would encompass your daily school curricula. Or if you are a church, this would include your Sunday school curricula for children as well as any weekend or weeknight programming for children. Have one person be in charge of compiling the list of curricula, but be sure to ask everyone in your group for ideas of what to include on it to make sure that you have the most accurate and comprehensive list as possible. For each curriculum (or program), give a brief, accessible description to remind children what it is.

Next, distribute the list of curricula to all the children. For each curriculum listed, have the children think about the following questions:

1. What do you like about the curriculum?
2. What do you dislike about the curriculum?
3. If you could make one change to improve the curriculum, what would it be?
4. If you could make one change to improve how the adults teach the curriculum to you, what would it be?

Give the children a week or two to come up with their answers. Encourage the children to answer the questions in whatever format is most comfortable to them. If they want to write down their answers on paper or use an electronic device, let them. Or if they want to just think about their answers, that is also acceptable. Additionally, give the children multiple avenues for returning their answers to you: on paper, through email, verbally in private, or verbally during a public event.

For this final and public piece, plan an event where all the adults and children come together to hear the children's answers and discuss how to move forward with the information you discover. Consider allowing children the opportunity to lead and moderate the event (of course, adults can provide guidance as needed). In an organized fashion, review each curriculum on your list and open the floor to the children to share their answers to each or any of the four questions. Remember to keep the focus on the children and their perspective. Even if the comments are critical or negative, avoid defensiveness and exercise humility and openness. Have someone be the event "scribe" to write down everyone's answers. After the event is over, compile the answers sent privately and those given during the public event and start thinking about how you can implement the changes in curricula and teaching that the children felt most passionate about.

thirteen

Seeing Children as Children

We conceive of an innate spiritual capacity
in childhood, but recognize that this may
focus in particular ways and take different
and changing forms as the child's other
capacities develop.

—Karl Rahner[1]

In chapters 10 through 12, I have argued that we need to see children as more than adults-in-the-making or incomplete adults. Children are "fully religious beings from birth."[2] We need to see children as Jesus saw them: God-to-us individuals who are capable of (1) prophetic speech against an adult world, (2) teaching and leading that adult world in profound, meaningful ways, and (3) actively creating their own theologies.

It would be very easy to misunderstand these points, so I want to be clear about what I am *not* saying. Imagine with me a seesaw. On one end of the seesaw is a church that excludes children. People in this church hate when infants are loud or cry during church services; young children are sent away from the adults to their own Sunday school where the least experienced pastors are responsible for their education; and adolescents are barely tolerated for exhibiting their growing pains and rebellious ways. The members of this church prefer to simply entertain the adolescents. This church is a church that disrespects children.

But there is the other side of the seesaw. An example of the other side comes from evangelical homeschooling. In that world, there is a popular movement called the family-integrated church.[3] In churches belonging to this movement, no distinction is made between children and adults. Children are required to sit through the adult services. Sunday schools are considered sinful. Youth groups are considered a breeding ground for rebellion.[4]

This type of church, like the first type, also disrespects children. Yes, children are not excluded *physically* from the religion of the adults. Yes, children are considered *capable* of understanding how adults talk about God. But children are still excluded. Why? They are excluded because these churches continue to value the *adult* way of doing things. Services are not changed to be accessible to children; children are not included in theological work; children are not considered teachers. Rather, adults require children to be silent and tolerate their existence in a world that does not include them. They are required to sit through age-inappropriate sermons and their developmental stages are not respected. Such churches may tolerate the cries of infant children in their services, but that does not mean those churches actually *welcome* children to the table in the way Jesus described.

Welcoming children does not mean we treat children as adults. In fact, treating children as adults is just another way we exclude children. It is a form of child abuse and neglect. When children act above their age or assume roles inappropriate for their age, it is actually a warning sign of trauma. Trauma specialists call this *parentification*.[5]

Welcoming children does not mean parentification. Welcoming children means that we see children *as children*. We respect their developmental processes and we create spaces for them to be prophets and priests *in age-appropriate ways*. We never lose sight of the fact that *they are still children*.

Seeing children as children requires at least four elements:

1. We need to be students of child development.
2. We need to respect children's developmental stages. This means respecting both children's developmental capabilities and children's developmental limits.
3. We need to make church for adults *and* children. This means thinking about "kid" activities (for example, drawing) as being equally worthy

to be considered worship as "adult" activities. In other words, we need to stop making distinctions between "kid" and "adult" activities when it comes to theology, specifically in a communal worship context.

4. Most importantly, we need to let children enjoy their childhood.

Understanding Child Development

I do not believe that every single member of the church needs to take a Child Development 101 class. (Though if they did, it would certainly not hurt.) It is important, however, for everyone who is interested in children's health and well-being—which should be almost everyone in the church—to have a basic understanding of how children develop. If we as Christians are called by Jesus to welcome children, then we ought to know how children are best welcomed, which means understanding them and what they need at various stages of their lives. This is where understanding child development comes into play.

In this section I present an overview of two of the most well-known theories of child development: the ages of humanity theory proposed by American psychologist Erik Erickson, and the cognitive development theory proposed by Swiss psychologist Jean Piaget. Fear not, I will not delve too far into the abstract while explaining these theories. They are worthy of discussion, though, because they are arguably the most influential theories about how children develop psychologically, socially, and mentally. Erickson's theory of the ages of humanity relates to how children develop *psychosocially*—how they develop in relationship to themselves, their family, and their peers. Piaget's theory, in contrast, concerns the development of *cognition*—how children think and create thought.

Why do we need to understand how children develop in relationship to themselves, their family, their peers, and their own thoughts? We need to understand because these concepts help us know how we can better relate to children, love children, and lift up children in age-appropriate ways. When we know, for example, that younger children have difficulties with symbolic thinking, we can make sure that our church services involve practical thinking as well so that younger children do not feel alienated. Knowing how children best learn and explore their worlds at different stages enables us to empower them in the most effective ways possible.

Relational Development

American psychologist Erik Erickson's theory of the ages of humanity relates to how children develop *psychosocially*—the fancy way of saying how children develop *relationally*—in relationship to themselves and others. Erickson breaks down his theory into eight different stages, or what he calls ages. Christian educators David Ng and Virginia Thomas give the following explanation for how Erickson's theory works: "Basic to Erikson's schema is the idea that at each age of development a central issue arises to challenge the person. In dealing with the issue, often with the help of parents or others close to the person, that person may develop certain strengths which accrue to his or her personality and prepare that person to meet the issue that will arise in the next stage of development."[6] Each stage does not have to happen sequentially; they can occur in random order, one can finish before another, one can begin before another ends, and so on. However, the stages build on each other.

The first five stages are most pertinent because they are the ages related to childhood and adolescence. (The last three stages concern adulthood.) We can visualize the first five stages in the following way (note that Erickson uses heteronormative language, which means that he assumes every child's primary caregiver will be a mother):[7]

Age	Strength	Challenge	Significant Relationship	Question(s)	Examples
Infancy (0–23 months)	Hope	Trust vs. mistrust	Mother	Can I trust the world?	Being fed, cuddling
Early childhood (2–4 years)	Will	Autonomy vs. shame and doubt	Parents	Is it okay to be me (and not you)?	Toilet training, clothing one's self

Age	Strength	Challenge	Significant Relationship	Question(s)	Examples
Preschool age (4–5 years)	Purpose	Initiative vs. guilt	Family	Is it okay for me to do, move, and act?	Exploring the world, using tools, making art
School age (5–12 years)	Compe-tence	Industry vs. infe-riority	Neighbors, school	Can I make it in the world of people and things?	School, sports
Adolescence (13–19 years)	Fidelity	Identity vs. role confusion	Peers, role models	Who am I? Who can I be?	Social relation-ships

Let us start at the beginning, the stage of infancy. During this stage, the child—a newborn infant—faces the challenge of learning to *trust*, which entails "the importance of a child learning that the world is reliable and will dependably meet one's needs."[8] The child interacts with her mother and, based on whether the mother helps the child meet her needs of feeding, sleeping, being held, and being changed, the child will either grow to trust or mistrust the world around her. In other words, the child is constantly asking the question (albeit nonverbally), *Can I trust the world?* If she ultimately learns that she can, she develops the strength of *hope*. Hope enables her to move on to the next stage with increased self-confidence.

The next stage spans early childhood, from two to four years old. This is the stage where the child hopefully gains the strength of *will*. Learning to have a will of one's own comes about from interacting with one's parents and learning to be autonomous instead of feeling shame and doubt about not being able to do things one's self. For example, learning to use the bathroom independently or dressing one's self. The child is learning to answer the question, *Is it okay to be me (and not you)?* The child is learning to differentiate himself from those around him, and learning to be his own person with his own will. As Christian educator Vivian L. Houk writes, "They develop in a way that lets them know that they are separate, autonomous individuals capable of relating to others in meaningful ways. This enables them to live in a community and to live out their lives, which came from God, with others."[9]

In the next stage, which spans the ages of four and five, the child learns to take initiative on her own. If she learns to do so, she gains a sense of *purpose*. This purpose inspires her to do, act, create, and imagine. She will explore the world around her and use tools and make art. As she does so, she will continually confront the question: *When is it okay for me to do, move, and act, and when is it not?*

From the ages of five to twelve, the child enters into the school age. Here the child interacts significantly with a world beyond his immediate family: with neighbors and peers and teachers at school. During this time, the child will wonder, *Can I make it in the world of people and things?* To find out, the child will learn how to be industrious with regard to school and sports; and if he fails at this, he can begin to develop a sense of inferiority. If he can conquer that sense, however, he will develop the strength of *competence*, gaining the belief that he really can make it in the world.

The final stage we will consider is that of adolescence, spanning the years of thirteen to nineteen. During this time of frenzied physical, hormonal, and neurological growth, the child enters an *identity crisis*, wondering, *Who am I? Who can I become?* Through significant interactions with peers and role models, the child has to decide who she *is* and what she wants to *be*. She will develop either a strong sense of *identity* or become confused about her identity in the world. Social relationships will have a significant influence on this process.

Cognitive Development

Children develop in more than relational ways. They also develop in their thinking, which is called *cognitive development*. To understand more about how children develop cognitively, we turn to Swiss psychologist Jean Piaget. Piaget is well known for his theory of cognitive development, which argues that children go through four stages. The official terms for each of these stages are: the *sensorimotor* stage, the *preoperational* stage, the *concrete operational* stage, and the *formal operational* stage. Christian educators David Ng and Virginia Thomas write, "A simplified way to summarize Piaget's description of children is to show that children work at four tasks of cognitive development: the creation of objects, then the creation of symbols, then the creation of rules, and finally the creation of thought." Let us consider each of the four stages in turn.[10]

The *sensorimotor* stage lasts from birth until a child acquires the skill of language. "Sensorimotor" refers to the nerves that control how a person's body functions. Child psychologist Laura E. Berk explains, "Its name reflects Piaget's belief that infants and toddlers 'think' with their eyes, ears, hands, and other sensorimotor equipment."[11] During this stage, children learn to manipulate objects around them. They learn to coordinate their experiences of seeing and hearing with the objects in their experiences by touching, tasting, and smelling them. Children gain knowledge of the world by using their five senses to interact with the objects around them, learning that they are separate from those objects. One key lesson children learn during this time is *object permanence*, which means that objects still exist even when they do not see them. When a parent plays peekaboo with a child, for example, the child learns that the parent does not cease to exist simply because the parent is not seen behind their hands. Through games like peekaboo, children learn that they and the objects around them have concrete existence.

The *preoperational* stage begins when a child starts speaking and lasts until around the age of seven. During this stage, Berk states that "the most obvious change is an extraordinary increase in representational, or symbolic, activity."[12] According to Piaget, children cannot think logically nor can they manipulate information mentally during this stage. However, they are exceptional at play, particularly make-believe or symbolic play. An example of such play is when a child pretends Legos are snacks and sheets of paper are fancy dining ware. Berk points out that "make-believe is another excellent example of the development of representation in early childhood. Piaget believed that through pretending, children practice and strengthen newly acquired representational schemes."[13] Children during this stage can also be very self-focused, or what psychologists refer to as *egocentric*. Life revolves around the child and the child's point of view can be the only point of view. Seeing life from other people's points of views can be difficult.

The *concrete operational* stage occurs during preadolescence, from the ages of seven to eleven. During this stage, children begin to master the rules of logic. Their thinking becomes more formal and, Berk says, "more closely resembling the reasoning of adults than that of younger children."[14] Piaget argues that such children cannot yet engage in abstract, hypothetical thinking but they can think logically about concrete objects and symbols. Inductive reasoning (reasoning from parts to a whole) occurs during this time. One particularly important skill children learn during this stage is classification. Piaget found that, starting at the age of seven, children began to successfully categorize things and think about the multiple relationships between those categories.[15]

The *formal operational* stage occurs from the ages of eleven until adulthood. Piaget believes children can begin to use abstract, hypothetical thinking during this stage—thinking *about* their thinking, in other words. They also begin to think about objects or ideas that have no necessary relation to reality. As Berk describes such children, "they no longer require concrete things or events as objects of thought. Instead, they can come up with new, more general logical rules through internal reflection."[16] This internal reflection enables deductive reasoning in children: evaluating the validity of propositions (statements of belief) using formal logic instead of concrete situations.[17] This in turn allows them to engage in philosophical and religious debates.

The Takeaway

These two theories are not the only ones or even the most accurate ones. There are certainly people who criticize Erickson and Piaget, and some of these criticisms are very important for our current discussion of child liberation theology. Edward Robinson, for example, argues that Piaget's theory sees children as incomplete human beings, because it focuses on how children do not yet see the world the way adults do—and the way adults see the world is supposedly the golden standard. But if we believe that children have wholly adequate insights into the universe at each and every developmental stage, then we cannot always compare children's capabilities to adults' capabilities. We must see children at each stage as being adequate thinkers—thinkers who have their own unique way of viewing the world that is entirely sufficient for them.[18]

Robinson argues that children have an "original vision" of the world, even though they are still developing. Robinson quotes from Edwin Muir, who says, "A child has a picture of human existence peculiar to himself, which he probably never remembers after he has lost it: the original vision of the world. I think of this picture or vision as that of a state in which the earth, the houses on the earth, and the life of every human being are related to the sky overarching them; as if the sky fitted the earth and the earth the sky."[19] Having been taught that children lack so many adult qualities, Robinson was startled when he studied the religious experiences of children to find that they have so many undetected positive qualities. Robinson writes, "[Piaget] is still accepted as orthodoxy in many quarters; there has been little fundamental change in recent years. The picture of childhood that emerges is a largely negative, not to say a patronizing one. So it was with considerable excitement that on joining this research project I found myself reading this sort of thing: 'The most profound experience of my life came to me when I was very young, between 4 and 5 years old.'"[20]

I believe this is a far better takeaway: children, at each of their developmental stages, are wholly capable of understanding the universe in their own unique, original ways—in ways that can lead to "the most profound experience" of their lives. God has made every child fully human at each stage of development. They may not have mastery of more "adult" functions such as abstract thinking, and that is okay. In fact, children have far more mastery of those functions than we likely realize, as Robinson discovered (and others like Robert Coles, whom we discussed in chapter 11, discovered, too). Even at very young ages, ages where children supposedly do not think abstractly, they are already thinking in profound and beautiful ways—sometimes even abstract ways. Children are continually surprising us with their original visions of God and the world.

Christian educator Karen Marie Yust summarizes the lesson here well: "The hierarchical nature of many developmental charts, with their linear construction and emphasis on upward movement toward 'optimal' adult functioning, has distracted us from the very real capabilities that children have *as children*. Instead of using human development theories to focus on children's deficiencies, as has been the tendency in contemporary parenting and religious education literature, we need to use this research to help us, as adults, understand how children can, in fact, be faithful throughout childhood."[21] We must use our knowledge of child development, in other words, to make faith and church accessible and empowering to children, rather than using it as an excuse for why we exclude or marginalize them.

Respecting Children's Developmental Stages

Being students of child development is only the beginning. Christians also need to apply what they learn about child development to how they interact with children at different stages. A key part of respecting those stages is respecting how children think about and interact with religion at any given age. In *The Children's God*, David Heller provides a helpful breakdown of how children of various ages think about God.

Heller examines how children in three different age categories—four to six years old, seven to nine years old, and ten to twelve years old—understand and relate to God. His most striking observation about the youngest children is that they relate to God in primarily playful ways. Even though the youngest children display "a clear absence of information concerning established religion and the sociology of religion," they "tend to maintain a positive and soft-mannered sense of a deity, frequently associating God with play and fun." Heller quotes four-year-old Marcie, who says, "God lives in a big castle, like our church; God also probably has a choir, and Christmas parties too!"[22]

Heller cautions us to not think about these youngest children's ideas about God as "simplistic." He writes, "There is no reason to assume that they have less of an idea of truth than conceptions of the deity which are more fully elaborated. There is something strikingly natural about the gay manner of these children, at the same time that developmental and socialization changes are also apparent" (41). Another interesting observation Heller makes about the youngest children is that "these fledgling theologians," as he calls them, have the ability to understand "that a certain duality in the universe must be addressed" (43). That is, young children realize that both good and bad exist in the world. They will relate that realization to God, sometimes thinking God can be both good and bad or that there is a good God and a bad God (e.g., Satan).

The next group of children, seven- to nine-year-olds, shows increasing knowledge and curiosity about God and religion. One of the driving forces behind this, Heller says, is their heightened awareness about being their own, independent persons. "They frequently ponder," Heller says, "whether they are alone or not in relation to a deity." This is seen in these children's play, where "aloneness is a common motif." Heller believes this is because, as children grow up, they realize that sometimes they will be alone—their family will not always be there for them, but perhaps God will be. Hence Heller says that, "The relationship between the child and the deity is heavily shaped by the child's current relation to the family. Loneliness seems to creep in as the child realizes that the family will not always act as a protective shield against the vast unknown of living" (47).

The oldest group of children, the ten- to twelve-year-olds, think most commonly upon two themes: doubt and pain. These children are beginning to think abstractly about philosophy and religion and, as a consequence, are beginning to question the religious traditions with which they grew up. Heller describes this process "as a kind of combat—a battle between the God of religion and the God of the child. The battle is begun by the children's budding recognition that this formal God does not always work so well. . . . As a consequence of this awareness, the child will begin to do much reshaping and rethinking as adolescence ensues" (50–51).

A key area around which these older children will reshape and rethink God and religion is that of pain, or suffering. Heller continues, "They are left asking two elemental questions: (1) What is God's role in suffering? (2) Why does God let one feel pain? The children were honest and wise enough to acknowledge that they really did not have answers to these questions" (52). These questions provoke older children to seek their own answers apart from their parents' and community's traditions and orthodoxies. They seek to make faith their own based on their own personal explanations.

Understanding where children are emotionally and mentally at each stage of their lives is so important for the church because "the expression of faith is affected by physical, cognitive, emotional, and social development."[23] Knowing this helps us identify what questions children are struggling with and when and can help us tailor the experiences and messages children have in a faith community to what they most need at any given time. We should be aware, for example, that older children are going to have questions about theodicy (why suffering exists) and not shy away from those hard discussions. And we should be encouraging young children's playfulness, because that is how they get in touch with their own ideas about God and the world.

We also need to know these things so we do not force children to "grow up" too quickly. Forcing very young children into propositional thinking about God—when in fact play is the best avenue for them to think about God—can have drastic consequences. As Vivian L. Houk explains, "When we ask children to deal with problems beyond their cognitive abilities, understanding, and control, they can become anxious, tune out, and develop a disassociation from the issues."[24] This is what happens when we force very young children to sit through hour-long sermons that are tailored only to adults. We communicate to children that being a child is inappropriate, and we also ignore the way God made those children to best learn about God. Only when we respect children's various developmental stages can we truly make church for adults *and* children alike, which is where we will turn next.

Designing Church for Adults and *Children*

Understanding how children grow emotionally, mentally, and physically enables us to make church for adults *and* children. When we know what children's needs, capabilities, and limitations are at each given developmental stage, we know how to cater to those within the context of church. And it is vital that we do so because the way in which we welcome (or do not welcome) children within the context of church gives a clear message to the world about the value we place on children. Christian educators David Ng and Virginia Thomas say, "The way we involve or separate our children in our liturgy is a clear statement of belief about who we are and what we believe."[25]

It is important that we place our current practices and intentions regarding children's roles in our churches under a microscope. Because even with the best of intentions, we can alienate or segregate children in ways that can have devastating effects—effects we may not even be aware of. When we shuffle children out of the general sanctuary week after week for children's church, for example, we are making clear that there are two different churches—one church is the "real" church, the "main" church, which is for adults, and the other, less "serious" one is for children. We start dividing the body of Christ and erecting boundaries between where each part of the body can be. This can create inappropriate power hierarchies within the congregation.

When we do this, the "real" or "main" church becomes an adults-only world. The sermon is geared toward adult ears, it uses adult vocabulary, it employs adult analogies, and engaging with it requires an adult attention span. Children and their noisiness and spontaneity are not welcome. (This is a shame, because children's noisiness and spontaneity can teach us adults to be more free in how we worship and instruct us to be playful in how we live out our lives according to the Holy Spirit.) When children *are* included in services, they are often shushed and scolded for being unable to pay attention or be quiet in a setting that lacks accommodations to engage children's attention or incorporate their enthusiastic sounds.

I would argue that such a church needs to radically rethink how it involves children in its corporate worship. For the church to be whole, children must be included in worship. The gospel does not discriminate. The grace of God does not segregate. The gospel and God's grace know no age boundaries; they are for adults and children alike. Children belong in corporate worship because the gospel and God's grace belong to children as much as adults.

How can we include children in corporate worship in age-appropriate ways? One obvious way would be to change the style and length of the sermon if the current model is a forty-minute detailed exegesis of a biblical text. We must be more creative in what and how we present so as to engage people of all ages and capabilities. Children are not the only population who would benefit from more diversity in teaching methods.

Another would be to include children in receiving the sacraments of the bread and wine (or grape juice). The sacraments belong to children as much as they belong to adults. At their core, they are tangible signs and symbols of God's outpouring love for humanity. As tangible signs and symbols, they are object lessons that children can physically touch, taste, smell, and hear. The Protestant reformer John Calvin, in his *Institutes of the Christian Religion*, writes, "The sacraments . . . lead us by the hand as tutors lead children."[26] In other words, they are the perfect avenues for children to interact with and know God more intimately. Why should we then exclude children from that which most appeals to them, that which is almost perfectly constructed to interest them?

Furthermore, when we allow children to participate in the sacraments, we are making the bold declaration that our faith is by the grace of God, not by the works of our own hands and minds. When children—who, according to their various developmental ages, may be unable to rationally assent to the cognitive propositions of the Christian faith—participate in the sacraments, we are making clear that the sacraments are God's *gift* to us. We do not deserve them according to how intellectually advanced we are. The gospel is God's *gift* to everyone; it does not require us to think a certain way according to some neurotypical adult standard. Thus the sacraments reveal the topsy-turvy kingdom that Jesus has implemented, where even the smallest of children are welcomed to the table with open arms. As Ng and Thomas write,

> When children partake of bread and wine the "tables are turned." Their participation in the sacrament of the Lord's Table teaches the rest of the church something very important about God and our relationship with God. We are prevented from a gnostic practice of our religion. The essence of gnostic religion is the right knowledge of certain secrets; thus is the path to salvation. . . . When children have the audacity to receive God's gifts, which they could in no way deserve on the basis of their knowledge or experience, the rest of the church can learn again the meaning of trust and faith. In the matter of a "right practice" of the sacraments, it is possible that the children shall lead us.[27]

How else can we better involve children in church, beyond the sacrament of communion? One immediate way to do this is to rethink how we collect tithes and offerings. Instead of restricting these gifts to money, we can reframe them as offerings of *one's self and the strengths or possessions one has.* Not everyone has money to give. Some people in our churches are poor. Some have disabilities and cannot earn salaries. Some are children and are thus too young to have money. We can allow people to offer up something that is valuable to them—their time, a piece of art, a favorite toy. This reminds the church that giving of one's self does not always have to involve finances. Giving of one's self is a holy contract between that self and God. It is supposed to be a joyous volunteering that one can do regardless of age or financial status. This also helps to remind the church that *all* parts of the body of Christ have something to contribute, which in turn empowers *all* people (children included) to participate.

Children can become involved in smaller ways, such as with the de-sign of the weekly bulletin or service leaflet. Many churches simply print a picture of their church on the front of the bulletin, the same picture week after week. Why not make the picture a drawing that children make about the previous week's sermon? This will not only encourage children to engage with the sermon each week; it also will make children feel like they are making a valuable contribution to the church. You can even allow adults to draw, too, which communicates to the body of Christ that play (in this case, through art) is a way we worship our creative God.

These are but a few suggestions for how we can better involve children in corporate worship.[28] Children can also be involved as ushers, as choir members, as youth group mentors, as service volunteers, and yes, even as *leaders.* In fact, wherever possible, I would urge you to include children as leaders. Include children on every committee that makes decisions for your church. You *need* a child's point of view, especially when it comes to decisions that affect children—but also in other matters as well. As Ng and Thomas rightly point out, "Children . . . are persons, not puppies—you don't pat them on the head and say how cute they are; you shake their hands and converse with them. You respect them and try to find out from them what they are thinking about and what issues confront them."[29] The child's point of view is unique and valuable, and it is a point of view that should be welcome in the church. The child's point of view is not to file "For Future Use Only." It is pertinent for the right-here and right-now. In the right-here and right-now, children have needs and wants just as adults do, and they deserve to have their needs and wants heard and valued.

Letting Children Enjoy Childhood

Of course, not every child *wants* to be a leader. This may surprise you, but that is okay.

Part of letting children enjoy their childhood is realizing that not every child wants to be a prophet, priest, or theologian. So while child liberation theology urges us to give children the space to fill these roles, it also urges us to allow children *not* to be in them. Children must decide for themselves. Not every child needs to be an activist. Not every child needs to speak prophetically. Especially as champions of child liberation, we need to accept that. Children have to figure out for themselves who they are and what they want to be. As adults, our responsibility is to empower them in their own endeavors.

Setting aside prophetic leadership roles in faith communities, what every child does need is a childhood that is full of joy and love. Every child needs—and has a right to—a loving caregiver, a supportive home environment, adequate food and water and shelter, and a supportive education. It is sometimes seen as anathema to speak of children having rights, but rights they do have. The Bible speaks to these rights: in Isaiah's commands to Israel, children have the right to adequate provision and care as well as safe childhoods (Isa. 1:17; 65:20, 23); in the household code commands to parents in Ephesus and Colossae (Eph. 6:4; Col. 3:21), children have the right to homes that are kind and loving.

In these and many other instances, the Bible sets standards of rights children have to a quality life. They are to enjoy their youth with play and merriment, like Wisdom played and made merry at God's side in Proverbs (Prov. 8:30–31). They are to have carefree youths, just as the children in Zechariah's vision of restored Zion played in the streets (Zech. 8:5). To those individuals who claim youth is nothing but a modern invention, I would point them to these images. These images show us God's holy plan for childhood as a time for play and imagination and recreation—a time for becoming the future of the church in the present moment, in other words.[30]

Unfortunately, not every child has the privilege of enjoying childhood. A child who experiences sexual abuse is abruptly thrown into a cruel, sadistic adult world. A child of color will grow up in a starkly racist world.

An LGBTQIA child might grow up in a home where they feel they must hide their true self or risk punishment and alienation.

The church must be aware of these realities and bravely speak into the silence many children experience around abuse, exploitation, and every kind of maltreatment. The church must be zealous in ensuring children have a childhood that is full of joy and love. And make no mistake, the church must *fight* for this. It cannot be lazy or apathetic. "At the heart of the gospel is a God who is the ultimate child advocate."[31] The church should be the champion for all children everywhere.

INCLUDING CHILDREN

The exercise for this chapter's "Including Children" is inspired by *Children in the Worshiping Community*, a book by Christian educators David Ng and Virginia Thomas. This exercise will help adults and children alike to think about ways that children can become more involved in your family, faith community, or religious organization. Every single person belongs to the body of Christ, regardless of capabilities and limitations. And every single person brings unique gifts to the body.

Ng and Thomas set up the exercise in the following manner:

> Read aloud Romans, chapter 12. This message of encouragement and exhortation to the church is as meaningful for children as for any age group. Read the chapter with some children. Are they not also called to sacrificial living, to transformation by the renewal of their minds, to what is good and acceptable and perfect? Are they not also members of the body of Christ, with differing gifts? Can they not show faith and serve and teach and show mercy? Children can love, show honor, be aglow with the Spirit, rejoice in hope, be patient in tribulation and constant in prayer. The church would not be whole without children.[32]

For this exercise, you will need one piece of paper per child, one crayon or pen per child, and one whiteboard or chalkboard or other way of displaying people's answers in front of a group.

Next, assemble the children in your family, faith community, or religious organization. Distribute the paper and writing utensils to all the children. Have one or several of the children read Romans 12 out loud. After the passage is read, ask the children to start identifying and naming the different gifts and ways people can serve their community as mentioned in Romans 12. For example, "prophesying," "serving," "teaching," "encouraging," "practicing hospitality," "being willing to associate with people of low position," and so on. Write down everyone's answers on the whiteboard. Once you have all the answers recorded, ask the children if they can think of any other ways in which people can serve their community that are *not* listed in Romans 12. Write down those answers, too.

After you and the children have thoroughly brainstormed the different ways in which people can serve their community, go through the list with the children. As you talk about each item, ask the group to consider how *children* can bring this gift or serve the community in this way. For example, ask the children: "How can *you* encourage people in your community?" "How can *you* practice hospitality in your everyday life?"

To conclude this exercise, give the children several minutes of silent time. During this time, have them privately reflect on and write down or draw representative pictures of their answers to the following two questions:

1. What gift(s) do I currently bring to my community?
2. What gift(s) can I offer my community that I do not offer already?

fourteen

All the Children of the World

Christ already has unambivalently welcomed
children. If the church and world want to
welcome Christ and the God who sent him,
then the church and the world best figure out
how to welcome children.

—Joyce Ann Mercer[1]

Probably the most well-known Bible verse in the United States is John 3:16: "For God so loved the world that he gave his one and only Son, that whoever believes in him shall not perish but have eternal life." Yet the most neglected part of this verse is God's love for *the world*. God does not love just one or another part of the world; God loves the entire world—including every single human being within it. Even conservative evangelical children sing about this in Sunday school when we sing, "Jesus loves the little children, *all the children of the world*."[2] Yes, our Lord and Savior loves not only certain children, but *all* children. All the children of the world! This is a universal claim and the love it speaks of washes over every shore, every country, every race, every gender, and every identity.

Child liberation theology similarly proclaims the love of Jesus for every single child. Child liberation theology should liberate not only the white cisgender male child in the United States. It should also liberate Black children, Asian children, queer children, poor children, female children—every single child you can think of. Our theology of child liberation, therefore, must consider how each child may face unique or specific challenges that other children may not. We must be *intersectional* in our approach to child liberation—that is, we must consider how sin impacts every child and every people group in different, overlapping, and contrasting ways.[3] In this chapter, I will consider how the process of child liberation can and must take unique forms for different children's groups. This is important for every faith community that desires to work toward child liberation, even if a particular faith community does not have children within certain marginalized groups.

Children's rights are human rights. Creating accessibility within our faith communities for *all* groups of children—even groups we do not have currently—will only help move society toward the goal of universal child liberation. To this end, let us discuss three different categorizations of children: children of color, children with disabilities, and neurodiverse children. We will consider how we can best advocate for each of these groups of children. We could easily include other categories of children (such as girls, children in poverty, LGBTQIA children, non-Christian children, etc.), but then this chapter would itself become the length of a book. Hopefully you can gather some tools here to apply to other issues of oppression and abuse that children encounter in their daily lives.

When it comes to child liberation theology, we must "go beyond the walls of the academy." We must go to the places where children "are actively resisting oppression of their families and community, that is, to the churches, community centers, and other local agencies and organizations."[4] Child liberation is not an abstract idea. It is a practical reality we can concretely implement in our day-to-day lives. By creating space for all children in our families, faith communities, and religious organizations, we ensure that every single child can feel welcome. While we learn to embrace all children, we will get a better perspective on how we can best help them liberate themselves. Thus child liberation must be something so tangible and concrete that even children themselves can understand it, can see its importance, and can work toward its realization in our right-here and right-now. Child liberation must speak directly to the daily struggles of all of God's children.[5] Let us turn our attention to some of those struggles now.

Children of Color

It is vitally important for white Christians and predominantly white churches today to do everything they can to understand the experience of people of color in the United States.[6] For centuries white Americans have closed their eyes to racial disparities, discrimination, segregation, and oppression. For too long white churches have feigned ignorance of their complicity in oppressive governmental policies and church practices that have harmed not only people of color in general but, even more personally, Christians of color. Our very brothers and sisters in Christ, our spiritual siblings, have been harmed by our actions and inaction.

If the parental rights agenda could be called the Golden Calf of the Christian Right, then liberalism's alleged superiority when it comes to children's rights should be called a Trojan Horse. The so-called liberal or leftist emphasis on children's rights has, all too often, been no more than a white fist in disguise. The liberal advocates oppress the exact same children, people of color, women, and LGBTQIA individuals who have been oppressed by the Christian Right. To understand how this occurs, let us consider the biggest accomplishment of the children's rights movement: the child protection system.

Before discussing the child protection system in the United States, let me be clear: *child protection* is absolutely an important task. It is a crucial part of, and maybe even the best criterion for, child liberation. However, there is a vast different between child protection as a *goal* and the child protection *system* that we have put in place legislatively through our government and the child protection *systems* we put in place corporately in our churches. Both sets of systems, while well intentioned, have some significant flaws. And we need to be brave in facing these flaws so that we can do better in the future.

Racism in the US Child Protection System

In her groundbreaking book, *Shattered Bonds: The Color of Child Welfare*, law professor Dorothy Roberts makes the startling claim that the US child protection system is an "apartheid institution." It is "a state-run program that disrupts, restructures, and polices Black families."[7] (Roberts focuses primarily on Black families, so this section will as well.) To understand these controversial statements, we must consider the facts about race and how it factors in America's foster care system.

There are more than half a million children currently in foster care in the United States. Black children are the most likely of any racial group to be disrupted by the foster care system. "Black children make up nearly half of the foster care population," Roberts points out, "although they constitute less than one-fifth of the nation's children. In Chicago," for example, "95 percent of children in foster care are Black."[8] In other words, Black children are disproportionately removed from their families compared to other groups of children. As Roberts puts it, "Black families are the most likely of any group to be disrupted by child protection authorities."[9] Other children of color, like Latino and Native American children, are also in the child welfare system in disproportionate rates.[10]

A major reason for the child protection system's disproportionate impact on families of color is because the system criminalizes *poverty*, and families of color are disproportionately represented according to that metric. By focusing so much on poverty instead of physical or sexual abuse, and focusing on *punishment* rather than *extending welfare* to poverty-stricken families, the child protection system hurts the very people who most need help.[11] Roberts explains, "Parental income is a better predictor of removal from the home than is the severity of the alleged child maltreatment or the parents' psychological makeup. After reviewing numerous studies on the reasons for child removal, Duncan Lindsey concludes, 'inadequacy of income, *more than any factor*, constitutes the reason that children are removed.' Child removal continues to relate more to saving children from poverty than protecting them from physical harm."[12]

Roberts makes an insightful comparison between the racial disparities in the child protection system and the same disparities in our nation's prisons. "The racial disparity of children in protective custody," she writes, "mirrors the far more publicized racial disparity in our nation's prison population."[13] This is an important observation. During the same decades when the number of Black children in protective custody exploded, so too did the number of Black youth and adults in prison.

Michelle Alexander explores the massive increase in incarcerated Black youth and adults in her bestselling book, *The New Jim Crow*. Alexander notes that, "In less than thirty years, the U.S. penal population exploded from around 300,000 to more than 2 million. . . . The United States now has the highest rate of incarceration in the world. . . . The racial dimension of mass incarceration is its most striking feature. No other country in the world imprisons so many of its racial or ethnic minorities. The United

States imprisons a larger percentage of its black population than South Africa did at the height of apartheid."[14] This increase in incarceration hits youth in particular: "America incarcerates more of its children than any country in the world."[15] But Black youth shoulder this burden more than any other group of children, as Alexander notes: "Youth of color are more likely to be arrested, detained, formally charged, transferred to adult court, and confined to secure residential facilities than their white counterparts. . . . African American youth account for 16 percent of all youth, 28 percent of all juvenile arrests, 35 percent of the youth waived to adult criminal court, and *58 percent of youth admitted to state adult prison*."[16] Latino and Native American children also face increased rates of incarceration.[17]

Children of color, therefore, stand in the crosshairs at nearly all points in their lives. The child protection system has them in its sights, as does the criminal justice system. Children of color are oppressed and marginalized from all sides. Is it any wonder, then, that suicide rates among Black children have nearly doubled since the 1990s?[18] That Native American children take their own lives at a rate of more than three to ten times the national average?[19] That over 10 percent of Latina girls attempt suicide every year?[20] The very systems that should be protecting these children are instead removing them from their families, often for no reason other than that those children's families *are* oppressed and marginalized—they are poor because of decades of systemic injustice. Instead of looking out for their best interests, the child protection system adds salt to their already-overwhelming wounds.

Ignoring Color in Church Child Protection Systems

Many Christians—conservative and liberal alike—believe that "colorblindness"[21] is the ultimate weapon for combating racism. If saying, "I don't see color" is the height of virtue, this is understandable. However, "I don't see color" more often than not simply means that one is ignoring the very real disparities in justice and mercy experienced by people of color. It means that one is unwilling to admit one's *inaction* concerning these racial disparities, and it means one is *complicit* in furthering the injustice of racism.

As Christians who are called to speak prophetically against abuse and oppression, we must see color. We must see color because our society is constructed in a way that *systemically hurts* people because of color; this includes the American church. Recognizing and understanding this is critical. We must acknowledge these injustices and speak out against them. One way is to acknowledge that many of our churches' child protection policies have not acknowledged that children of color face higher rates of abuse and maltreatment. These policies do not acknowledge that racism itself is abuse. And until we acknowledge these facts, we are going to miss the opportunity to help the children who most desperately need protection.

Consider the following facts about child abuse and neglect more broadly:

- Girls are five times more likely to be abused than boys.[22]
- Black children face almost twice the risk of sexual abuse than white children.[23]
- Black girls face an even higher risk, as 60 percent of Black girls experience sexual assault by the age of 18.[24]
- Native American children face two times the rate of abuse.[25]
- Children in low socioeconomic status households are three times as likely to be victimized.[26]
- Children with disabilities are 2.9 times more likely to be victims of sexual violence.[27]
- Deaf children are particularly at risk for abuse, with Deaf girls reporting childhood sexual abuse twice as often as the hearing population and Deaf boys reporting it three times as often as the hearing population.[28]
- LGBTQIA children are more likely to be sexually assaulted than heterosexual and cisgender children.[29]

As you can see from these statistics, children who face intersecting oppression (and not only the intersecting oppression of racism) also face increased risk for abuse and maltreatment. These forces are correlated. The more marginalized a child is, the more likely it is that the child will be hurt by an adult or other figure in the child's life. Marginalization is a breeding ground for oppression and abuse.

This is as true for children of color as it is for any other group of children who face marginalization. Children of color face almost twice the risk of sexual abuse than white children, and girls of color face even higher risk, as demonstrated by 60 percent of Black girls experiencing sexual assault by the age of eighteen. Until the child protection policies we institute in our churches make this sort of intersectionality explicit in their wording, until we acknowledge racism as abuse and make anti-racism part of our child protection and liberation efforts, we will have continue to have significant holes in our safety nets. The most vulnerable children in our congregations and faith communities will fall through the cracks.

What, then, can our families, faith communities, and religious organizations do to advocate for, learn from, and empower children of color? Here are a few suggestions:

1. Make anti-racism part of your lives and ministries.

Racism—prejudice and discrimination against people of color, including children of color—is antithetical to Jesus's teachings. It is antithetical to living as followers of Jesus. Yet racism pervades life in the United States, with children of color being torn from their families, forced into an abuse-ridden foster care system, and then targeted by mass incarceration. Christians cannot be complacent toward racism. Christians must actively take an anti-racist position in a world where white supremacists and white nationalists feel increasingly comfortable in the public square.[30]

Anti-racism means putting in the work of undoing both systemic racism as well as the effects of it.[31] This anti-racist position must extend to our faith communities, both the families involved and the leadership that guides those families. Our faith communities must make anti-racism an integral part of what it means to be a Christian and what it means to follow Jesus today.

Start addressing race and racism as a family and faith community. Talk openly about how race and racism function in the United States. Talk openly about our country's history of enslavement and the Ku Klux Klan and segregation and redlining (and how Christians were often at the forefront of these evils). Determine how you as a family or faith community can commit to fighting white supremacy and countering the effects of racism. Being "not racist" will not suffice in an actively racist world. In an actively racist world, Christians must be actively anti-racist.

2. Make anti-racism part of your children's lives and children's ministries.

Children begin to internalize racial bias in preschool. By the ages of four and five, children of all colors are already viewing people with darker skin less favorably than people with lighter skin. Researchers have found that this is because children are "astute observers of the social world," and that even at early ages they become "increasingly attuned to social category labels, social status, and the biases exhibited by family members."[32] In other words, children are absorbing messages from their families and communities about race and racism from the moment they can begin sorting and categorizing people. Reformed chaplain Melissa Kuipers writes, "We live in a society marred by sin, entrenched in the evil of racism, and our children are not immune to the subtle ways in which it influences us. Even if our congregations are welcoming to all people, we need to be intentional about emphasizing the anti-racist direction of the gospel."[33] If your family, faith community, or religious organization is going to be anti-racist, your anti-racist efforts must extend to children. In this chapter, I underscore how children experience the effects of white supremacy and racism just like adults.

Unfortunately, many faith communities and religious organizations are silent on these issues.[34] Kuipers offers several suggestions for changing this, pointing out, "We need to be creating children's ministries that are anti-racist, and we can do that in many small, and sometimes big, ways." Kuipers suggests, for example, increasing representation of children of color in church imagery—making sure that the images of children used in your church bulletins, flannelgraph kits, coloring pages, and Sunday School curricula include children of color. She also suggests increasing diversity by encouraging and inviting people of color to participate in your children's lives and children's ministries, encouraging the children to read books and enjoy art and music created by people of color, and educating children to understand and address racist acts (like hate crimes) and racism as a system of abuse from a Christian perspective—from the perspective of every human being made in the image of God.[35]

3. Make anti-racism part of your child protection and liberation efforts.

To make your child protection and liberation efforts anti-racist means several things. First, if you are a faith community or religious organization, your child protection policy should specifically name and describe racism as one form of abuse children experience—white children through the damaging impacts of white supremacy and Black children and other children of color through the many impacts of personal and systemic racism. Second, your child protection policy should make clear how your community or organization will be fighting against racism for the protection and liberation of children specifically. And third, intentionally seek out and include children of color and their families in this entire process. Make sure you listen to, highlight, and amplify their voices and treat them as equal partners who have the firsthand knowledge of and experience with racism.

Treating children of color and their families as partners is key to ensuring that you are not approaching anti-racism with a "white savior" complex.[36] (A white savior complex is when a white person attempts to help a person of color from a position of superiority.)[37] Black children do not need white people to protect them; they need white people to stop harming them and their families. They need white people to stop breaking apart Black families in the name of child protection. They need white people to acknowledge that racism is child abuse and remember that children experience racism just like adults do.

Children with Disabilities

Americans and Christians in America have long discriminated against people with disabilities,[38] especially children with disabilities.[39] In fact, Brett Webb-Mitchell points out, "While many mainline denominations have eloquent position papers stating that all people should be welcomed, individual congregations have been scandalously inhospitable to children with disabilities."[40] As touched on briefly above, children with disabilities already face higher rates of abuse and neglect than children without disabilities, so children with disabilities face a world that is far scarier and challenging than other children face. The fact that churches—places that should be refuges from life's hardships—remain closed to so many children with disabilities only adds insult to injury.

Throughout history, children with disabilities have suffered greatly due to ableism, the systemic prejudice and discrimination against people with disabled bodies.[41] Ableism is why children with disabilities were locked up in asylums with death rates over 80 percent in the first year of imprisonment; these children were often naked or clothed only in rags and forced to sleep on the floor.[42] Ableism is why it was legal to deny children with disabilities access to an education until 1975.[43] Ableism is why it was legal to forcibly sterilize children with disabilities in more than thirty states throughout the twentieth century.[44] First legalized in 1907, forced sterilizations continued into the 1980s, and over eighty thousand individuals with disabilities were subjected to them.[45] As of 2022, seventeen states still permit the practice with regard to children with disabilities.[46] Ableism is why people can write the following about people with disabilities and be lauded rather than criticized: "Their life is absolutely pointless. . . . They are a terrible, heavy burden upon their relatives and society as a whole. Their death would not create even the smallest gap."[47]

Ableism persists to this day. More than 20 percent of the general population in the United States have a disability,[48] and one in four families includes someone with a learning difference.[49] Ableism has plenty of opportunities to burn brightly and luridly. Even today, many parents reject children with disabilities.[50] Many children with disabilities are sent to live in institutions.[51] In the United States, approximately 67 percent of fetuses with prenatally diagnosed Down syndrome are aborted.[52] In many parts of Europe, including the United Kingdom, that percentage rises to more than 90 percent.[53]

People with disabilities also face increased rates of sexual abuse. People with disabilities are twice as likely as the general population to experience sexual assault.[54] Worse still, women with disabilities are four times more likely to experience a sexual assault than other women.[55]

Considering Jesus's ministry to people with disabilities, one would think that the church would be a refuge for people with disabilities. Unfortunately, this is often not the case. For many people with disabilities, church remains inaccessible. In fact, "more than half of parents of children with disabilities report that their children have been excluded at church because of their disability."[56] This is for a number of reasons. First, many Christian traditions have equated—and still equate—disability with sin.[57] (Quite ironic, since Jesus directly decouples disability from sin during his ministry in John 9:1–6.) People with disabilities are thus blamed for their disabilities and told that their disabilities are the result of demonic possession or rebellion against their Creator. Second, many Christians assume that people with disabilities do not have spiritual lives. The Protestant reformer Martin Luther, for example, "referred to children with intellectual disabilities as 'a mass of flesh with no soul who were "filled with Satan," the father of idiots.'"[58] Third, many churches have constructed, both intentionally and unintentionally, barriers that prevent people with disabilities from participating fully in faith communities.

These barriers to participation are many and worth dwelling on for a moment. One of the most significant barriers remains because churches successfully lobbied to be exempt from the Americans with Disabilities Act (ADA) in 1990—and they remain exempt to this day. Religious organizations or entities controlled by religious organizations (such as summer camps and vacation Bible schools) are thus under no legal obligation to make their spaces open and accessible to people with disabilities.[59] Other barriers to participation include architectural barriers, such as whether a church is wheelchair-accessible; attitudinal barriers, such as demeaning, condescending, or paternalistic attitudes from congregants toward people with disabilities; communication barriers, such as not providing sermons in multiple formats (for example, offering a written transcript or simultaneous interpretation into American Sign Language); programmatic barriers, such as not providing extra support in Sunday school to a child with high support needs; and finally, liturgical barriers, such as excluding children with intellectual disabilities from communion because "they cannot understand it."[60]

Aside from the sheer meanness of this kind of exclusion of people with disabilities from churches, it directly contradicts the image of hospitality we see in Jesus. Jesus welcomes people with disabilities. He loves them and lays his hands on them. Jesus is, in fact, disabled himself: the resurrected Jesus still bears the holes in his hands and feet and side from his crucifixion (John 20:19–29). He is visibly disabled, the disabled God-Child.[61] When we exclude people with disabilities, therefore, we are excluding our very Lord and Savior.

How can we move toward a world where faith communities welcome and lift up children (and adults) with disabilities? The first and most important step is to simply involve children with disabilities. But simply involving children is not enough. Children with disabilities must be able to participate *fully* in their faith community. This is the difference between *integration* and *inclusion*. We don't want to merely *integrate* children with disabilities into our faith communities; we want to *include* them in *all* aspects of communal life. We should move beyond understanding particular traits associated with disabilities and create community around each child. We want each child to be a *part* of a community, not just *in* a community. Inclusion is *fellowship side-by-side*.[62]

How do we fully include children with disabilities in our faith communities? Here are a few suggestions:

1. Affirm children's disabilities as positive parts of their identities. Weave children with disabilities into your faith community.

Each and every person bears the image of God—and they bear God's image not in spite of impairments but through them.[63] Each and every person has a gift to bring to the body of Christ. Each and every child is unique. Look beyond the labels of disability and look to the child before you instead. What does this individual child need? What does this individual child like? What gift(s) does this individual child bring to your faith community? Affirm and assure that child that God's image is reflected through their disability, not in spite of it.

Then start weaving children with disabilities into your faith community. Begin by highlighting children with disabilities in your faith community's pictures and lessons—anywhere you have images of children (promotional materials, sermon PowerPoint presentations, etc.), make sure children with disabilities are represented. Do not segregate children with disabilities. Think about how to include children with disabilities beyond the corporate worship service on Sunday by extending your home visitation program to families with children with disabilities or by inviting children with disabilities to participate in mentorship programs. Think about how to include children with disabilities in all aspects of your church's internal ministries.[64]

2. Talk to and listen to children with disabilities. Let them tell their own stories.

Children with disabilities have stories to tell. Talk to these children and listen to their stories. Let them develop their own voices and listen to them when they tell us how we can better minister with them. "One of the first steps [to better include people with disabilities]," writes Kevin Timpe, "is to realize that we need to change some of our social dynamics. We need to listen to those who have disabilities when they tell us what we can do to improve. But it is difficult to listen to those who aren't in our lives."[65] We need to make extra efforts as faith communities, then, to welcome and listen to children with disabilities. "There is a long history," Timpe adds, "of people with disabilities not being able to tell their own stories."[66] Resist repeating that history as a faith community. Children with disabilities are not only capable of telling their own stories; they are also capable of worshiping and thinking about God. Let children with disabilities create their own theologies. Let them be the budding theologians they are.

> *3. Abide by the ADA even though your faith community is exempt legally. Be above reproach.*

Christians and faith communities should be on the front lines of advocating for the rights of people with disabilities. Without question, this should include advocating for disability rights and abiding by the ADA. As Erik W. Carter points out, "Your building offers one of the first pronouncements of your congregation's theology." Carter asks, "What do your facilities communicate about the commitments and values you hold?"[67] Do they declare that all are welcome to participate or that you will only do what is required explicitly by law?

The ADA protects the bare minimum of what society owes to people with disabilities. Christians and faith communities should be going above and beyond what is required by any given government when it comes to the treatment of people with disabilities. They should be working fervently to ensure that those who live on the margins of society—and this includes people with disabilities—are protected from abuse and oppression. Recognizing and enforcing disability rights is a holy task.[68]

How can Christians and faith communities exceed the requirements of the ADA? Think about the ways you can change or adapt your community's practices to ensure that everyone can participate. If you are a faith community, for example, make sure your greeters and ushers are comfortable welcoming people with disabilities. Offer training so that they know how to extend a polite greeting, offer any needed assistance, and make introductions to other key individuals in your community. Talk to the children in your faith community, too, and help them practice how to welcome and include peers when their peers have disabilities. Think about how to engage all five main senses during worship services; do not merely rely on information being relayed through speech and received by hearing. This kind of reassessment helps not only people with disabilities participate more fully, but also children in general, elderly people, and anyone who learns better through non-aural approaches.[69] If you are able to design your community such that *everyone* can participate from the beginning, you will find that more people will actually participate.

> *4. Empower children with disabilities to be leaders in your faith community. Minister alongside children with disabilities, not to children with disabilities.*

Children with disabilities deserve more than integration and inclusion. Like all children, they deserve the chance to become whoever or whatever they dream they can be—and that includes being leaders. Children with disabilities, like all children, do not need to be viewed as targets of conversion. They are capable themselves of ministering, of sharing the gospel with others, of leading their faith communities toward righteousness and justice. We must, therefore, approach ministry surrounding children with disabilities as something we do *alongside* those children, not something we do to or for those children. Children with disabilities are capable of expressing themselves (if only we would pay attention). Children with disabilities are capable of being leaders (if only we would humble ourselves and be led). The question is, will we allow and welcome them into all levels of participation and decision-making in our faith communities?[70]

This principle holds true beyond our faith communities and extends to all social justice movements. Disability and sexual assault survivor advocate Shannon Dingle explains, "Your justice is unjust if disabled people aren't included. We know our place, and it isn't on the margins of your movement. No, we belong, and we'll fight to be seen."[71] Children with disabilities deserve to be in the front and center of our social justice movements.

5. Think about how to include children with disabilities beyond corporate worship settings.

There are many other parts of life besides church from which children with disabilities are excluded. Start thinking about the points of contact between your faith community and parts of your larger community, and determine how you can fight against ableism in other contexts as well. "Efforts toward improving physical accessibility," Carter observes, "must extend beyond the worship space to all aspects of shared congregational life. . . . Consider the many other locations in which ministries, fellowships, celebrations, and other activities occur, including classrooms, gymnasiums, community centers, summer camps, retreat centers, and members' homes. People who can participate in only a small fraction of congregational activities are unlikely to ever feel like full members of the community."[72] To ensure children with disabilities feel like full members of the community, extend your welcome and inclusion of them beyond the walls of your faith community.

Neurodiverse Children

Neurodiversity refers to autists, the preferred term for individuals on the autism spectrum.[73] One out of every sixty-eight children is an autist.[74] As opposed to people with disabilities in general, autists—like Deaf people— prefer identity-first language rather than person-first language.[75] They see their autism as something to celebrate and champion, so they put it front and center. They believe that they are simply wired differently than non-autistic people, also known as "neurotypicals" or "allists." They do not believe there is anything wrong with themselves; they are "different, not less."[76] They reject the language of disability and instead see themselves as *neurodiverse*.[77]

Autism is "a neurological, or brain, difference."[78] It was first discovered by Leo Kanner in 1943, who described it as a form of childhood schizophrenia. A year later, Hans Asperger—who never saw Kanner's work— published a paper describing four children who had similar traits. Both Kanner and Asperger referred to what they discovered as "autism," which comes from the Greek word for "self," *autos*—because the children they observed seemed withdrawn into themselves.[79] It wasn't until the 1980s that Lorna Wing—the mother of an autistic child herself—proposed that autism is a spectrum.[80]

Autistic children exhibit a variety of behaviors and thoughts that make them different from other children. These differences involve: linguistic understanding, social skills, repetitive themes and behaviors, desire for routine, perspective-taking ability, and sensory responses.[81] For example, some autistic children find speaking and listening to spoken words difficult; they may prefer sign language or printed words. Many autistic children find social settings difficult, especially the expectation of eye contact. They often prefer routine and repetition and can get anxious and overwhelmed when schedules or actions are interrupted without warning. They also may have sensory problems, finding certain types of sounds, sights, smells, and textures overwhelming. Because autism is a spectrum, some children will display these differences in more notable ways and some children will display them in more subtle ways.

Autistic children vary in how much support they need. Some people refer to this spectrum of needs as "low functioning" versus "high functioning," but autists themselves say those classifications are stigmatizing and unhelpful. Autists suggest using the phrases "low support needs" and "high support needs" instead.[82]

Autistic children experience increased risk and rates of abuse and neglect and discrimination. They are up to three times more likely to suffer bullying, physical abuse, and sexual abuse compared to neurotypical children.[83] Autistic girls are particularly at risk; nine out of every ten autistic women are sexually victimized, most of whom are first victimized as children.[84] Autists have historically suffered significantly, as documented in Steve Silberman's book, *NeuroTribes*. Autists have been subjected to cruel, degrading, and terrorizing practices such as forced sterilization, live surgical experimentation, and euthanasia during the times of Hitler. Asperger himself recommended that dozens of the autistic children he studied be transferred to Am Spiegelgrund in Vienna, where they were murdered by the Nazis.[85]

Today, we are becoming aware increasingly of the fact that autists are just as human as neurotypicals and they deserve the same basic human rights the rest of us have. We are moving to a place of seeing autists not as diseased or in need of cures but rather as different (hence the term "neuro*diverse*") and in need of acceptance and support.[86] Unfortunately, Christian faith communities often remain closed to autistic children. The odds of an autistic child never attending religious services are nearly twice as high as compared to other children.[87]

It does not have to be this way, though. Churches can become places where autistic children are loved and accepted, rather than judged and excluded. Here are a few suggestions on how to do so.

1. Realize each child is unique and has unique needs and gifts. Get to know each child individually.

No two autists are the same. A common saying in the autist community is, "If you've met one individual with autism, you've met just that one individual with autism."[88] While autistic children often share certain characteristics, every autistic child has unique support needs. Every autistic child has different thoughts, feelings, longings, and existential and religious struggles. Don't make assumptions about a child just because of a diagnostic label. Get to know each child and find out their specific needs and gifts.

One way to determine a child's needs and gifts is to ask how the child learns best.[89] This is a great question to ask about every child, not just autistic children. But it is especially important for autistic children because they may prefer different ways of learning (seeing, hearing, doing, etc.) from the other children who are participating. Figure out how they best learn in other contexts, such as home or at school. Then, create community around each child that fosters support of their learning preferences. Belonging to a community is something everyone needs, but it is especially important for autistic people: 46 percent of autists have no friends who are also peers.[90] Peer support is vital for humans' well-being. Strategize to create a community of loving and supportive peers around each child in your faith community.[91]

2. Use visual aids when communicating.

Neurodiverse children sometimes have difficulties with paying attention to and tracking along with spoken words. It can be really helpful to use visual aids to better communicate with neurodiverse children. Episcopal priest Susan Richardson explains, "Vision is often a very stable sensory system, so using picture or word schedules, devising behavior systems using visual supports, and illustrating a biblical concept with pictures or real objects can often enhance communication."[92] As you implement more visual aspects to your communication methods, be sure to solicit feedback from your neurodiverse participants and their caregivers to make sure the aids are working well.

Note, too, that using visual aids to enhance communication is helpful for many people, not just autistic children. Visual aids can also help people with learning differences, people with hearing difficulties, Deaf people, and more.

3. Be sensitive to sensory needs.

Autistic children may process information differently than non-autistic children. For example, they may experience sounds as being louder than non-autistic children; lots of loud noises can be overwhelming. Or they may experience sounds softer than non-autistic children, and thus need extra volume to get their attention.

Being aware of the sensory needs of the children in your congregation promotes maximum welcome within your faith communities. A great example of how to make a space accessible to autists comes from the Oregon Zoo. In 2019, the Zoo launched a new "sensory-inclusive program" in order to "help guests with sensory needs." According to the zoo, their "staff received training on how to recognize guests with sensory needs and how to handle a sensory-overload situation. Bags equipped with noise canceling headphones, fidget tools, verbal cue cards and weighted lap pads will be available to guests."[93] This is a wonderful example of how to intentionally make space for neurodiverse children, and one that Christians could replicate in their own faith communities.

4. Educate your faith community about neurodiversity.

One of the best ways you can support neurodiverse children in your faith community is to educate community members about neurodiversity. As you implement ideas to support neurodiverse children, explain to your faith community why you are doing so. Educate them about the history of neurodiversity and how neurodiverse individuals have been treated cruelly and inhumanely. Bring awareness to the early signs of neurodivergence so that families in your faith community know how to identify them and can secure any supports children need as soon as possible. Early identification and support are key to help autistic children thrive.[94]

5. Fight for the rights of neurodiverse children as a faith community.

As mentioned in the previous section about children with disabilities, faith communities should be on the front line of advocating for children with differences and disabilities. This includes neurodiverse children. Neurodiverse children in our world are often extremely marginalized and are still treated cruelly and inhumanely by many families and institutions. These children deserve to be protected and to have their rights defended.

Fighting for the rights of neurodiverse children means listening to both autistic children *and* autistic adults; autistic children grow up and become adults.[95] By listening to autistic adults, we know now that certain practices previously used to "cure" or "help" autistic children—like ABA (Applied Behavior Analysis)—are actually abusive. In fact, the most influential practitioner of ABA, Ole Ivar Lovaas, is the same person who inspired conversion therapy for LGBTQIA people.[96] That alone should be reason enough to stay away from it. If that negative association were not enough, though, autists speak to the many horrific abuses they have experienced during ABA, including beatings, electrocution, and starvation.[97] This is the end result of approaching autism as if it is a disease we must eradicate. Autism is not a disease; like left-handedness, it is a normal difference among human beings that deserves ready acceptance and full support—and our faith communities should be leading the way in this regard.[98]

All Children

The examples in this chapter only scratch the surface of what it means to truly be a welcoming faith community for all children. We must think intentionally, methodically, and transparently about the children at the margins of our society. We must figure out how to lift up and empower *those* children, not only the children who look like us. If Jesus truly loves all the children of the world, it is time to stop singing it and start living it.

To live it, we cannot let child liberation theology remain academic and theoretical. It must become something practical and tangible. This is why child liberation theology requires focus on praxis, or action. By doing so, we can make a concrete difference in the lives of children in our community and around the world. Start with the multiple examples given in this chapter of how this can be accomplished in our faith communities in the United States. By moving from academic contemplation into concrete practice, we unlock the liberation that is inherent to the gospel message. The gospel is *good news* for children.

By including and advocating for the children at the margins of our society, we help the gospel message reach its fullest potential. We fight to realize the kingdom of God in our right-here and right-now. Thus we place children at the center of our praxis, just as Jesus himself once did. The kingdom of God is a kingdom for *all* children.

INCLUDING CHILDREN

Children, just like adults, have multiple layers of identity. We identify by family, by race, by class, by gender, by sexuality, by ability, by nationality, by religion, and so forth. The phrase *identity politics* is often thrown about pejoratively by evangelicals and other members of the Christian Right. The fact remains: everyone has multiple layers of identity and these layers impact how we experience the world and how the world experiences us. Everyone engages in identity politics because humans are storytelling beings who find meaning in their identities.

Ask the children in your family, faith community, or religious organization to think about their own layers of identity. What aspects of themselves do they most identify with? What aspects of themselves do they least identify with? Help the children think through these two questions by listing for them the various possibilities (family, race, class, gender, sexuality, ability, nationality, religion, etc.). After the children have time to think about these questions and discuss them in a small group format, read to them Galatians 3:26–29. After reading, challenge the children to think about verse 28 in particular, where the epistle writer declares, "There is neither Jew nor Gentile, neither slave nor free, nor is there male and female, for you are all one in Christ Jesus." Ask the children: Does the fact that we are "all one in Christ Jesus" mean that we should ignore our differences? Does Jesus erase our identities and what makes each of us who we are? Or, does this verse mean that we are all equally worthy of community and love? That we participate in the body of Christ through our differences, not in spite of them?

Ask the children to consider ways in which our differences can make it harder or more difficult for us to be in community with and love one another. Then, discuss how we can overcome those obstacles to better love our neighbors. Challenge the children to think about one way every day that they can better care for and love another child who is different from them in a significant way.

conclusion

A Kingdom of Children

Let the little children come to me, and do not
hinder them, for the kingdom of God belongs
to such as these.

—Jesus, Mark 10:14

W hat a powerful, radical sentiment! *The kingdom of God belongs to
children.* Jesus declared that about children, not adults. I appreciate
how Presbyterian theologian Eugene H. Peterson paraphrases this verse
in *The Message*: "Don't push these children away. Don't ever get between
them and me. These children are at the very center of life in the kingdom."
Children are the beating heart of the good news that Jesus brings.

If children are at the center of life in the kingdom, can we go so far
as to say God loves children more than adults? I am not convinced this is
wise. I think it is dangerous and unhealthy to create a false binary between
children and adults. Both children and adults are equally human and
equally image bearers of God. But despite this equal imaging, God made
a point to declare their kingdom belongs to and champions children—and
that point is undeniable and striking.

I have tried to communicate something equally radical in this book
to parallel Jesus's bold welcome and inclusion of children. In the United
States, we need to reimagine everything when it comes to how we think
about, talk about, and interact with children—most especially in Christian
families, faith communities, and religious organizations. The end goal is
to create space for children to unfold into their own beautiful selves and

empower them to take up theological tasks themselves. We do not want to speak for children. We want children to find and use their own voices. We want to welcome and equip children so that the children can tell us how the American church can improve how it thinks about, talks about, and interacts with them.

I think that is a radical change from the way we currently do many things. But I also hope that I have communicated that radical change does not require an extremist movement. I have not proposed that we abolish families. While most child abuse happens in families, families are nonetheless deeply important for child liberation and protection. I have not proposed that we give infants the right to vote. While I do support lowering the voting age, I believe certain age restrictions (like laws concerning the age of consent) are similarly deeply important for child liberation and protection. To avoid extremism, we must always balance child liberation on the one hand and child protection on the other hand. Key to that balancing act is respecting the developmental stages of children. Ignoring children's developmental needs is just another form of child abuse and neglect.

I am conservative in the sense that I believe we should respect institutions that work, but I am progressive in the sense that I believe we need to radically alter the practices and values of those institutions when they inflict abuse and harm. We should not abolish families, but we should reject authoritarianism in families. We should not give infants the right to vote, but we should respect infants' inherent human rights and urge the government to protect those rights. These suggestions may seem radical, but I would argue they are not extreme. They are necessary antidotes in a country that is extreme in being anti-child, in a country where it is still legal for teachers to strike children, legal for parents to deny their children lifesaving medicine, and legal for the government to forcibly sterilize children just because they have a disability. In such an extreme world, we *must* be as radical as Jesus. We must love and protect children with abandon.

Part of that love and protection means radically rethinking how we approach the Bible as both a text and a model for action. We need to place children at the center of every passage we read. What I propose is a fundamental change to how many people approach the Bible, and I believe it is a change that is modeled on Jesus's own actions. Just as Jesus put a child in the middle of a group of disciples while they debated the technicalities of divorce, we, too, must put children in the middle of our theologies and our ideologies and our teaching philosophies and our politics. We must lift up children and consider them like Jesus would.

We must also truly think about what it means, as the first child liberation theologian Janet Pais suggested, that Jesus is not just God incarnate. Jesus is the God-*Child*. It is a child that will come to judge us all. It is a child who rules in the kingdom of God—not only because that kingdom belongs to the children, but also because *the God-Child himself rules*. The implications of this image should challenge and transform our ideas about parenting and discipline and many other subjects.

As I have argued throughout this book, one significant implication of this image is that adultism is a lie. Adults are not inherently better than or superior to children. Children are not less than adults. Adulthood is not the destination with childhood a mere stage to outgrow. At every stage of development, children are fully human, fully vested with human rights, and fully reflective of God's image. At every age, children have the exact same worth and value as adults.

When we see children as being made in the same image of God as adults are, I would argue we can no longer treat children as anything less than equals. Call it age egalitarianism perhaps, but at every stage of development and age, children must be seen as they truly are: fellow travelers on the path toward God. Every child is a sibling in Christ. Brett Webb-Mitchell writes the following regarding children with disabilities, but I believe his points are equally applicable to all children:

> To guide these young people on, [we] need to be co-pilgrims with these young people, guiding them along the way of the sacred story learned in Christian communities and lived out in the world. As co-pilgrim, the task is to share and walk with them, to be the good companion who does not abandon the pilgrim, even in the face of great temptations and death, like the friend "Faithful" to Bunyan's pilgrim, Christian. As companion, [we] are to be present as storytellers, retelling the sacred story because the sacred story is the map for life's journey. For it is in the sacred story of God's love, recorded in Scripture, and the telling of God's story, that one discovers and unleashes

the reservoir of God's gift of faith, hope, and love that alone can heal, nurture, and guide these young people's spirits.[1]

One practical result of viewing children as our spiritual siblings and fellow pilgrims on the path toward God emerges from our discussion. We must break free from thinking about the parent-child relationship as a ruler-subject relationship. Children are not the servants or slaves of their parents. Children are their own human beings. Children have their own relationship with God that must be tended to, not forced. Children's wills are right and good and they deserve to have their wills respected, not broken or crushed. Parents should be strengthening, not clipping, their children's wings.

We must also acknowledge the capabilities of children as fellow human beings. Children are capable of speaking truth about the times we live in. They are prophets. They can be leaders and teachers and they can think about God and the universe in deep and profound ways when they are given the space and tools they need. It is time to end our patterns of disempowering and marginalizing children.

We change these patterns by beginning with the fundamental principle that children are not only image bearers of God but are also, in our right-here and right-now, appointed by Jesus as God-to-us. Every child presents us with the question and charge Peter received from Jesus after the resurrection: "Do you love me? Then feed my sheep" (see John 21:15–17 for the full exchange).

The challenge we now face is to extend that principle of equality to how we parent in families, how we care for and teach children in school and church, and how we guide children toward health and happiness as they grow older. Do you parent in such a way that your children feel the assuredness of God's image and feel comfortable confronting you when they believe you are in the wrong? Does your Sunday school offer room for children to be God-to-us, asking questions and pushing back like twelve-year-old Jesus in the temple? Does your religious organization allow children to be image bearers of God, serving in leadership and guiding your ministry? If not, it is time to change.

As we make the necessary adjustments, we must remember two things: first, children are still children, not adults. As I stated earlier, liberating children requires us to respect children's developmental stages, not ignore them. This is because adultification and parentification are real phenomena. They are devastating to children's health and well-being.

Second, we cannot make changes that help only certain children and leave other children behind. Far too often, efforts to protect some children come at the neglect or expense of other children. Child liberation theology must speak to and be formed by the struggles of every child, especially the most marginalized. We find the kingdom of God at the margins of society precisely because the margins are where we find such children.

The kingdom of God belongs to children because the kingdom of God is a kingdom of children. It is the kingdom ushered into life by Jesus the God-Child. A topsy-turvy kingdom where the first are last, the last are first, the meek shall inherit the earth, and a little child shall lead us. This is the meaning of the incarnation, the significance of salvation. The kingdom of God is at hand, it is good news, and it belongs to children. Will we follow Jesus's example and lift up and center children? Will we do the hard work of making our homes, our families, our churches, our schools, and our communities accessible to and supportive of every child? Will we speak out prophetically against adultism and childism, naming them as the direct threats to the gospel of Jesus that they are?

I began this book by noting that we live in extreme times. Child liberation theologian Rebecca Stevens-Walter says we live in "biblical times"—a modern timeline marked by plagues and widespread disregard for the welfare of children.[2] This is true as well. Really, we live in apocalyptic times. Not apocalyptic in the sense of the end of the world (though some days it certainly seems that way) but rather apocalyptic in the sense of *revelatory*. As theology professor David Dark writes about the word *apocalypse*, "In its root meaning, it's not about destruction or fortune telling; it's about revealing. . . . Apocalyptic shows us what we're not seeing."[3]

Our days—marked by extreme climate change, extreme wealth disparities, and extreme prejudice against marginalized people—are apocalyptic because they reveal the desires of our hearts in stark terms. As we grow numb to the sounds of mass shooters massacring children in schools, as we shrug off children's hospitals shutting down from bomb threats, as parents watch their children suffer through formula shortages and school shutdowns and empty medicine aisles in the midst of a worldwide pandemic, it's becoming strikingly clear how little our world values the lives of children. Our days reveal how much abuse and violence the powers-that-be will allow children to experience, provided it enriches their pockets or furthers their agendas to benefit adults.

Yet there is also hope in apocalypse. There is hope because apocalypses remind us that abuse and oppression do not have to have the final word. They do not have to be forever. Dark writes, "If these powers are the boot that, to borrow Orwell's phrase, presses down upon the human face forever, apocalyptic is the speech of that human face. Apocalyptic denies, in spite of all the appearances to the contrary, the 'forever' part."[4] We can, if we choose, say *no!* to those who want us to silence and mistreat children. We can, if we choose, create space for children to find their voices, share their voices, and improve the world as a result of their voices. We can, if we choose, dismantle the powers-that-be and the oppressive systems in place to deny children their God-given right to be the unique image bearers of God that they are. An apocalypse does not have to be the end. An apocalypse can be the beginning, too.

This is why I refuse to give up hope. I refuse to give up hope because I believe the kingdom of God is for our right-here, right-now world of extremes. The kingdom of God is the radical statement that even the smallest among us are worthy of bearing God's image and worthy of being appointed God-to-us. Even the smallest among us can teach us, can lead us, and can change the course of history toward justice and peace. In every child, an image of God is born anew.

INCLUDING CHILDREN

For this final "Including Children" activity, ask both the children and the adults in your family, faith community, or religious organization to work together to create an action plan to continue your efforts to protect and liberate the children in your lives. If your faith community or religious organization did not have a child protection policy prior to reading this book, hopefully you rectify that as soon as possible. Your child protection policy will be the foundation of your efforts to equip and empower the children in your community. So if you do not yet have a child protection policy, please make one and consider including the following ideas in your policy. If you have a policy already, consider modifying it to include the following ideas. If you are a family, consider how to work these ideas into your family meetings.

Gather all the children and adults and hold an open forum on the topic of children and issues that confront them. Ask everyone to think about the following: (1) how many times each year they would like to meet to discuss this topic (children and issues that confront them); (2) what issues most confront the children in your immediate community; and (3) what your immediate community can do to better uplift and empower its children. Build this feedback process into your child protection policy. Regularly check in with the children around you whom you are parenting or serving or teaching and directly ask them how you can be better adults to them. This kind of feedback collection should be just as regular as having child abuse awareness days to educate your immediate community about the child protection policy and the warning signs of grooming and abuse.

Let's say everyone agrees to meet twice a year to check in about the topic of children and issues that confront them. Add a clause to your child protection policy specifying the number of required meetings to be held each year. If you are a family, add check-in dates to your family calendar or make this kind of check-in a standing agenda item for family meetings. Follow through on this commitment to meet and discuss with both the children and the adults. Consider appointing—or voting for—several children and several adults to serve together on a planning committee to schedule, outline, and run the meetings.

Notes

Epigraph

1. Judith M. Gundry-Volf, "The Least and the Greatest: Children in the New Testament," in *The Child in Christian Thought*, ed. Marcia J. Bunge (Grand Rapids: Eerdmans, 2001), 60.

Introduction

1. Chung Hyun Kyung, "Following Naked Dancing and Long Dreaming," in *Inheriting Our Mothers' Gardens: Feminist Theology in Third World Perspective*, ed. Letty M. Russell et al. (Louisville: Westminster Press, 1988), 69.

2. BBC News, "COVID Map: Coronavirus Cases, Deaths, Vaccinations by Country," July 5, 2022, https://tinyurl.com/24ju3dvc.

3. William A. Haseltine, "COVID-19 Has Orphaned 5.2 Million Children," *Forbes*, March 1, 2022, https://tinyurl.com/3yhpkzuj.

4. Centers for Disease Control and Prevention, "Global Orphanhood Associated with COVID-19," June 2, 2022, https://tinyurl.com/yzuejhfm.

5. NPR, "About 200,000 Kids Were Orphaned by COVID-19," January 13, 2022, https://tinyurl.com/mtwavwd.

6. There are many analyses and studies of how COVID-19 policies around the world reflect childism and adultism. See, for example: Rebecca Adami and Katy Dineen, "Discourses of Childism: How COVID-19 Has Unveiled Prejudice, Discrimination and Social Injustice against Children in the Everyday," *The International Journal of Children's Rights*, June 15, 2021, https://tinyurl.com/2d48cdvm; Nisreen A. Alwan, "We Must Call Out Childism in

COVID-19 Policies," *BMJ*, October 29, 2021, https://tinyurl.com/n29zm968; Minsun Shin, "Confronting Childism and Prioritizing a Holistic Approach during the COVID-19 Crisis," *Contemporary Issues in Early Childhood*, February 18, 2022, https://tinyurl.com/ysr3ryyp; and Katy Dineen, Bengt Autzen, and Nisreen A. Alwan, "Children, Intersectionality, and COVID-19," *The Lancet*, February 16, 2022, https://tinyurl.com/ybxusatc.

7. "Violent far-right extremism surged in the United States during Donald Trump's presidency and has grown deadlier since converging with the mass shootings epidemic." Mark Follman, "Violent Far-Right Extremism Is Fueling Mass Shootings in America," *Mother Jones*, May 16, 2022, https://tinyurl.com/3y273vkf.

8. More than 311,000 American children have experienced gun violence at school since the Columbine High School massacre in 1999. See the *Washington Post*, "More Than 311,000 Students Have Experienced Gun Violence at School since Columbine," May 27, 2022, https://tinyurl.com/5xzdpfra.

9. Sarah Mehta, "There's Only One Country That Hasn't Ratified the Convention on Children's Rights: US," ACLU, November 20, 2015, https://tinyurl.com/2h23ab9t.

10. Childhelp, "Child Abuse Statistics," https://tinyurl.com/2mtyxyu8, accessed July 26, 2022.

11. Katherine Kaufka Walts, "An Introduction to Child Trafficking in the United States," American Bar Association, January 9, 2012, https://tinyurl.com/46cdb7ur.

12. United Nations Office on Drugs and Crime, *Global Report on Trafficking in Persons*, 2020, https://tinyurl.com/bdfhnrkx.

13. Childhelp, "Child Abuse Statistics," https://tinyurl.com/2mtyxyu8, accessed July 26, 2022.

14. Elisabeth Young-Bruehl, *Childism: Confronting Prejudice against Children* (New Haven: Yale University Press, 2012), 2.

15. Ronda Racha Penrice, "Ending the Sexual Abuse to Prison Pipeline for Black and Brown Girls," NBC News, July 17, 2015, https://tinyurl.com/f4w694dy.

16. US Department of Labor, "Child Labor, Forced Labor & Human Trafficking," https://tinyurl.com/yw3mk89w, accessed July 30, 2022.

17. Alana Semuels, "How Common Is Child Labor in the U.S.?," *The Atlantic*, December 15, 2014, https://tinyurl.com/5bch6jm4.

18. The Child Welfare League of America and Lambda Legal Defense and Education Fund, "Out of the Margins: A Report on Regional Listening Forums Highlighting the Experiences of Lesbian, Gay, Bisexual, Transgender, and Questioning Youth in Care," 2006, https://tinyurl.com/yc796wb3.

19. Alicia VanOrman and Beth Jarosz, "Suicide Replaces Homicide as Second-Leading Cause of Death Among U.S. Teenagers," Population Reference Bureau, June 9, 2016, https://tinyurl.com/h4ddrvc3.

20. National Alliance on Mental Illness, "What You Need to Know about Youth Suicide," https://tinyurl.com/32dpm8s5, accessed July 30, 2022.

21. David K. Li, "Youth Suicide Attempts Soared during Pandemic, CDC Report Says," NBC News, June 11, 2021, https://tinyurl.com/47x8d7wc.

22. Boz Tchividjian and Shira M. Berkovits, *The Child Safeguarding Policy Guide for Churches and Ministries* (Greensboro: New Growth Press, 2017), 11.

23. Tchividjian and Berkovits, *Child Safeguarding Policy*, 11.

24. National Center for Health Statistics, "National Survey of Children's Health," 2007, https://tinyurl.com/2p8rhv8m.

25. Tony Morgan, "Measuring Church Health: How Many Kids Will Attend?," The Unstuck Group, https://tinyurl.com/yrtkb9vd, accessed November 25, 2022.

26. Pew Research Center, "Religious Affiliation among American Adolescents," September 10, 2020, https://tinyurl.com/4br2bw9c.

27. Paul Finkelman, *Defending Slavery: Proslavery Thought in the Old South: A Brief History with Documents* (Boston: Bedford/St. Martin's, 2003).

28. American Indian Relief Council, "History and Culture: Boarding Schools," https://tinyurl.com/yckvbnbp, accessed May 18, 2016.

29. Jason Wilson, "Letting Them Die: Parents Refuse Medical Help for Children in the Name of Christ," *Guardian*, April 13, 2016, https://tinyurl.com/yhzdp3ut.

30. Cotton Mather, *A Family Well-Ordered, or, AN ESSAY to Render PARENTS AND CHILDREN Happy in One Another*, 1699, https://tinyurl.com/3k8pncvt, p. 4.

31. Jonathan Edwards, *Thoughts on the Revival of Religion in New England*, 1742, https://tinyurl.com/23z56nnz, accessed November 25, 2022.

32. Sarah Childress, "What's the State of the Church's Child Abuse Crisis?," PBS, February 25, 2014, https://tinyurl.com/52dbvsz5.

33. Kathryn Joyce, "By Grace Alone," *American Prospect*, May 5, 2014, https://tinyurl.com/4kmxshvf.

34. See, for example, Sarah Pulliam Bailey, "How Christian Home-Schoolers Laid the Groundwork for 'Parental Rights,'" *Washington Post*, June 11, 2022, https://tinyurl.com/y6mrn5n9.

35. "For fourteen years I was a youth worker who identified as a progressive Christian and served in progressive churches. I quickly realized that the vast majority of the youth ministry publishing and conference world was monopolized by more conservative evangelicals. With every book I read and every conference I attended, I found myself having to constantly translate and filter content in order to tease out nuggets of material that would be transferable to my context. When a few youth ministry books and events started to ride the emerging church wave, I felt that they were rarely as unabashedly progressive as I wanted to be." John Vest, "Welcome to Progressive Youth Ministry," *Patheos*, March 8, 2016, https://tinyurl.com/3s8wmewy.

36. "The efforts of religious conservatives such as Dobson and others to address issues of childhood and parenting from within their perspective of the Christian faith has developed into a popular movement and a multi-billion dollar industry. Interestingly, though, some of the literature, if not the theology supporting it, now finds its way onto the shelves of mainline church libraries and in mainline and theologically liberal parents' homes. Bendroth contends that this crossover happened as a result of the vacuum left by mainline theology's inability to say anything directly about sex and theology. In this vacuum, she says, even the more rule-oriented take on sex and family life became a welcome alternative to 'the randomness of mainline parenting.'" Joyce Ann Mercer, *Welcoming Children: A Practical Theology of Childhood* (St. Louis: Chalice Press, 2005), 140.

37. There are many notable exceptions on all sides, of course. The gentle parenting movement is transforming how conservatives approach parenting through visionaries like L. R. Knost and Samuel Martin. On the liberal side, visionaries like Joyce Ann Mercer and Cindy Wang Brandt are challenging liberal and progressive Christians to create practical resources to help parents and their children.

38. The church does not need to "do anything new but rather something very old. Specifically, we need to return to the message of Jesus and center our responses to child abuse on the words and actions of Jesus." Victor Vieth,

On This Rock: A Call to Center the Christian Response to Child Abuse on the Life and Words of Jesus (Eugene: Wipf and Stock, 2018), 3.

39. Naim Stifan Ateek, *Justice and Only Justice: A Palestinian Theology of Liberation* (Maryknoll: Orbis Books, 2003), 6.

40. "The criterion to judge the different styles of theologizing is not codified in the Bible, and the norm of theology is not determined by whether it smells something like that of Augustine and Aquinas—or Tillich and Barth, for that matter. Instead, it lies in the praxis of the religious communities struggling for the liberation of humankind. All theologies must be judged as to how far they contribute to the liberation and humanization of the human community." Kwok Pui-lan, "Mothers and Daughters, Writers and Fighters," in *Inheriting Our Mothers' Gardens: Feminist Theology in Third World Perspective*, ed. Letty M. Russell et al. (Louisville: Westminster Press, 1988), 32.

41. Ateek, *Justice and Only Justice*, 6.

42. Peruvian liberation theologian Gustavo Gutiérrez writes, "The intention is to recognize the work and importance of concrete behavior, of deeds, of action, of praxis in the Christian life. . . . Theology as a critical reflection on Christian praxis in the light of the Word does not replace the other functions of theology, such as wisdom and rational knowledge; rather it presupposes and needs them. But this is not all. We are not concerned here with a mere juxtaposition. The critical function of theology necessarily leads to a redefinition of these other two tasks. Henceforth, wisdom and rational knowledge will more explicitly have ecclesial praxis as their point of departure and their context." *A Theology of Liberation* (Maryknoll: Orbis Books, 2014), 8, 11.

43. The mujerista theology of Ada María Isasi-Díaz "insists on and aids Latinas in defining our preferred future," as Isasi-Díaz writes on page 63 in *Mujerista Theology: A Theology for the Twenty-First Century* (Maryknoll: Orbis Books, 1996). Like Peruvian liberation theologian Gustavo Gutiérrez and Black liberation theologian James H. Cone, Isasi-Díaz believes self-determination is a prerequisite to true and full liberation. "Liberation is not something one person can give another"; rather, liberation is something in which the oppressed must become active participants, "a process in which the oppressed are protagonists." *Mujerista Theology*, 1.

44. In *Mujerista Theology*, Isasi-Díaz begins with Hispanic women's experiences and struggles for survival. These, rather than biblical texts, are the foundation of mujerista theology's hermeneutics. She writes on page 148:

"Hispanic women's experience and our struggle for survival, not the Bible, are the source of our theology and the starting point for how we should interpret, appropriate, and use the Bible."

45. "At the center of the unfolding of the kin-dom is the salvific act of God. Salvation and liberation are interconnected. Salvation is gratuitously given by God; it flows from the very essence of God: love. Salvation is worked out through the love between God and each human being and among human beings. This love relationship is the goal of all life. . . . The word 'kin-dom' makes it clear that when the fullness of God becomes a day-to-day reality in the world at large, we will all be sisters and brothers—kin to each other, we will indeed be the family of God." Isasi-Díaz, *Mujerista Theology*, 89, 103.

46. "To sin is to refuse to love one's neighbor and, therefore, the Lord himself. Sin—a breach of friendship with God and others—is according to the Bible the ultimate cause of poverty, injustice, and the oppression in which persons live. . . . Behind an unjust structure there is a personal or collective will responsible—a willingness to reject God and neighbor." Gutiérrez, *Theology of Liberation*, 24.

47. Mercy Amba Oduyoye, "Be a Woman, and Africa Will Be Strong," in *Inheriting Our Mothers' Gardens: Feminist Theology in Third World Perspective*, ed. Letty M. Russell et al. (Louisville: Westminster Press, 1988), 52.

48. E.g., Gustavo Gutiérrez's Latin American liberation theology.

49. E.g., James H. Cone's Black liberation theology.

50. E.g., Minjung theology. Chung Hyun Kyung describes Minjung theology in the following manner: "*Minjung* means 'grassroot people' in Korea. Minjung theology arose out of the Korean people's experiences of suffering and liberation under the political dictatorship and economic exploitation of the 1970s." "Following Naked Dancing and Long Dreaming," in Russell, *Inheriting Our Mothers' Gardens*, 161.

51. E.g., Mujerista theology and Womanist theology.

52. E.g., Queer theology.

53. E.g., see Nancy L. Eiesland, *The Disabled God: Toward a Liberatory Theology of Disability* (Nashville: Abingdon Press, 1994).

54. The data here comes from two sources: Children's Assessment Center, "Child Sexual Abuse Facts," https://tinyurl.com/y5eh5jnd, accessed November 26, 2022; and World Health Organization, "Violence against Adults and Children with Disabilities," https://tinyurl.com/5n76pypc, accessed November 26, 2022.

55. Janet Pais, *Suffer the Children: A Theology of Liberation by a Victim of Child Abuse* (Mahwah: Paulist Press, 1991), 17–18.

56. Pais, *Suffer the Children.*

57. See, for example, Brendan Hyde, *The Search for a Theology of Childhood – Essays by Jerome W. Berryman from 1978–2009* (Brisbane: Connor Court, 2013); David H. Jensen, *Graced Vulnerability: A Theology of Childhood* (Cleveland: Pilgrim Press, 2005); or the previously mentioned Mercer, *Welcoming Children.*

58. The most notable example of this is the Child Theology Movement website: https://tinyurl.com/bdejxbs8. Other examples include Haddon Willmer and Keith J. White, *Entry Point: Towards Child Theology with Matthew 18* (London: WTL Publications, 2015) and William C. Prevette, *Child, Church and Compassion: Towards Child Theology in Romania* (Eugene: Wipf and Stock, 2012).

59. I am not alone in building on Pais's work on child liberation theology. Other wonderful thinkers in this field include Craig Nessan, Rebecca Stevens-Walter, and Samantha Field.

60. Isasi-Díaz, *Mujerista Theology*, 67–68.

61. Women of Color, in Solidarity, "What Is 'Mujerista,' and What Is 'Mujerista Theology?,'" October 6, 2013, https://tinyurl.com/3x8s3r72.

62. See, for example, Alanna Weissman, "I Hate Your Kids. And I'm Not Sorry," *Salon*, October 7, 2015, https://tinyurl.com/th42an3m.

63. This assessment is inspired by and adapted from Youth Infusion's "Youth Adult Engagement Readiness Assessment," https://tinyurl.com/2wnnnrpy, accessed May 17, 2016.

Chapter One

1. Jacqueline E. Lapsley, "'Look! The Children and I Are as Signs and Portents in Israel': Children in Israel," in *The Child in the Bible*, ed. Marcia J. Bunge (Grand Rapids: Eerdmans, 2008), 86–87.

2. Marcia J. Bunge, "The Vocation of the Child: Theological Perspectives on the Particular and Paradoxical Roles and Responsibilities of Children," in *The Vocation of Children*, ed. Patrick McKinley Brennan (Grand Rapids: Eerdmans, 2008), 33.

3. Elisabeth Young-Bruehl, *Childism: Confronting Prejudice against Children* (New Haven: Yale University Press, 2012).

4. James St. James, "7 Harmful Ways Parents Often Wield Adultism against Their Kids," *Everyday Feminism*, March 27, 2016, https://tinyurl.com/47aue8w4.

5. Dan Shewan, "Conviction of Things Not Seen: The Uniquely American Myth of Satanic Cults," *Pacific Standard*, September 8, 2015, https://tinyurl.com/5n7d9dfc.

6. Anna North, "How #SaveTheChildren Is Pulling American Moms into QAnon," *Vox*, September 18, 2020, https://tinyurl.com/2p9hs92a.

7. Patrick McKinley Brennan, "Introduction," in *The Vocation of the Child*, ed. Patrick McKinley Brenna (Grand Rapids: Eerdmans, 2008), 4.

8. "Theology is language about God. . . . A theologian needs to be much more than a historian or a systematic logician. If the fundamental experience is not present to this person, then the reference point for the whole language system cannot be understood. Without the original vision theology becomes mere words about words." Jerome W. Berryman, *Godly Play* (Minneapolis: Augsburg Fortress, 1995), 153.

9. Jacqueline Howard, "Among 20 Wealthy Nations, US Child Mortality Ranks Worst, Study Finds," CNN, January 8, 2018, https://tinyurl.com/58yejt2c.

10. Laura E. Berk, *Child Development* (London: Pearson Education, 2013), 118.

11. Roosa Tikkanen, Munira Z. Gunja, Molly FitzGerald, and Laurie Zephyrin, "Maternal Mortality and Maternity Care in the United States Compared to 10 Other Developed Countries," *The Commonwealth Fund*, November 18, 2020, https://tinyurl.com/276xy7ck.

12. Joshua Cohen, "U.S. Maternal and Infant Mortality: More Signs of Public Health Neglect," *Forbes*, August 1, 2021, https://tinyurl.com/yckvrnxs.

13. Population Reference Bureau, "Black Women Over Three Times More Likely to Die in Pregnancy, Postpartum Than White Women, New Research Finds," December 6, 2021, https://tinyurl.com/4thsa457.

14. Berk, *Child Development*, 119, emphasis original. Hereafter, page citations will be in the text.

15. Boston National Public Radio, "Study: Paid Maternity Leave Reduces Infant Mortality Rates," April 6, 2016, https://tinyurl.com/43thjk86.

16. Childhelp, "Child Abuse Statistics and Facts," https://tinyurl.com/2mtyxyu8, accessed August 1, 2022.

17. Polaris, "Labor Trafficking," https://tinyurl.com/2pycjnek, accessed April 22, 2016.

18. Human Rights Watch, "Tobacco's Hidden Children: Hazardous Child Labor in United States Tobacco Farming," May 13, 2014, https://tinyurl.com/y8ax3t3t.

19. US Department of Labor, "List of Goods Produced by Child Labor or Forced Labor," https://tinyurl.com/5bdb2sv8, accessed April 22, 2016.

20. Abby Haglage, "Lawsuit: Your Candy Bar Was Made by Child Slaves," *Daily Beast*, September 29, 2015, https://tinyurl.com/ydp9mmr8.

21. Polaris, "Sex Trafficking."

22. National Center for Missing and Exploited Children, "Child Sex Trafficking," https://tinyurl.com/yx5td8uw, accessed April 22, 2016.

23. Liberals and progressives can be guilty of this. See, for example, *Oregon Live*, "Readers Respond: Americans Are Not Barbaric," January 16, 2020, https://tinyurl.com/2p8a2nfp.

24. Emma Batha, "U.S. Toughens Ban on 'Abhorrent' Female Genital Mutilation," Reuters, January 7, 2021, https://tinyurl.com/ycxs4863.

25. Maniza Habib, "Female Genital Mutilation Isn't Just a Foreign Issue," *Ms. Magazine*, April 21, 2022, https://tinyurl.com/4zf8dtfn.

26. Emma Batha, "U.S. Woman Says Strict Christian Parents Subjected Her to FGM," Reuters, April 1, 2019, https://tinyurl.com/3w366w3r.

27. Kelly Weill, "Sheriff Covered Up Mormon Child Marriage," *Daily Beast*, February 8, 2016, https://tinyurl.com/2dzztzmh.

28. Fraidy Reiss, "America's Child-Marriage Problem," *New York Times*, October 13, 2015, https://tinyurl.com/39tbyj5f.

29. Libby Anne, "Child Marriage and the Rest of the Maranatha Story," *Patheos*, December 2, 2013, https://tinyurl.com/bdcukbpk.

30. Kristin Rawls, "Queer People Don't Groom Kids, Evangelicals Do!—Part II: Evangelicals and an Epidemic of Child Marriage," *Illuminations*, July 25, 2022, https://tinyurl.com/29bk4xk9.

31. Victoria Richards, "Child Marriage Chart Reveals Girls Can Wed at 12 in Some Parts of the US—as Lawmakers Battle to Raise Age to 16," *Independent*, March 9, 2016, https://tinyurl.com/4pc6yj28.

32. Jerry A. Coyne, "Faith Healing Kills Children," *Slate*, May 21, 2015, https://tinyurl.com/yc2ukcm7.

33. Aleksandra Sandstrom, "Most States Allow Religious Exemptions from Child Abuse and Neglect Laws," Pew Research Center, August 12, 2016, https://tinyurl.com/cwh2wmhy.

34. Betsy Z. Russell, "Lawmakers Scrutinize Idaho's Faith-Healing Ex-

emption from Child Neglect, Manslaughter Charges," *The Spokesman-Review*, August 4, 2016, https://tinyurl.com/3b9a7p4k.

35. Jerry Markon, "Can a 3-Year-Old Represent Herself in Immigration Court? This Judge Thinks So," *Washington Post*, March 5, 2016, https://tinyurl.com/36u2hwhm.

36. Mark Keierleber, "'It's Barbaric': Some US Children Getting Hit at School Despite Bans," *Guardian*, May 19, 2021, https://tinyurl.com/4js8dnr2.

37. Sarah Carr, "Why Are Black Students Facing Corporal Punishment in Public Schools?," *The Nation*, April 8, 2014, https://tinyurl.com/38vbjubp.

38. Associated Press, "Paddling in NC Schools Up Despite More Bans," March 14, 2016, https://tinyurl.com/msuw6f9m.

39. Lisa Wade, "U.S. Schools Are Teaching Our Children That Native Americans Are History," *Pacific Standard*, December 3, 2014, https://tinyurl.com/ye2ayu2j.

40. Human Rights Watch, "US: Students with Disabilities Face Corporal Punishment at Higher Rates," August 10, 2009, https://tinyurl.com/5t8393fw.

41. Heather Vogell, "Violent and Legal: The Shocking Ways School Kids Are Being Pinned Down, Isolated against Their Will," *ProPublica*, June 19, 2014, https://tinyurl.com/2cu9r9z6.

42. Homeschooling's Invisible Children, "Some Preliminary Data on Homeschool Child Fatalities," https://tinyurl.com/2p9e9jwr, accessed November 26, 2022.

43. Homeschooling's Invisible Children, "Themes in Abuse," https://tinyurl.com/3xjh53be, accessed November 26, 2022.

44. Coalition for Responsible Home Education, "Protections for At-Risk Children," https://tinyurl.com/3vedn2s6, accessed November 26, 2022.

45. Jessica Huseman, "Small Group Goes to Great Lengths to Block Homeschooling Regulation," *ProPublica*, August 27, 2015, https://tinyurl.com/bde7cy7x.

46. Coalition for Responsible Home Education, "Homeschool Notification," https://tinyurl.com/2jcu4kvt, accessed November 26, 2022.

47. Huseman, "Homeschooling Regulation."

48. Huseman, "Homeschooling Regulation."

49. Kay Bell, "When Teens Owe Money to Uncle Sam," Fox Business, July 21, 2014, https://tinyurl.com/yc7ewdcb.

50. Jim Dwyer, "A Life That Frayed as Bail Reform Withered," *New York Times*, June 9, 2015, https://tinyurl.com/39x7ysec.

51. Jillian Keenan, "Paying Taxes and Going to Jail Like Adults; Teens Deserve the Right to Vote, Too," *The Daily Beast*, September 6, 2014, https://tinyurl.com/wfmfs5td.

52. Phillip Holloway, "Should 11-Year-Olds Be Charged with Adult Crimes?," CNN, October 15, 2015, https://tinyurl.com/3xwynrx5.

53. Marlene Martin, "Twenty-First Century Barbarism," *Jacobin*, July 2, 2015, https://tinyurl.com/yfphnkk9.

54. Alex Morris, "The Forsaken: A Rising Number of Homeless Gay Teens Are Being Cast Out by Religious Families," *Rolling Stone*, September 3, 2014, https://tinyurl.com/mvcc8ptm.

55. Katy Steinmetz, "Why Transgender People Are Being Murdered at a Historic Rate," *Time*, August 17, 2015, https://tinyurl.com/4hwes2wn.

56. US Office for Victims of Crimes, "Responding to Transgender Victims of Sexual Assault," June 2014, https://tinyurl.com/42pf42z4.

57. Elizabeth Weil, "What if It's (Sort of) a Boy and (Sort of) a Girl?," *New York Times*, September 24, 2006, https://tinyurl.com/56y9r47j.

58. Associated Press, "Surgery to Choose Gender No Longer Only Option for Intersex Children," April 17, 2015, https://tinyurl.com/3s337d23.

59. Jonathan Merritt, "3 Reasons Conservative Christians Will Lose the Transgender Debate," *Religion News Service*, May 14, 2016, https://tinyurl.com/563exc7y: "In 2013, I asked Russell Moore about why he failed to mention intersex persons and he said he doesn't believe their existence is relevant to this discussion because 'only a minuscule number of cases involve persons of indeterminate gender.' Sorry, but ignoring the existence of millions of humans around the globe will not cut it."

60. Lianne Simon, "Why Christians Should Oppose Bathroom Bills," March 12, 2015, https://tinyurl.com/y2xcnwcp; and The Intersex Roadshow, "When Intersex People Are Collateral Damage in Transphobic Battles," February 25, 2015, https://tinyurl.com/58w2a7zz.

61. Sharon Bernstein, "Abortions in U.S. Rise, Reversing a 30-Year Trend, New Data Show," Reuters, June 15, 2022, https://tinyurl.com/435c9e2h.

62. Jacqueline E. Lapsley, "'Look! The Children and I Are as Signs and Portents in Israel': Children in Israel," in *The Child in the Bible*, ed. Marcia J. Bunge (Grand Rapids: Eerdmans, 2008), 85.

63. "The failure is not one of charity, as is commonly perceived in popular thought, but a failure of justice at the systemic level." Lapsley, "Children in Israel," 85.

64. Lapsley, "Children in Israel," 86.

65. Lapsley, "Children in Israel," 88.

Chapter Two

1. Cindy Wang Brandt, "Cyntoia Brown Reminds Us That Children Exist in Every Intersection of Oppression," *Sojourners*, January 9, 2019, https://tinyurl.com/bddk8x39.

2. Judith M. Gundry-Volf, "The Least and the Greatest: Children in the New Testament," in *The Child in Christian Thought*, ed. Marcia J. Bunge (Grand Rapids: Eerdmans, 2001), 33: "Children had no rights of their own and were legally subject to their father, who had almost absolute power over them. According to Dionysius of Halicarnassus, 'the law-giver of the Romans gave virtually full power to the father over his son, whether he thought proper to imprison him, to scourge him, to put him in chains, and keep him at work in the fields, or to put him to death.' The Roman father's authority was supremely demonstrated in his 'power of life and death' over his children. He could decide whether to recognize a newborn and raise it, or to expose it (cast it out in a public place)."

3. "Intersectionality" is a term coined by American civil rights advocate and law professor Kimberlé Crenshaw. Crenshaw first articulated her theory of intersectionality in 1989 in a paper she wrote for the University of Chicago Legal Forum, "Demarginalizing the Intersection of Race and Sex: A Black Feminist Critique of Antidiscrimination Doctrine, Feminist Theory and Antiracist Politics." Crenshaw explained how Black women face overlapping systems of oppression because they stand at the intersection of race and gender. She later expanded her analysis beyond Black women and looked at how various individuals face intersecting oppressions: for example, poor people with disabilities, trans women, immigrants of color, etc. Thus, intersectionality now is used to communicate the ways diverse systems of oppressions overlap and how advocates must advocate for *everyone*, not merely the most visible members of marginalized groups.

Chapter Three

1. Keith J. White and Haddon Willmer, *An Introduction to Child Theology*, The Child Theology Movement Limited, 2006, https://tinyurl.com/bdhbyeyr.

2. "The text is our situation." Hugo Assmann, *Theology for a Nomad Church* (Maryknoll: Orbis Books, 1975), 104.

3. "Experience and our struggle for survival, not the Bible, are the source of our theology and the starting point for how we should interpret, appropriate, and use the Bible." Ada María Isasi-Díaz, *Mujerista Theology: A Theology for the Twenty-First Century* (Maryknoll: Orbis Books, 1996), 149.

4. Rosemary Radford Ruether argues that "there has been a tendency to treat this principle of 'experience' as unique to feminist theology (or, perhaps to liberation theologies) and to see it as distant from 'objective' sources of truth of classical theologies. This seems to be a misunderstanding of the experimental base of all theological reflection. What have been called the objective sources of theology, Scripture and tradition, are themselves codified collective human experience." *Sexism and God-Talk* (Boston: Beacon Press, 1993), 12.

5. "As human beings, we must inevitably see the universe from a centre lying within ourselves and speak about it in terms of a human language shaped by the exigencies of human intercourse. Any attempt rigorously to eliminate our human perspective from our picture of the world must lead to absurdity." Michael Polanyi, *Personal Knowledge* (Chicago: University of Chicago Press, 1974), 3.

6. Mercy Amba Oduyoye, "Be a Woman, and Africa Will Be Strong," in *Inheriting Our Mothers' Gardens: Feminist Theology in Third World Perspective*, ed. Letty M. Russell et al. (Louisville: Westminster Press, 1988), 38.

7. "Generations of evangelical Sunday School students are well familiar with the flannelgraph, a board covered with flannel fabric and usually resting on an easel. Sunday School teachers, especially at the elementary level, use the flannelgraph to illustrate stories from the Bible. They move representations of Moses or Noah or the pillar of fire, all of which are also backed with flannel, around the board in an attempt to bring the stories to life for young audiences." Randall Herbert Balmer, *Encyclopedia of Evangelicalism* (Louisville: Westminster John Knox, 2002), 221.

8. "We use the term *childist* to describe interpretation that focuses on the agency and action of children and youth in the biblical text, instead of seeing them primarily as passive, victimized, or marginalized." Kathleen Gallagher Elkins and Julie Faith Parker, "Children in Biblical Narrative and Childist Interpretation," *The Oxford Handbook of Biblical Narrative*, ed. Danna Nolan Fewell (Oxford: Oxford University Press, 2016), 425.

9. "The first step of childist interpretation is simply to read against the

grain of the text and notice child characters. Since life for children is rarely the concern of the biblical writers, children's appearances in the text are often brief, making it easy to gloss over their presence. To explore these characters, we draw on narrative critical methods and place the child(ren) at the center of attention." Elkins and Parker, "Children in Biblical Narrative," 425.

10. This parallels Jesuit liberation theologian Juan Luis Segundo's *hermeneutics of suspicion*, in which traditional interpretations of the Bible are challenged in order to lift up people from the margins of those interpretations. Child liberation theology also employs a hermeneutics of suspicion. Child liberation theologian Janet Pais writes that the theology "assert[s] the right . . . to question basic assumptions of traditional interpretation that may result from and perpetuate oppressive systems. In relation to children, such assumptions might be called 'adultist.'" *Suffer the Children* (Mahwah: Paulist Press, 1991), 15.

11. Just as feminist theologian Elisabeth Schüssler Fiorenza suggests a hermeneutics of suspicion ought to be applied to the text and also to the social conditions from which the text arose, child liberation theology demands that we give full consideration to the child's role in each narrative and the social conditions surrounding that child. We must make that child the priority in how we exegete the passage in every way possible. "Unlike Gutiérrez, Fiorenza is not satisfied with new ways of looking at the text. She wants to analyze not only the text itself but also the social conditions at the time." Ann-Cathrin Jarl, *In Justice: Women and Global Economics* (Minneapolis: Fortress Press, 2003), 60. Jarl offers extensive discussion of the hermeneutics of liberation theologians on pages 58–60.

12. This parallels the sentiment of Black liberation theologian James H. Cone: "Black Theology is not prepared to discuss the doctrine of God, man, Christ, Church, Holy Spirit—the whole spectrum of Christian theology— without making each doctrine an analysis of the emancipation of black people." *Black Power and Black Theology* (Maryknoll: Orbis Books, 1997), 121.

13. For an analysis of how the eunuch story relates to LGBTQIA acceptance, see Lawrence Richardson, "The Biblical Case for Embracing Transgender," The Salt Collective, https://tinyurl.com/39unvntc. Also see Lianne Simon, "Testimony of a Happily Married Intersex Eunuch," *Patheos*, October 5, 2013, https://tinyurl.com/yrcxkeja.

14. Peruvian liberation theologian Gustavo Gutiérrez declares in his con-

clusion, "All the political theologies, the theologies of hope, of revolution, and liberation, are not worth one act of genuine solidarity with exploited social classes. They are not worth one act of faith, love, and hope, committed—in one way or another—in active participation to liberate humankind from everything that dehumanizes it." *A Theology of Liberation* (Maryknoll: Orbis Books, 2014), 174.

15. "Jesus commands us to 'Love the Lord your God with all your heart, all your soul, and all your mind.' He goes on to command us to, 'Love your neighbor as yourself.' The children in our families, our churches, and the communities where we live and work are our 'neighbors.'" Jeanette Harder, *Let the Children Come: Preparing Faith Communities to End Child Abuse and Neglect* (Scottdale: Herald Press, 2010), 16.

16. Jeffrey Brown, "I Is for Infant: Reading Aloud to Young Children Benefits Brain Development," PBS, June 24, 2014, https://tinyurl.com/4uhcuceb.

17. "Of particular importance for this paper is the idea that children are sources of revelation. The issue of changing the gaze when it comes to children and to respect them as a new mission hermeneutic, has to do with the challenge to accept the witness, prophecy and revelation from children as representatives of Jesus." Nico Botha, "Children as Theological Hermeneutic: Is There a New Epistemological Break Emerging?," Association for Education and Research in Europe (GBFE) in South Africa, November 2012, https://tinyurl.com/3986uma6.

18. "As children grow in their cognitive capabilities, one of the best questions parents can ask is 'What do you think?' This is an underappreciated power phrase. To take seriously children's opinions is to honor them as full human beings, giving them the dignity of contributing meaningfully to conversations. Respecting children's thoughts empowers them to believe their voices matter, their ideas matter, and ultimately that they matter. They deserve to be fully present to take up space in our world despite their small stature and young age." Cindy Wang Brandt, *Parenting Forward: How to Raise Children with Justice, Mercy, and Kindness* (Grand Rapids: Eerdmans, 2019), 53.

19. "I want to suggest that the emergence of children worldwide as agents of mission, necessitates a new epistemology. One of the building blocks of such an epistemology is the suggestion by Strachan (2011: 283) of 'joining children in their world.' She implies quite strongly a shift in paradigm in hinting a 'redress in favour of the children.' The new missiological epistemology can

only come to the fore if we start in the world of children and learn from their experiences." Botha, "Children as Theological Hermeneutic."

20. "In a theology from below, the very first act is commitment. And therefore a theology from below is a 'with' theology. In concrete terms, and in the context of the paper, a theology where purportedly children are the interpretive key, cannot be a theology about or for children, but a theology 'with' children." Botha, "Children as Theological Hermeneutic."

21. "[We must] shift our attention from the Bible and tradition to people's stories. The exclusiveness of the Christian claim often stems from a narrow and mystified view of the Bible and church teaching. . . . Our religious imagination cannot be based on the Bible alone, which often excludes women's experience." Kwok Pui-lan, "Mothers and Daughters, Writers and Fighters," in *Inheriting Our Mothers' Gardens: Feminist Theology in Third World Perspective*, ed. Letty M. Russell et al. (Louisville: Westminster Press, 1988), 29.

22. "The images and metaphors we use to talk about God are necessarily culturally conditioned, and biblical ones are no exception." Pui-lan, "Mothers and Daughters," 30.

23. "Opening this treasure chest is the first step to doing our own theology. With full confidence, we claim that our own culture and our people's aspirations are vehicles for knowing and appreciating the ultimate. This would also imply that our Christian identity must be radically expanded. Instead of fencing us from the world, it should open us to all the rich manifestations that embody the divine." Pui-lan, "Mothers and Daughters," 30.

24. Oduyoye, "Be a Woman," 49.

25. "We have to move from a passive reception of the traditions to an active construction of our own theology." Pui-lan, "Mothers and Daughters," 30.

26. Pui-lan, "Mothers and Daughters," 31.

27. Pui-lan, "Mothers and Daughters," 31.

Chapter Four

1. Danna Nolan Fewell, *The Children of Israel: Reading the Bible for the Sake of Our Children* (Nashville: Abingdon Press, 2003), 27.

2. While Christianity has a long history of teaching that children are parental property and children's wills are evil and need to be crushed, Judaism has a long history of protecting and promoting children's rights. For

introductions to how Jewish people think about children, children's rights, and child advocacy, see Rabbi David Rosen's two articles, "How Children Are Valued in the Jewish Tradition," October 12, 2004, https://tinyurl.com/yys7rkax; and "The Rights of the Child—Jewish Perspective," https://tinyurl.com/2p8duwdm, accessed August 7, 2022. See also Michael Shire, "Learning to Be Righteous: A Jewish Theology of Childhood," *Nurturing Child and Adolescent Spirituality: Perspectives from the World's Religious Traditions*, ed. by Karen Marie Yust, Aostre N. Johnson, Sandy Eisenberg Sasso, and Eugene C. Roehlkepartain (Oxford: Rowman & Littlefield, 2006), 43–52.

3. Examples of defenses include: Glen Scrivener, "'Kill Me a Son': The Beautiful Scandal of Abraham's Sacrifice," *The Gospel Coalition*, November 27, 2018, https://tinyurl.com/yrs2cpr2; Tremper Longman III, "Abraham and Isaac: A Test of Faith," *Zondervan Academic*, September 4, 2018, https://tinyurl.com/uwtpbmkc; and Felix Fernandez, "Sacrificing Isaac," *The Banner*, May 2, 2022, https://tinyurl.com/vsr7vbux. Examples of critiques include: Carol Delaney, "Should We Admire Abraham's Willingness," Santa Clara University, April 18, 2002, https://tinyurl.com/2p83jrhy; Andrew Arndt, "Revisiting the Sacrifice of Isaac," *Mere Orthodoxy*, February 2, 2022, https://tinyurl.com/yddm8dsy; and Richard Dawkins, *The God Delusion* (Boston: Mariner Press, 2008), 242–43.

4. In his book *Fear and Trembling*, Kierkegaard argued that Abraham's faith is "a paradox which is capable of transforming a murder into a holy act, well-pleasing to God," as cited by Carol Delaney, *Abraham on Trial: The Social Legacy of Biblical Myth* (Princeton: Princeton University Press, 2020), 123.

5. Terence E. Fretheim, "'God Was with the Boy' (Genesis 21:20): Children in the Book of Genesis," in *The Child in the Bible*, ed. Marcia J. Bunge (Grand Rapids: Eerdmans, 2008), 14.

6. Qur'an 37:101–3.

7. "Isaac (so it seems) has been left behind on the mountain, as the text notes that Abraham returned with his servants to Beersheba (22:19)—no mention made of the nearly-immolated Isaac, who sinks into shadows as the patriarchal narratives progress." Andrew Arndt, "Revisiting the Sacrifice of Isaac," *Mere Orthodoxy*, February 2, 2022, https://tinyurl.com/yddm8dsy.

8. Carol Delaney, "Should We Admire Abraham's Willingness," Santa Clara University, April 18, 2002, https://tinyurl.com/2p83jrhy.

9. Fretheim, "'God Was with the Boy,'" 22–23.

10. Fretheim, "'God Was with the Boy,'" 23.

11. Tamar Kadari, "Lot's Daughters: Midrash and Aggadah," Jewish Women's Archive, https://tinyurl.com/47bvnyp4, accessed February 18, 2017.

12. Solomon Schechter and Julius H. Greenstone, "Marriage Laws," *Jewish Encyclopedia*, https://tinyurl.com/4xsb2rtu, accessed February 18, 2017.

13. R. L. Stollar, "How We Marginalize Abuse Survivors: The Spirit of Ham," Homeschool Alumni Reaching Out, October 31, 2014, https://tinyurl.com/2s3d6ks9: "What Ham did was not simply see his father naked — nor was it telling his brothers that his father was naked. . . . The problem is what 'nakedness' means in the context. Namely, 'seeing' or 'uncovering' nakedness is a biblical euphemism for a sexual act. One sees this euphemism used repeatedly in Leviticus 18. This has long been a recognized interpretation within both Judaism and Christianity." See also David Frankel, "Noah, Ham and the Curse of Canaan: Who Did What to Whom in the Tent?," TheTorah.com, October 18, 2017, https://tinyurl.com/2p9yf72w: "The sin, in the original narrative, is not homosexual sex itself, but forced incest of a son with his father in a situation in which the father has no ability to defend himself; this would explain the harshness of the father's curse."

14. Some notable interpretations include: Origen, "Homily 5 on 1 Samuel," *Origen: The Early Church Fathers*, ed. by Joseph W. Trigg (London: Routledge, 1998), 200; Ligonier Ministries, "Lot and His Daughters," November 10, 2006, https://tinyurl.com/yekb2tmv; Wil Gafney, "Lot Sexually Manipulates His Two Daughters," TheTorah.com, October 19, 2021, https://tinyurl.com/5b775nz4; and Jonathan Hadjdamach, "Lot and His Daughters: A Troubling Tale of Sin and Seduction," Art UK, May 27, 2022, https://tinyurl.com/mtkmaemf.

15. Ilan Kutz, "Revisiting the Lot of the First Incestuous Family: The Biblical Origins of Shifting the Blame onto Female Family Members," *BMJ*, December 24, 2005.

16. 12News, "Pro-Rape Pastor Defends Church's Hiring of Child Rapist," April 15, 2016, https://tinyurl.com/yp3449re.

17. Elizabeth Breau, "Teaching Rape and Incest," *thirdspace: a journal of feminist theory & culture*, November 2003, https://tinyurl.com/2m67vvy5.

18. Herbert Lockyer, "Lot's Daughters," *All the Women of the Bible* (Grand Rapids: Zondervan, 1988), as cited at https://tinyurl.com/2p9853tc.

19. Darkness to Light, "Child Sexual Abuse Statistics: The Magnitude of the Problem," December 22, 2015, https://tinyurl.com/muhcvdp8.

20. Darkness to Light, "Child Sexual Abuse Statistics: Perpetrators," December 22, 2015, https://tinyurl.com/yew8cv7z.

21. Darkness to Light, "Child Sexual Abuse Statistics: Perpetrators," December 22, 2015, https://tinyurl.com/yew8cv7z.

22. RAINN, "Victims of Sexual Violence: Statistics," https://tinyurl.com/39ry7ue7, accessed December 11, 2022.

23. Kutz, "First Incestuous Family."

24. Here are just three of many examples: Homeschooling's Invisible Children, "Girl by Rob and Marie Johnson," August 13, 2015, https://tinyurl.com/khs76rn9; Homeschooling's Invisible Children, "K. B. by Robert Sanders," March 22, 2015, https://tinyurl.com/4z4yw78c; and Homeschooling's Invisible Children, "Lindsay Tornambe and Others by Victor A. Barnard," April 17, 2014, https://tinyurl.com/2p8bnrd9.

25. Kadari, "Lot's Daughters."

26. Paul Baxter writes that evangelical scholar Walter C. Kaiser Jr. declared, "Unfavorable assessments of this incident have brought more criticism of the Bible than almost any other narrative." From "Why Would God Send a Bear to Maul Children?," *The Christian Index*, February 4, 2022, https://tinyurl.com/mrymcbnz.

27. An example of how the passage is used to scare children into obedience comes from Chad Bird, who says he was taught "the moral of the Bible story from 2 Kings 2:23–25 was this: pay honor to your elders, your church leaders, or you too might suffer a similar fate from the God who will not be mocked—or let his prophets be mocked." "The Misunderstood Story of Bear Attacks, a Bald Prophet, and Forty-Two Mouthy 'Kids,'" *1517*, February 25, 2020, https://tinyurl.com/24znd8tj.

28. Several prominent examples of evangelical interpretations include: Baxter, "Why Would God Send a Bear?"; Bird, "Misunderstood Story"; Elizabeth Mitchell, "Elisha, Little Children, and the Bears," Answers in Genesis, November 12, 2010, https://tinyurl.com/5xxdmtuz; Vance Bradley, "Elisha and the 42 Children," United Church of South Royalton, September 8, 2019, https://tinyurl.com/45tw28eb; and Henry M. Morris, "Elisha's Bears," Institute for Creation Research, February 23, 2009, https://tinyurl.com/yckphb27.

29. "In 2015, just under 60% of evangelical churches espoused a literal interpretation of Scripture, data from Pew Research showed. In 2019, Pew Research also noted that some 61% of Southern Baptists, who tend to express

higher levels of religious commitment than Americans overall, accepted the Bible as the literal Word of God. This share exceeded the share of those who hold this belief among all U.S. adults—31%—and among other Evangelical Protestants, which had fallen to 53%." *Decision Magazine*, "Gallup: Less Than Half of Evangelicals Believe Bible Is 'Actual Word of God,'" July 12, 2022, https://tinyurl.com/t96py2nz.

30. A few examples follow: Paul Baxter describes the children as "a gang of young teenagers" in "Why Would God Send a Bear?" Chad Bird says the children are "young men" in "Misunderstood Story." Vance Bradley writes, "Instead of children, it's more appropriate to say mature adolescents or young men," in "Elisha and the 42 Children."

31. Mitchell, "Elisha, Little Children, and the Bears."

32. This parallels the sentiment expressed by evangelical homeschool leader Voddie Baucham concerning Michael Brown, the Black teenager shot by a white police officer. Baucham wrote for the Gospel Coalition that "Brown reaped what he sowed." See Voddie Baucham, "Thoughts on Ferguson," The Gospel Coalition, November 26, 2014, https://tinyurl.com/547bt55a.

33. "The basic idea of [a projective test] is that when a person is shown an ambiguous, meaningless image (i.e. an inkblot) the mind will work hard at imposing meaning on the image. That meaning is generated by the mind. By asking the person to tell you what they see in the inkblot, they are actually telling you about themselves, and how they project meaning on to the real world." Mike Drayton, "What's behind the Rorschach Inkblot Test?," *BBC*, July 25, 2012, https://tinyurl.com/kcknvckn.

34. Here are some examples: Paul Baxter writes that the children were "a gang of young teenagers" and cites Gleason Archer's description of the children as "a serious public danger, quite as grave as the large youth gangs that roam the ghetto sections of our modern American cities" in "Why Would God Send a Bear?"; Elizabeth Mitchell describes the children as "young hoodlums" in "Elisha, Little Children, and the Bears"; and Henry M. Morris similarly says the children are "a gang of young hoodlums" in "Elisha's Bears."

35. For a helpful summary of adultification bias, see Shehnal Amin and Abigail Black, "Adultification Bias of Black Children: Q&A with Jahnine Davis," Farrer & Co, March 29, 2022, https://tinyurl.com/2kkxvjth.

36. "Examining patterns of police treatment towards Black youth highlights a prominent issue: the adultification bias, which is the phenomenon where adults perceive Black youth as being older than they actually are." Janice

Gassam Asare, "How the Adultification Bias Contributes to Black Trauma," *Forbes*, April 22, 2021, https://tinyurl.com/4uwktr6e.

37. Bradley, "Elisha and the 42 Children."

38. *The William Davidson Talmud*, Sotah 47a, https://tinyurl.com/4yux4nru, accessed December 10, 2022.

39. "The rabbis of the Talmud are struck and deeply troubled by this violence—against teasing children, no less. One strand of rabbinic thought attempts to minimize Elisha's apparent overreaction. Rabbi Eleazar suggests that the offenders were not children at all, but rather individuals of little faith and no observance of the commandments, and so their punishment was commensurate with their intentional wickedness. But even so, the rabbis of the Talmud cannot exonerate Elisha for obscene overreaction, and imagine he was indeed punished by God for his actions." Sara Ronis, "Elisha," My Jewish Learning, https://tinyurl.com/mwrm99uj, accessed July 29, 2022.

40. "Children learn violence-related behaviors . . . by watching peers and adults acting aggressively." Sally Kuykendall and Maria DiGiorgio McColgan, "Bullying as a Behavior Learned Through Trauma," International Bullying Prevention Association, https://tinyurl.com/yc37wta8.

41. The idea of not harming God's anointed people (i.e., prophets) is certainly one found in the Bible. For example, the phrase "Do not touch my anointed ones; do my prophets no harm" appears twice: in 1 Chronicles 16:22 and Psalm 105:15. However, this phrase has also been twisted by some Christians to imply senior leaders in faith communities and organizations are above reproach, leading one author to declare the phrase "one of the most abused verses in the entire Bible." Ron Cantor, "'Touch Not God's Anointed': One of the Most Abused Verses in the Entire Bible," *Charisma Magazine*, July 17, 2018, https://tinyurl.com/yr82rrx4.

42. Even evangelicals recognize that this belief has taken hold and are trying to counter its influence in their own communities. Writing for the Reformed organization Ligonier Ministries, Augustus Nicodemus Lopes states, "David's reluctance to kill Saul because Saul was the Lord's anointed has been interpreted by many evangelicals as a biblical principle that applies to pastors of modern-day churches." "Do Not Touch the Lord's Anointed," October 19, 2019, https://tinyurl.com/d4adwf4m.

43. Ron Henzel, "Trapped in the Shadow of 'God's Anointed': Breaking Free from an Unbiblical Concept," Recovering Grace, May 5, 2014, https://tinyurl.com/tf2nnuyx.

44. Bryan Smith, "The Cult Next Door," *Chicago Mag*, June 20, 2016, https://tinyurl.com/ysr8hfr2.

45. The two most notable examples would be: Søren Kierkegaard's *Fear and Trembling*, trans. Howard V. Hong and Edna H. Hong (Princeton: Princeton University Press, 1983), the entirety of which is on the topic of Abraham's inner turmoil; and Immanuel Kant's *The Conflict of the Faculties*, trans. Mary J. Gregor (Lincoln: University of Nebraska Press, 1992), especially 113–15.

46. The name AWANA is an acronym for Approved Workmen Are Not Ashamed, a phrase from 2 Timothy 2:15. AWANA as an organization serves "133 countries worldwide through 66,000 churches, reaching over 4.9 million kids." AWANA, "Awana Announces Matt Markins as New CEO," January 11, 2022, https://tinyurl.com/596kpzj8.

47. "It is time that the Christian community come to terms with the heartbreaking reality that those who pose the greatest risk to our children are within our families, churches, and circle of friends." Boz Tchividjian, "Sex Offenders, Faith Communities, and Four Common Exploitations," *Religion News Service*, April 26, 2014, https://tinyurl.com/bdfwvjmh.

48. Justin and Lindsey Holcomb, *God Made All of Me: A Book to Help Children Protect Their Bodies* (Greensboro: New Growth Press, 2015).

Chapter Five

1. Jeanette Harder, *Let the Children Come: Preparing Faith Communities to End Child Abuse and Neglect* (Scottdale: Herald Press, 2010), 37.

2. This valuing of the marginalized and the oppressed literally runs in Jesus's blood, as his family history demonstrates. "Jesus is the descendant of not one but three victims of sexual exploitation [Tamar, Rahab, and Bathsheba]—a clear indication that God's kingdom includes the marginalized, the oppressed, and victims of abuse." Victor Vieth, *On This Rock: A Call to Center the Christian Response to Child Abuse on the Life and Words of Jesus* (Eugene: Wipf and Stock, 2018), 20.

3. Judith M. Gundry-Volf, "The Least and the Greatest: Children in the New Testament," in *The Child in Christian Thought*, ed. Marcia J. Bunge (Grand Rapids: Eerdmans, 2001), 47.

4. Nissan Mindel, "Miriam," Chabad.org, https://tinyurl.com/2p8h723t, accessed September 23, 2022.

5. "She was also called Puah, meaning 'Whisperer,' for she was whispering words of prophecy." Mindel, "Miriam."

6. Tamar Meir, "Miriam: Midrash and Aggadah," Jewish Women's Archive, https://tinyurl.com/4pssfxbd, accessed September 23, 2022.

7. Mindel, "Miriam."

8. Meir, "Miriam."

9. Meir, "Miriam: Midrash and Aggadah."

10. Pesikta Rabbati 43.

11. Maggy Whitehouse, *A Woman's Worth: The Divine Feminine in the Hebrew Bible* (Winchester: John Hunt Publishing, 2013), 126.

12. Gundry-Volf, "Least and the Greatest," 47.

13. "When I went East and came to the place where these things were preached and done, I learned accurately the books of the Old Testament, and send them to you as written below. Their names are as follows: Of Moses, five books: Genesis, Exodus, Numbers, Leviticus, Deuteronomy; Jesus Nave, Judges, Ruth; of Kings, four books; of Chronicles, two; the Psalms of David, the Proverbs of Solomon, Wisdom also, Ecclesiastes, Song of Songs, Job; of Prophets, Isaiah, Jeremiah; of the twelve prophets, one book; Daniel, Ezekiel, Esdras. From which also I have made the extracts, dividing them into six books. Such are the words of Melito." Eusebius, *Church History*, 4.26.14 (*NPNF*[2] 1:206).

14. "As Eli ages, he continues to lose control over his sons. He hears rumors that they take advantage of the naïve masses, particularly that they have been sleeping with the women who congregate at the gate of the sanctuary. These women, whose trusting naivete contrasts so mightily with Hannah's defiance, are the same women who donated their mirrors to forge the laver in God's sanctuary (Exodus 38:8), women who came to Shiloh seeking to cleave to God, and who were duped into confusing proximity to God with proximity to the priests. Whether or not the rumors were true matters little; they were rooted in the reality of a priesthood that monopolized access to God and used its power to take advantage of the people." Rabbi Elli Fischer, "Perversion of the Priesthood: The Decline and Fall of the House of Eli in the Talmud," in *To Stand & Serve: On Being a Kohen—Essays in Memory of Marc Weinberg*, ed. Aviad Tabory and Elli Fischer (Jerusalem: Koren Publishers, 2015), 80.

15. Alexander MacLaren, "Commentary on 1 Samuel 3," https://tinyurl.com/yc5pkycf, accessed January 3, 2023, emphasis added.

16. Josephus, *Jewish Antiquities* 5.10.4, in *The New Complete Works of Josephus*, trans. William Whiston (Grand Rapids: Kregel Academic, 1999), 194.

17. "[A father] may assume the primary role—or only role—in family or tribe decision making. In extreme cases the father as head of the family (and therefore head of the wife) may also have the final say between life and death. Israel's patriarchal society during those centuries in which the Pentateuch was produced understood the father—that is, the adult male head of the family—as possessing both power and prestige. He could, for example, sell his daughter as a servant (Exod. 21:7)." Alice L. Laffey, *An Introduction to the Old Testament: A Feminist Perspective* (Minneapolis: Fortress Press, 1988), 16.

18. *The William Davidson Talmud*, Berakhot 31b, Sefaria.org, https://tinyurl.com/4kwc3tzy, accessed December 10, 2022.

19. *The William Davidson Talmud*, Berakhot 31b, https://tinyurl.com/ykrpv4a4, accessed December 10, 2022.

20. Fischer, "Perversion of the Priesthood," 88.

21. Josephus, *Jewish Antiquities*, 5.10.4, in *The New Complete Works of Josephus*, trans. by William Whiston (Grand Rapids: Kregel Academic, 1999), 194.

22. Laurel Koepf, "Inside Out: The Othered Child in the Bible for Children," *Text, Image, and Otherness in Children's Bibles: What Is in the Picture?* (Atlanta: Society of Biblical Literature, 2012), 19.

23. J. Hampton Keathley III, "The Healing of Naaman (2 Kings 5:1–19)," *Studies in the Life of Elisha*, 2004, https://tinyurl.com/bp9d89bc.

24. Laffey, *Introduction to the Old Testament*, 136.

25. Walter Brueggemann, "A Brief Moment for a One-Person Remnant (2 Kings 5:2–3)," *Biblical Theology Bulletin: Journal of Bible and Culture* 31, no.2 (May 1, 2001): 53–59.

26. Heather Farrell, "The Little Maid," *Women in the Scriptures*, January 28, 2009, https://tinyurl.com/skf24vb7.

27. Lois Wilson, *Stories Seldom Told: Biblical Stories Retold for Children and Adults* (Kelowna: Wood Lake Publishing, 1997), 105.

28. To learn more about *inclusios*, see https://tinyurl.com/2pn84ydw.

29. Koepf, "Inside Out."

30. Robin Cohn, "The Luminous Servant," *Women in the Bible for Thinkers*, May 11, 2010, https://tinyurl.com/3d8pyt9d, accessed February 8, 2017.

31. *The William Davidson Talmud*, Sotah 47a, https://tinyurl.com/35a3r8wv, accessed December 10, 2022.

Chapter Six

1. Kristin Johnston Largen, *Baby Krishna, Infant Christ: A Comparative Theology of Salvation* (Maryknoll: Orbis Books, 2011), 101.

2. Largen, *Baby Krishna, Infant Christ*, 19.

3. "Christians, like the Ptolemies with Serapis, sought to convert followers of [Isis] by using popular iconography and liturgy of [Isis] to create similarities between the systems. The Virgin Mary is a visible vestige of [the Kemetic System] in Christianity as witness in various Madonna with Child images. The icon is analogous to the seated [Isis] with [Horus] that was widely distributed during the Late Kingdom." Jennifer Williams, "From Aset to Jesus: The History of the Goddess Aset in Ancient Kemet from Circa 3000 BCE until the Removal of Feminine Salvation Circa 400 CE," *Journal of Black Studies* 45, no. 2 (2014): 118–19.

4. Emma Swan Hall, "Harpocrates and Other Child Deities in Ancient Egyptian Sculpture," *Journal of the American Research Center in Egypt* 14 (1977): 55–58.

5. *Encyclopedia Britannica Online*, s.v. "Izanagi and Izanami," https://tinyurl.com/2p9ycb75, accessed July 1, 2016; and *Encyclopedia Britannica Online*, s.v. "Ebisu," https://tinyurl.com/38sh2npn, accessed July 1, 2016.

6. Sonia Narang, "Nepal's Living Goddess Who Still Has to Do Homework," BBC, June 18, 2014, https://tinyurl.com/66xr3bmb.

7. Laura Amazzone, *Goddess Durga and Sacred Female Power* (Lanham: Hamilton Books, 2010), 73–74.

8. The background information on Hinduism presented in this chapter comes from Largen, *Baby Krishna, Infant Christ*.

9. Largen, *Baby Krishna, Infant Christ*, 1.

10. Largen, *Baby Krishna, Infant Christ*, 5.

11. *Krishna: The Beautiful Legend of God*, trans. Edwin F. Bryant (London: Penguin Books, 2003), 39.

12. Largen, *Baby Krishna, Infant Christ*, 37.

13. Largen, *Baby Krishna, Infant Christ*, 80.

14. Thich Nhat Hanh, *The Heart of the Buddha's Teaching: Transforming Suffering into Peace, Joy, and Liberation* (New York: Broadway Books, 1999), 3.

15. Nhat Hanh, *Heart of the Buddha's Teaching*, 3.

16. Thich Nhat Hanh, *Touching Peace: Practicing the Art of Mindful Living* (Berkeley: Parallax Press, 1992), 121.

17. Nhat Hanh, *Living Buddha, Living Christ*, 34.

18. Nhat Hanh, *Touching Peace*, 38.

19. Nhat Hanh, *Living Buddha, Living Christ*, 45–47.

20. Nhat Hanh, *Living Buddha, Living Christ*, 45–47.

21. Nhat Hanh, *Living Buddha, Living Christ*, 48–49.

22. "Siddhartha Gautama was twenty-nine years old when he left his family." Nhat Hanh, *Heart of the Buddha's Teaching*, 6.

23. "The idea of suffering is a central thought in Buddhist practice. The original word in Pali is dukkha, which is most often translated as suffering, but is sometimes translated simply as 'unsatisfactoriness' or as 'stress.' Dukkha refers to the psychological experience—sometimes conscious, sometimes not conscious—of the profound fact that everything is impermanent, ungraspable, and not really knowable." Norman Fischer, "Suffering Opens the Real Path," *Lion's Roar*, January 20, 2017, https://tinyurl.com/bdfptexf.

24. "Jesus' life is not primarily a precursor to, a movement toward some far-off salvation in the future, but rather an unfolding of the salvation that has happened in the incarnation." Largen, *Baby Krishna, Infant Christ*, 207.

25. Qur'an 6:14, 6:163, 39:12. Abdullah Yusuf Ali, *The Holy Qur'an* (New Delhi: Kitab Bhavan, 1996).

26. The background information on Muhammad in this chapter comes from Lesley Hazleton, *The First Muslim: The Story of Muhammad* (New York: Riverhead Books, 2013), 7, emphasis original. Hereafter page citations will be in the text.

27. Alice Walker, *In Search of Our Mothers' Gardens* (San Diego: HBJ Publishers, 1983), xi, emphasis original.

28. For example, "A controlled child is one who has submitted his will to his parents. When they speak to him he obeys them quickly and with a good attitude—even when they are not watching. He has self control, and so obeys them without sass or complaint." Reb Bradley, *Child Training Tips* (Fair Oaks: Family Ministries Publishing, 1996), 37. Another example comes from John MacArthur, *What the Bible Says about Parenting* (Nashville: Thomas Nelson,

2000), 115–16: "Even Jesus *learned* obedience. In His humanity, obedience was something He had to be taught. Scripture says, 'He learned obedience by the things which He suffered' (Hebrews 5:8)." Here MacArthur implies that God the Parent used pain (corporal punishment) to teach Jesus the God-Child obedience.

29. Largen, *Baby Krishna, Infant Christ*, 85. Hereafter page citations will be in the text.

30. Bart Ehrman, *Lost Scriptures: Books That Did Not Make It into the New Testament* (Oxford: Oxford University Press, 2003), 58.

31. Saint Irenaeus, cited in Denis Minns, *Irenaeus* (Washington, DC: Georgetown University Press, 1994), 91.

32. "While the Gospels do not include such details, we can be sure that Jesus cried when he was hungry and got angry at his mother when she did not pick him up as quickly as he would have liked. Certainly, he would have been fussy, even irritable, and he probably fought nap time tooth and nail like all children do at one time or another. Imagine him teething, being potty-trained, being spanked. Imagine him learning to speak, learning to walk, learning to read and write. We usually do not consider these things when we think about God, but infancy narratives in scripture encourage us to do so. Jesus' humanity is not *sui generis*, it is our humanity." Largen, *Baby Krishna, Infant Christ*, 119.

33. Tarja S. Philip, *Menstruation and Childbirth in the Bible: Fertility and Impurity* (Frankfurt: Peter Lang, 2006), 91.

34. Elizabeth A. Johnson, *Dangerous Memories: A Mosaic of Mary in Scripture* (New York: Bloomsbury, 2004), 126–27.

35. John A. Beck, *The Baker Illustrated Guide to Everyday Life in Bible Times* (Ada: Baker Books, 2013).

36. Terence E. Fretheim, "'God Was with the Boy' (Genesis 21:20): Children in the Book of Genesis," in *The Child in the Bible*, ed. Marcia J. Bunge (Grand Rapids: Eerdmans, 2008), 6.

37. "Almost 200 texts about violence against children in the Hebrew Old Testament, another fifty from the deutero-canonical writings." Andreas Michel, "Sexual Violence against Children in the Bible," in *The Structured Betrayal of Trust*, ed. R. Ammicht-Quinn, H. Haker, and M. Junker-Kenny (London: SCM Press, 2004), 51–71.

38. "Even as an infant, he was not less than the savior of the world, not less than God's only begotten son, not less than fully divine, and certainly not less

than fully human. He did not 'become' the Son of God at some point in his early adulthood, nor did he 'develop' his identity as savior, realizing it gradually over the years. Instead, from the moment he was born, he was completely and totally the one whom the disciples proclaimed him to be after the resurrection, the one whom Paul wrote and preached about all through Asia Minor, the one in whom countless Christians have professed their faith for millennia. Thus, we might as well say that at the moment of his incarnation the world was changed forever, and the chasm between the Divine and the human was overcome." Largen, *Baby Krishna, Infant Christ*, 122.

Chapter Seven

1. Janet Pais, *Suffer the Children: A Theology of Liberation by a Victim of Child Abuse* (Mahwah: Paulist Press, 1991), 15. Hereafter page citations will be in the text.

2. "God took on all the powerlessness, weakness, and neediness of human childhood for our salvation." Pais, *Suffer the Children*, 15.

3. "In the incarnation we can glimpse the inner divine relationship between the first and second persons of the Trinity, Father and Child." Pais, *Suffer the Children*, 58.

4. "The doctrine of the Trinity tells us that the Child aspect of God, the Son, was not created, but is eternally begotten of the Father." Pais, *Suffer the Children*, 74.

5. "Revealing God as Child and revealing the Father in relationship with the Child, the incarnation reveals the inner nature of God is relational." Pais, *Suffer the Children*, 85.

6. This is in line with what we read in Mark 3:35, where Jesus states, "Whoever does God's will is my brother and sister and mother."

7. The age of discernment, also known as the age of accountability, is the age at which children allegedly become morally culpable for sin in their lives. The actual age depends on who is making the argument. Here is one example: "Biblically, it will be sometime before twenty years of age (Deut. 1:39 with Num. 14:29–31). Observation seems to suggest that some children may be accountable as early as five, while others may not be fully accountable until nineteen. The mentally impaired may never develop to the point of moral re-

sponsibility." Michael Pearl and Debi Pearl, *To Train Up a Child* (Pleasantville: No Greater Joy Ministries, 1994), 17–18.

8. Kate Wong, "Why Humans Give Birth to Helpless Babies," *Scientific American*, August 28, 2012, https://tinyurl.com/3ceypc8e.

9. James H. Cone, *The Cross and The Lynching Tree* (Maryknoll: Orbis Books, 2011), 22.

Chapter Eight

1. Janet Pais, *Suffer the Children: A Theology of Liberation by a Victim of Child Abuse* (Mahwah: Paulist Press, 1991), 72.

2. Gustavo Gutiérrez, *A Theology of Liberation* (Maryknoll: Orbis Books, 2014), 125.

3. "Our love for God is demonstrated by how we love and 'receive' children. . . . Loving, protecting, and advocating for children is an essential component of our overall worship of God." Boz Tchividjian, *Protecting Children from Abuse in the Church* (Greensboro: New Growth Press, 2013), 4.

4. Voddie Baucham, *Family Shepherds* (Wheaton: Crossway, 2011), 118.

5. "Johnny doesn't disobey because he's cranky, tired, or hungry, or because he hasn't been conditioned properly; he does it because he's a descendant of Adam." Baucham, *Family Shepherds*, 119.

6. James Dobson, *The New Strong-Willed Child* (Carol Stream: Tyndale House, 2004), 1–3.

7. Michael Pearl and Debi Pearl, *To Train Up a Child* (Pleasantville: No Greater Joy Ministries, 2006).

8. "The most enduring and influential source for the widespread practice of physical punishment, both in this country and abroad, has been the Bible." Philip Greven, *Spare the Rod: The Religious Roots of Punishment and the Psychological Impact of Physical Abuse* (New York: Vintage Books, 1992), 6.

9. Janet Heimlich, *Breaking Their Will: Shedding Light on Religious Child Maltreatment* (Amherst: Prometheus Books, 2011), 80–82.

10. Pearl and Pearl, *To Train Up a Child*.

11. Reb Bradley, *Child Training Tips: What I Wish I Knew When My Children Were Young* (Fair Oaks: Family Ministries Publishing, 1996).

12. Pearl and Pearl, *To Train Up a Child*.

13. J. Richard Fugate, *What the Bible Says about . . . Child Training* (Tempe: Aletheia, 1980); and Baucham, *Family Shepherds*.

14. Dobson, *New Strong-Willed Child*.

15. Pearl and Pearl, *To Train Up a Child*.

16. Tedd Tripp, *Shepherding a Child's Heart* (Wapwallopen: Shepherd Press, 2005).

17. "[A police officer] does what he can to resist the criminal and restrain him, knowing that his duty—while limited in its ultimate effectiveness—is necessary. It's the same for parents." Baucham, *Family Shepherds*, 126.

18. "I am just thankful that one-year-olds don't weigh two hundred pounds, or a lot more mothers would be victims of infant 'momicide.'" Pearl and Pearl, *To Train Up a Child*, 14.

19. R. L. Stollar, "The Child as Viper: How Voddie Baucham's Theology of Children Promotes Abuse," Homeschoolers Anonymous, January 16, 2015, https://tinyurl.com/4kfefc8w.

20. "Horsley describes the issue in terms of children's social status: 'In ancient Palestine, as in most any traditional agrarian society, children were the human beings with the lowest status. They were, in effect, not-yet-people.' The [language that] "the kingdom of God" belongs to children sharpens the agenda of the whole Gospel story that the kingdom of God is present for the people, the peasant villagers, as opposed to the people of standing, wealth, and power.' In the patriarchal honor/shame society being described, children were quite literally the possession of their fathers. Thus in this story the child's low social standing accentuates Jesus' message that [we should] lift up the lowliest." Joyce Ann Mercer, *Welcoming Children: A Practical Theology of Childhood* (St. Louis: Chalice Press, 2005), 51.

21. "A father is the head of his house, its lord, its master, its ruler. . . . It's a chain of authority, which is a chain of command." Philip Lancaster, *Family Man, Family Leader* (San Antonio: Vision Forum, 2011), 159.

22. Recovering Grace, "The Umbrella of Oppression," May 9, 2014, https://tinyurl.com/kynnyewr.

23. Institute in Basic Life Principles, "What Is an 'Umbrella of Protection'?," https://tinyurl.com/yckjtcch, accessed April 23, 2016.

24. Recovering Grace, "The Leaky Umbrella," October 6, 2011, https://tinyurl.com/2p99btys.

25. Wende Benner, "Gothard's ATI and the Duggar Family's Secret," Homeschoolers Anonymous, May 23, 2015, https://tinyurl.com/yusyj594.

26. Recovering Grace, "There Is No Victim: A Survey of IBLP Literature on Sexual Assault and Abuse," April 25, 2014, https://tinyurl.com/4y3druax.

27. "*We* are the ones in charge of the home. We owe no apologies for the exercise of our authority. We are not answerable or accountable to our children." Bradley, *Child Training Tips*, 44, emphasis original.

28. Stollar, "The Child as Viper."

29. Bradley, *Child Training Tips*, 37.

30. One example touted by the Pearls: "After a little instruction about consistent training and the proper use of the rod, [the parents] went home and gave it a try. Two weeks later they were in a church meeting where I was speaking. Their children all sat on the bench with them, never making a stir. Afterward, the father, eyes filled with wonder, exclaimed, 'There was a miracle here tonight, and no one seemed to notice.' As I was looking around for discarded crutches, he continued, 'A whole service and not a peep out of them! I can't believe it!' A little training and a little discipline with the rod, and the children gave their parents 'rest' and 'delight.'" *To Train Up a Child*, 47.

31. Pearl and Pearl, *To Train Up a Child*, 61.

32. "You exercise authority as God's agent. . . . You must direct your children on God's behalf for their good." Tripp, *Shepherding a Child's Heart*, xix.

33. "The Lord has placed parents over the child. Their authority derives from Him. Therefore when children rightly obey they do it as unto the Lord (cf. Colossians 3:23–24). In a sense, then, the parents stand in the place of the Lord, and children are to obey them." John MacArthur, *What the Bible Says about Parenting* (Nashville: W Publishing Group, 2000), 121.

34. "Parents are the symbol and representative of God's authority to their children." Fugate, *Child Training*, 41.

35. Mercy Amba Oduyoye, "Be a Woman, and Africa Will Be Strong," in *Inheriting Our Mothers' Gardens: Feminist Theology in Third World Perspective*, ed. Letty M. Russell et al. (Louisville: Westminster Press, 1988), 44.

36. For more information on dominionism and its more extreme form of Christian reconstructionism, see Julie Ingersoll's book *Building God's Kingdom: Inside the World of Christian Reconstructionism* (Oxford: Oxford University Press, 2015).

37. George Grant, *The Changing of the Guard: Biblical Blueprints for Political Action* (Fort Worth: Dominion Press, 1987), 50–51.

38. George Grant, *Bringing in the Sheaves* (Powder Springs: American Vision Press, 1985), 98.

39. Michael Farris, *The Joshua Generation: Restoring the Heritage of Christian Leadership* (Nashville: B&H Publishing Group, 2005), 9–11.

40. See, for example, the story of the Sharp Family Singers in Julie Turkewitz, "Family Gospel Band Provided Soundtrack for Oregon Refuge Standoff," *New York Times*, January 28, 2016, https://tinyurl.com/3zm3dw9v.

41. Mary Pride, *The Way Home: Beyond Feminism, Back to Reality* (Fenton: Home Life Books, 2010), 77–78.

42. Charles D. Provan, *The Bible and Birth Control* (Monongahela: Zimmer Printing, 1989).

43. Pride, *Way Home*, 57.

44. "Quiverfull-minded Christians point to biblical texts that show how God opens the womb (i.e., God allows impregnation, full-term gestation, and successful birth to occur) as a blessing and closes the womb (i.e., God causes infertility) as a curse. For example, in Deuteronomy 28:4 and 11 God explains that if Israel is obedient to Him, they will be blessed with children, but in verse 18, He warns that disobedience will result in infertility." Juliana Denson, "Quiverfull: Conservative Christian Women and Empowerment in the Home," *LUX: A Journal of Transdisciplinary Writing and Research from Claremont Graduate University* 2, no. 1 (2013): 6.

45. Charles J. Reid Jr., "The Rights of Children in Medieval Canon Law," in *The Vocation of the Child*, ed. Patrick McKinley Brennan (Grand Rapids: Eerdmans, 2008), 245.

46. For a summary and history of the contemporary parental rights movement, see Sarah Pulliam Bailey, "How Christian Home-Schoolers Laid the Groundwork for Parental Rights," *Washington Post*, June 11, 2022, https://tinyurl.com/y6mrn5n9.

47. Rick Santorum, "Children Belong to Parents, Not Government," *Townhall*, April 16, 2013, https://tinyurl.com/yckddhad.

48. Fugate, *Child Training*, 31. "Parental authority delegates to parents the right to rule the children under their control. No other institution or person has rulership rights over children. Neither society, school personnel, nosey individuals, nor even other institutions have any authority over children. . . .

There is no such thing as 'child rights' sanctioned by the Word of God. The child has only the God-given right to be raised by his parents without the intervention of any other institution."

49. Helen Cordes, "Battling for the Heart and Soul of Home-Schoolers," *Salon*, October 2, 2000, https://tinyurl.com/bdey76ts. "HSLDA's sustained lobbying against the United Nations Convention on the Rights of the Child—the top issue cited in an 'issues alert' sent by the HSLDA to all members of Congress last fall—is necessary because 'if children have rights, they could refuse to be home-schooled, plus it takes away parents' rights to physically discipline their children,' says Klicka. He had a similar explanation for the group's opposition to increased federal child abuse laws."

50. "Three children's rights—the right to self-determine education, the right not to be physically hit by parents, and the right to self-determine one's medical treatment—are consistently targeted by HSLDA. In fact, nearly every statement HSLDA has made in the past (and continues to make to-day) against the UN Convention of the Rights of the Child—or any other declaration of children's rights—calls out these three rights negatively." R. L. Stollar, "Children as Divine Rental Property: An Exposition on HSLDA's Philosophy of Parental Rights," Homeschoolers Anonymous, January 5, 2015, https://tinyurl.com/mr23p7sh.

51. "The establishment of a stable personal identity is a significant mile-stone indeed—one that helps pave the way for positive psychological adjust-ment and the growth of deep and trusting emotional commitments that could conceivably last a lifetime. What may be most painful or 'crisis-like' about identity seeking is a long-term failure to establish one. . . . Indeed, many adolescents who are stuck in the diffusion status are highly apathetic and do express a sense of hopelessness about the future, sometimes even becoming suicidal." David R. Shaffer, *Social and Personality Development* (Boston: Cengage Learning, 2009), 191–92.

52. Shaffer, *Social and Personality Development*, 192. "Adolescents in the identity foreclosure status are often extremely close to and may sometimes fear rejection from relatively controlling parents (Berzonsky & Adams, 1999). Foreclosed adolescents may never question parental authority or feel any need to construct a separate identity. . . . By contrast, adolescents who move easily into the moratorium and identity achievement statuses appear to have a solid base of affection at home combined with considerable freedom to be indi-

viduals in their own right (Grotevant & Cooper, 1998). In family discussions, for example, these adolescents experience a sense of closeness and mutual respect while feeling free to disagree with their parents and to be individuals in their own right."

53. In his foundational text on capitalism, Scottish economist Adam Smith famously argued, "It is not from the benevolence of the butcher, the brewer, or the baker, that we expect our dinner, but from their regard to their own interest. We address ourselves, not to their humanity but to their self-love, and never talk to them of our own necessities but of their advantages." *An Inquiry into the Nature and Causes of the Wealth of Nations* (Carmel: Liberty Fund, 1981), I.ii.2.

54. Mercer, *Welcoming Children*, 73. Hereafter, page citations will be in the text.

55. "'Many popular songs today are written in intentional collaborations as part of a highly competitive industry,' said Anneli Loepp Thiessen, the study's author and a PhD candidate at the University of Ottawa. 'As the contemporary worship music industry has developed, it has become increasingly commercialized, with men subsequently coming to dominate the Top 25 list.'" Kelsey Kramer McGinnis, "Study: Female Songwriters Are Dropping Off the Worship Charts," *Christianity Today*, June 10, 2022, https://tinyurl.com/46b2yxbv.

56. "Is the poor, destitute child factored into Latin American liberation theology? Is feminist or womanist theology informed by the context of the lowly, marginalised girl child? Is Black theology based on the experiences of the black, hungry, dis-eased, illiterate township child? Are these mere rhetorical questions? Academic questions for that matter? No, these are life and death questions and the categorical answer to them is, NO!" Nico Botha, "Children as Theological Hermeneutic: Is There a New Epistemological Break Emerging?," Association for Education and Research in Europe (GBFE) in South Africa, November 2012, https://tinyurl.com/3986uma6.

57. Seeing children as innocents did not originate with contemporary progressive Christians. This belief can be traced back at least to early Christian theologian Pelagius (condemned as a heretic by Augustine's Council of Carthage in 418) and his followers. See Martha Ellen Stortz, "'Where or When Was Your Servant Innocent?' Augustine on Childhood," *The Child in Christian Thought* (Grand Rapids: Eerdmans, 2001), 91: "The Pelagian Celestius announced that infants were born in exactly the same state as Adam before the Fall."

58. Pais, *Suffer the Children*, 37.

59. "The wholeness of the young child, which if left intact might indeed allow growth and development in God's image, is instead broken. . . . Human perfection can grow only out of the already existing perfection of the image of God in the whole individual, born literally as a new creation." Pais, *Suffer the Children*, 32–33.

60. Tori Rodriguez, "Descendants of Holocaust Survivors Have Altered Stress Hormones," *Scientific American*, March 1, 2015, https://tinyurl.com/2jchn6ba.

61. "Maternal stress hormones also cross the placenta, causing a dramatic rise in fetal stress hormones (evident in the amniotic fluid) and in fetal heart rate, blood pressure, blood glucose, and activity level (Kinsella & Monk, 2009; Weinstock, 2008). . . . Excessive fetal stress may permanently alter neurological functioning as well, thereby heightening stress reactivity in later life. In several studies, infants and children of mothers who experienced severe prenatal anxiety displayed cortisol levels that were either abnormally high or abnormally low, both of which signal reduced physiological capacity to manage stress." Laura E. Berk, *Child Development* (London: Pearson Education, 2013), 105.

62. Billy Collins, *Sailing Alone around the Room* (New York: Random House, 2001), 38.

63. "Innocence in this sense tends to deny children any status other than their need to be protected as utterly vulnerable and malleable creatures. So it renders them, in their own reality, absent." William Werpehowski, "In Search of Real Children: Innocence, Absence, and Becoming a Self in Christ," in *The Vocation of the Child*, ed. Patrick McKinley Brennan (Grand Rapids: Eerdmans, 2008), 63.

64. "Even a vision of children as naturally and ideally 'open' to the divine can rob them of their agency; their blessed privilege of being an instance of 'childhood' is purchased at the cost of their real being in the world." Werpehowski, "In Search of Real Children," 63–64.

65. Bonnie J. Miller-McLemore, *Let the Children Come* (San Francisco: Jossey-Bass, 2003), 150.

66. Whereas representatives are means to an end (the end being whoever or whatever is being represented), substitutes are ends in themselves. Representatives serve as paths to a final destination, but substitutes are the final destination.

67. Kristin Johnston Largen, *Baby Krishna, Infant Christ: A Comparative Theology of Salvation* (Maryknoll: Orbis Books, 2011), 207.

68. In liberation theology, salvation is a communal and relational reality to achieve in the present, not a supernatural contract between God and an individual to ensure a place in a future heaven. "Salvation is not something otherworldly, in regard to which the present life is merely a test. Salvation— the communion of human beings with God and among themselves—is something which embraces all human reality, transforms it, and leads it to its fullness in Christ. . . . The struggle for a just society is in its own right very much a part of salvation history." Gutiérrez, *Theology of Liberation*, 85, 97.

69. David Ng and Virginia Thomas, *Children in the Worshiping Community* (Louisville: John Knox Press, 1981), 50.

70. Alice Miller makes this argument: "Jesus grew into a strong, aware, empathic, and wise person able to experience and sustain strong emotions without being engulfed by them. He could see through insincerity and mendacity and he had the courage to expose them for what they were. Yet to my knowledge no representative of the church has ever admitted the patent connection between the character of Jesus and the way he was brought up. Would it not make eminent sense to encourage believers to follow the example of Mary and Joseph and regard their children as the children of God (which in a sense they are) rather than treating them as their own personal property?" *The Truth Will Set You Free* (New York: Basic Books, 2001), 190–91.

71. Johnston Largen, *Baby Krishna, Infant Christ*, 129.

72. Kirsten Weir, "The Lasting Impact of Neglect," American Psychological Association, June 2014, https://tinyurl.com/2p83e5ah.

73. "Temper tantrums are a way a young child lets out strong emotions before he or she is able to express them in socially acceptable ways. Although a child may seem totally out of control, these fits of rage, stomping, screaming, and throwing himself or herself to the floor are a normal part of childhood development." John Hopkins Medicine, "Temper Tantrums," https://tinyurl.com/3auazmyz, accessed July 28, 2016.

74. Pais, *Suffer the Children*, 123–24.

75. "Every child is an individual with unique needs, which adults can know only in relationship with that child. Therefore, the ultimate child care rule is to relate to each child as an individual, letting relationship with the child keep you informed about her or his needs." Pais, *Suffer the Children*, 124–25.

Chapter Nine

1. Gustavo Gutiérrez, *A Theology of Liberation* (Maryknoll: Orbis Books, 2014), 174.

2. Ada María Isasi-Díaz, *Mujerista Theology: A Theology for the Twenty-First Century* (Maryknoll: Orbis Books, 1996), 1.

3. Isasi-Díaz, *Mujerista Theology*, 119–20.

4. "We have all been socialized to embrace patriarchal thinking, to embrace an ethics of domination which says the powerful have the right to rule over the powerless and can use any means to subordinate them. In the hierarchies of white supremacist capitalist patriarchy, male domination of females is condoned, but so is adult domination of children." bell hooks, *Feminism Is for Everybody* (Cambridge: South End Press, 2000), 74.

5. Bonnie J. Miller-McLemore, *Let the Children Come* (San Francisco: Jossey-Bass, 2003), 143.

6. Janet Pais has a provocative chapter on this subject titled "Letting the Child-Self Heal the Inner Adult-Child Split." See her book *Suffer the Children* (Mahwah: Paulist Press, 1991), 88–104.

Chapter Ten

1. Kathleen Gallagher Elkins and Julie Faith Parker, "Children in Biblical Narrative and Childist Interpretation," in *The Oxford Handbook of Biblical Narrative*, ed. Danna Nolan Fewell (Oxford: Oxford University Press, 2016).

2. Rosemary Radford Ruether, "Religion and Society: Sacred Canopy vs. Prophetic Critique," in *The Future of Liberation Theology: Essays in Honor of Gustavo Gutiérrez*, ed. Marc H. Ellis and Otto Maduro (Maryknoll: Orbis Books, 1989), 172–73.

3. For a full articulation of the sacred canopy concept, see Peter L. Berger, *The Sacred Canopy: Elements of a Sociological Theory of Religion* (New York: Anchor Books, 1967), 3–28.

4. Radford Ruether, "Religion and Society," 172–73.

5. To aid our interpretation, I would like to draw attention to the fact that Jesus was himself Jewish and this was a religious disagreement within Judaism. This is not a story of a Christian Jesus condemning Jewish merchants for greed—a trope that is anti-Semitic. See Marvin Perry and Frederick M. Sch-

weitzer, *Antisemitism* (New York: Palgrave Macmillan, 2002), 32, 120: "Prominent and primary to economic antisemitism, from patristics to Hitler and beyond, is the New Testament story of Jesus' expulsion of the moneylenders; it is invoked to show that Judaism is a materialist, amoral, profane religion, that the Jewish mentality is one of haggling and huckstering, and much else of the same kind. . . . The belief that the Temple worship was desecrated by sordid trade and profiteering and that purity was restored by the expulsion of the money changers became a leitmotif of our culture." A better interpretation of this passage, according to Malka Simkovich, is that "Jesus is not fighting Judaism. He's working within it and foregrounding what he views as being Jewish values. That's not to imply that all Pharisees or all Temple administrators are corrupt." Menachem Wecker, "AOC's Favorite Biblical Story Is Mired in a Dark, Anti-Jewish Past," *National Catholic Reporter*, November 21, 2020, https://tinyurl.com/mr3xheae.

6. W. J. C. Weren, *Studies in Matthew's Gospel: Literary Design, Intertextuality, and Social Setting* (Leiden: Brill, 2014), 56.

7. "Jesus recognizes, with gladness and thankfulness, that although the 'wise and prudent' have rejected him, he has found a welcome among the simple-hearted. . . . Jesus has spoken of the 'wise and prudent'—the arrogant doctors of the Law; and the 'babes' whom he contrasts with them can be no other than the unlearned multitude." Ernest F. Scott, "An Exegetical Study of Matt. 11:25–30," *The Biblical World*, University of Chicago Press, 35, no. 3 (March 1910): 187.

8. "In 11:25, 'little children,' Jesus is speaking figuratively, as in 18:3, where he says to adults, 'Unless you change and become like little children, you will never enter the kingdom of heaven.' . . . Why are they blessed? Jesus is not implying that little children are innocent. . . . It is not innocence but teachability that Jesus has in view. This is not the same as intellectual capacity. In the school of God, attitude is the all-important factor. . . . Only when the 'wise and learned' become like children—i.e. stop depending on their unaided reason—do they begin to be truly wise (1 Cor 3:18). Then, as teachable children, they are ready to receive the true riches—knowledge of God." Knox Chamblin, "The Revelation of God: Matthew 11:25–30," The Gospel Coalition, https://tinyurl.com/y6y66une.

9. "Divine wisdom does not rest with the wise or intelligent—with the Pharisees and scribes as one would expect—but it is found among the lowly,

the infants of society who have little knowledge, power, or wealth yet have embraced Jesus' proclamation of the kingdom." Israel Diaz, "Jesus, the True Interpreter of Torah: A Look at Matthew 11:25–30," March 2, 2011, https://tinyurl.com/3kerp7nt.

10. "The blessings of salvation aren't a reward to those who are smart and wise in their own eyes. It is not there for those who are talented and skillful but they are given to those who are humble, children as He says. They are not given except by unmerited favor to those who come to Him as little children. Those who come to Him may be very smart and scholarly or simple and uneducated. That's not the point. The point is that they come to humble reliance to the Lord Jesus Christ and He by His grace and mercy pours out salvation into their lives." Mark Cushman, "The Main Thing," Briarwood Presbyterian Church, PCA, August 11, 2013, accessed June 27, 2015, https://tinyurl.com/mr3mz8aw.

11. "Those who would follow Jesus are asked to be humble like the child —vulnerable, threatened, and dependent upon others and God. Indeed, for the Gospel of Matthew, to become like the child is to become like Jesus." Sharon Betsworth, "The Child and Jesus in the Gospel of Matthew," *Journal of Childhood and Religion* 1, no. 4 (June 2010): 14.

12. "In Matthew, the focus of each [narrative containing children] is on faith and discipleship rather than on the children themselves." Sharon Betsworth, *Children in Early Christian Narratives* (London: Bloomsbury Publishing, 2015), 75.

13. Joyce Ann Mercer, *Welcoming Children: A Practical Theology of Childhood* (St. Louis: Chalice Press, 2005), 18.

14. "Indigenous cultures of the young became tabula rasa for the universalization of the 'western child'. This hegemonic force of western notions of childhood and youth . . . had in particular two lasting consequences. One was that all issues relating to childhood—whether subsumed under discourses of legality or normality—would from the nineteenth century onwards be framed by the notion of a universal (western) child. Another was that the everyday lives of non-western children and young people would be judged against a yardstick that was frequently senseless in relation to their own worlds." Sheila Brown, *Understanding Youth and Crime: Listening to Youth?* (New York: McGraw-Hill Education, 2005), 21.

15. "[Jesus's] provocative teaching about children as recipients of divine

insight and representatives of Jesus seems to have had the least *Wirkungs-geschichte* [history of interpretations]." Judith M. Gundry-Volf, "The Least and the Greatest: Children in the New Testament," in *The Child in Christian Thought*, ed. Marcia J. Bunge (Grand Rapids: Eerdmans, 2001), 59.

16. For example, "At Delphi there were three kinds of cult personnel: the Pythia, a priestess whose official title was *promantis* or *prophetis*; two prophetic priests, appointed for life, who were probably identical with the two *prophetai* mentioned by Plutarch; and a board of five *Hosioi* ('holy ones'). The Pythia was an oracular prophetess who sat upon a tripod (representing the throne of Apollo) where she delivered oracular responses inspired by Apollo. . . . In Plutarch's time the young chosen to be the Pythia was taken from the lower class of farmers." David E. Aune, *Prophecy in Early Christianity and the Ancient Mediterranean World* (Grand Rapids: Eerdmans, 1983), 28.

17. Gundry-Volf, "Least and the Greatest," 47.

18. "Isis wandered everywhere at her wits' end; no one whom she approached did she fail to address, and even when she met some little children she asked them about the chest. As it happened, they had seen it, and they told her the mouth of the river through which the friends of Typhon had launched the coffin into the sea. Wherefore the Egyptians think that little children possess the power of prophecy, and they try to divine the future from the portents which they find in children's words, especially when children are playing about in holy places and crying out whatever chances to come into their minds." Plutarch, "Isis and Osiris," *Moralia*, Loeb Classical Library (Cambridge: Harvard University Press, 1936), 39, 356E.

19. Dio Chrysostom, "The Thirty-Second Discourse: To the People of Alexandria," *Discourses*, Loeb Classical Library (Cambridge: Harvard University Press, 1940), 185.

20. "I was saying these things and weeping in the most bitter contrition of my heart, when suddenly I heard the voice of a boy or a girl I know not which—coming from the neighboring house, chanting over and over again, 'Pick it up, read it; pick it up, read it.' Immediately I ceased weeping and began most earnestly to think whether it was usual for children in some kind of game to sing such a song, but I could not remember ever having heard the like. So, damming the torrent of my tears, I got to my feet, for I could not but think that this was a divine command to open the Bible and read the first passage I should light upon. For I had heard how Anthony, accidentally coming into church while the gospel was being read, received the admonition

as if what was read had been addressed to him: 'Go and sell what you have and give it to the poor, and you shall have treasure in heaven; and come and follow me.' By such an oracle he was forthwith converted to thee." Augustine, *Confessions*, trans. and ed. Albert C. Outler (Louisville: Westminster John Knox, 1955), 8.12.29.

21. "It seems as if an awkward, possibly fearful silence has replaced the earlier Hosannas. But no, children continue to acknowledge the Chosen One: 'Hosanna to the Son of David!' Jesus is confronted by indignant leaders and points them to Psalm 8: 'From the lips of children and infants you have ordained praise.' This is the climax of this section of the narrative of the life of Jesus, in which children and the kingdom have been inextricably linked." Keith J. White, "'He Placed a Little Child in the Midst': Jesus, the Kingdom, and Children," in *The Child in the Bible*, ed. Marcia J. Bunge (Grand Rapids: Eerdmans, 2008), 366.

22. Nick Harding and Sandra Millar, *Ready to Share One Bread: Preparing Children for Holy Communion* (London: Society for Promoting Christian Knowledge, 2015).

23. "Children have a capacity for knowledge of God and Matthew knows this. He depicts them as intuiting who Jesus is, and he depicts their intuition as prophesied by scripture and warranted by Godself." Adrian Thatcher, "The Teaching of Jesus About Families and Children," *Theology and Families* (Hoboken: John Wiley & Sons, 2008), 62–63.

24. "After centuries of marginalization, we should be careful not to render children marginal to the point of invisibility, particularly where and when Jesus chose to place them in the midst, as signs of kingdom of heaven and of welcoming him. We must beware lest for whatever seemingly good reason we find ways of losing the significance of what God in Christ is seeking to communicate to us." White, "'He Placed a Little Child in the Midst,'" 368.

25. Craig S. Keener, *The Gospel of Matthew: A Socio-Rhetorical Commentary* (Grand Rapids: Eerdmans, 2009), 503.

26. Christopher Rim, "How Student Activism Shaped the Black Lives Matter Movement," *Forbes*, June 4, 2020, https://tinyurl.com/23rydufs.

27. Bruno Moguel Gallegos, "My Death Needs to Mean Something," *Harvard Crimson*, January 6, 2015, https://tinyurl.com/8fw5vfzp.

28. Alex Morris, "The Forsaken: A Rising Number of Homeless Gay Teens Are Being Cast Out by Religious Families," *Rolling Stone*, September 3, 2015, https://tinyurl.com/mvcc8ptm.

29. Elizabeth Picciuto, "They Don't Want an Autism Cure," The Daily Beast, April 14, 2017, https://tinyurl.com/4bherttx.

30. Linda Kay Klein, *Pure: Inside the Evangelical Movement That Shamed a Generation of Young Women and How I Broke Free* (New York: Touchstone, 2018).

31. Eve Ettinger and Nylah Burton, "Homeschooling Regulations Must Prioritize the Needs of Students," *Teen Vogue*, September 1, 2021, https://tinyurl.com/25mxetc2.

32. Andrew Marantz, "The Youth Movement Trying to Revolutionize Climate Politics," *The New Yorker*, February 28, 2022, https://tinyurl.com/3djx88t2.

33. ParentalRights.org, "Parental Rights Amendment (HJRes. 38) Introduced in Congress," March 1, 2023, https://tinyurl.com/425a7n5c.

34. R. L. Stollar, "Children as Divine Rental Property: An Exposition on HSLDA's Philosophy of Parental Rights," Homeschoolers Anonymous, January 5, 2015, https://tinyurl.com/mr23p7sh.

35. Stollar, "Children as Divine Rental Property."

36. Institute in Basic Life Principles, "What Is an 'Umbrella of Protection'?," https://tinyurl.com/yckjtcch, accessed April 23, 2016.

37. "Although almost all theologians today and in the past would emphasize that children should honor and obey their parents, they often neglect a third and corresponding responsibility of children that is also part of the tradition: children have a responsibility and duty not to obey their parents if their parents or other adult authorities would cause them to sin or to carry out acts of injustice." Marcia J. Bunge, "The Vocation of the Child: Theological Perspectives on the Particular and Paradoxical Roles and Responsibilities of Children," in *The Vocation of Children*, ed. Patrick McKinley Brennan (Grand Rapids: Eerdmans, 2008), 42.

38. For an extended analysis of Ezekiel 20:18–19, see R. L. Stollar, "Children, Disobey Your Parents in the Lord, for This Is Right," *Patheos*, May 9, 2016, https://tinyurl.com/z7fdnmmj.

39. "In the late twelfth century and the first half of the thirteenth century, new ecclesiastical policies dictated that oblates who wished to leave the monastic life be released at puberty, before taking solemn vows. Thomas agrees, adding that children who have reached puberty may also, against their parents' wishes, break a betrothal or enter marriage or holy orders." Cristina L. H. Traina, "A Person in the Making: Thomas Aquinas on Children and

Childhood," in *The Child in Christian Thought*, ed. Marcia J. Bunge (Grand Rapids: Eerdmans, 2001), 107–8.

40. Thomas Aquinas, as quoted by Traina, "Person in the Making," 108.

41. Traina, "Person in the Making," 109.

42. Jane E. Strohl, "The Child in Luther's Theology: 'For What Purpose Do We Older Folks Exist, Other Than to Care for . . . the Young?,'" in *The Child in Christian Thought*, ed. Marcia J. Bunge (Grand Rapids: Eerdmans, 2001), 136.

43. Strohl, "Child in Luther's Theology," 138.

44. Martin Luther, as quoted by Strohl, "Child in Luther's Theology," 155.

45. Karl Barth, as quoted by William Werpehowski, "Reading Karl Barth on Children," in *The Child in Christian Thought*, ed. Marcia J. Bunge (Grand Rapids: Eerdmans, 2001), 397.

46. See, for example, Summit Ministries (https://tinyurl.com/4esdjb75), Worldview Academy (https://tinyurl.com/yeyjbhcc), and Worldview Weekend (https://tinyurl.com/54bsdfaz).

47. Kwok Pui-lan, "Mothers and Daughters, Writers and Fighters," in *Inheriting Our Mothers' Gardens: Feminist Theology in Third World Perspective*, ed. Letty M. Russell et al. (Louisville: Westminster Press, 1988), 23–24.

48. Becky Little, "How Boarding Schools Tried to 'Kill the Indian' Through Assimilation," History.com, August 16, 2017, https://tinyurl.com/bdz447vj.

49. Stephen Magagnini, "Long-Suffering Urban Indians Find Roots in Ancient Rituals," *Sacramento Bee*, June 30, 1997, https://tinyurl.com/4a4vxzbv.

50. Charla Bear, "American Indian Boarding Schools Haunt Many," NPR, May 12, 2008, https://tinyurl.com/4vawak9m.

51. Sari Horwitz, "The Hard Lives—and High Suicide Rate—of Native American Children on Reservations," *Washington Post*, March 9, 2014, https://tinyurl.com/bdzd7xjj.

52. If you do not already have a regular family meeting time, consider this encouragement to do so! Plan a time once a week for all the adults and children in your family to meet together. Keep the day and time consistent week to week so everyone knows exactly when it will be. Having a consistent meeting time will also help everyone to prioritize attending the meeting. What you do during the meeting is flexible. At the very least, give everyone a chance to share about something important going on in their lives. While each person shares, ensure that everyone else gives that person their full attention. Other ideas for family meetings include: reviewing the schedule for the next week, letting

people air out grievances with each other and discussing them in a constructive manner, reading the Bible and praying together, playing a video game or board game as a group, or doing meditation or grounding exercises together.

Chapter Eleven

1. David Heller, *The Children's God* (Chicago: University of Chicago Press, 1986), 4.

2. Robert Coles, *The Spiritual Life of Children* (Boston: Houghton Mifflin Company, 1990), xvi.

3. "Children do not use adult language to speak of their encounters with the existential boundaries to life. . . . This makes it all the more important for us to notice such issues in the lives of children and to give them religious language to name, value, and express their ultimate concerns so they can cope with them now and prepare for a more healthy and creative life later." Jerome W. Berryman, *Godly Play* (Minneapolis: Augsburg Fortress, 1995), x.

4. R. Havighurst and B. Keating, "The Religion of Youth," in *Research on Religious Development*, ed. M. Strommen (New York: Hawthorn Books, 1971), 697.

5. "Accidents, illnesses, bad luck—such moments of danger and pain prompt reflection in children as well as adults." Coles, *Spiritual Life of Children*, 109.

6. "For children, even those quite healthy and never before seriously sick, death has a powerful and continuing meaning." Coles, *Spiritual Life of Children*, 109.

7. Berryman, *Godly Play*, x.

8. Coles, *Spiritual Life of Children*, 101.

9. Coles, *The Spiritual Life of Children*, 102–3.

10. Alvin Plantinga, *God, Freedom, and Evil* (Grand Rapids: Eerdmans, 1974), 10.

11. Coles, *Spiritual Life of Children*, 104.

12. Coles, *Spiritual Life of Children*, 107, 108.

13. "There is no reason to assume that [children] have less of an idea of truth than conceptions of the deity which are more fully elaborated." Heller, *Children's God*, 41.

14. Brett Webb-Mitchell, *God Plays Piano, Too: The Spiritual Lives of Disabled Children* (New York: Crossroad Publishing Company, 1993), 89.

15. Webb-Mitchell, *God Plays Piano, Too*, 53.

16. Webb-Mitchell, *God Plays Piano, Too*, 53.

17. Webb-Mitchell, *God Plays Piano, Too*, 88.

18. Webb-Mitchell, *God Plays Piano, Too*, 90.

19. Laura E. Berk, *Child Development* (London: Pearson Education, 2013), 10.

20. Coles, *Spiritual Life of Children*, xv.

21. Coles, *Spiritual Life of Children*, 19–20.

22. Wendy L. Haight, *African-American Children at Church: A Sociocultural Perspective* (Cambridge: Cambridge University Press, 2002), 10–11, 15, 3.

23. Webb-Mitchell, *God Plays Piano, Too*, 99.

24. Webb-Mitchell, *God Plays Piano, Too*, 99.

25. Webb-Mitchell, *God Plays Piano, Too*, 95–96.

26. Webb-Mitchell, *God Plays Piano, Too*, 107.

27. Coles, *Spiritual Life of Children*, 25.

28. Berryman, *Godly Play*, 142–43.

29. Coles, *Spiritual Life of Children*, 99.

30. Berryman, *Godly Play*, 144.

31. Robb McCoy, "Six Reasons I Share Communion with Kids," The Fat Pastor, March 7, 2014, https://tinyurl.com/3wfbbe3u.

32. Kristin Johnston Largen, *Baby Krishna, Infant Christ: A Comparative Theology of Salvation* (Maryknoll: Orbis Books, 2011), 119–20.

33. "What does emancipation of children's bodies look like? Is it enough to simply stop assaulting their bodies? Certainly, that is a crucial change and one in which we must continue the momentum in turning the societal tide, but the paradigm change to release our power over children will manifest in the transformation of myriad parenting practices. The opposite of domination is building a strong and steady current that supports a child's agency over her own body. We want our children to confidently proclaim, 'My body is my body. It belongs to me.'" Cindy Wang Brandt, *Parenting Forward* (Grand Rapids: Eerdmans, 2019), 37.

34. For additional ideas about what emotional and mental child protection could look like, see Cindy Wang Brandt, "7 Spiritual Child Protection Policies," *Patheos*, August 25, 2017, https://tinyurl.com/yyb4fwym.

35. Brandt, "7 Spiritual Child Protection Policies."

36. *Children Are Like That* (Omaha: John Day Company, 1930), 37.

37. Haight, *African-American Children at Church*, 33–34.

38. "Why are youth disengaged? There is not one easy answer. It is clear

however, that part of the solution in combating ageism lies in creating mean-ingful opportunities for youth engagement where young voices are heard, and where ideas lead to action." Ilona Dougherty, ed., *The Youth-Friendly Guide to Intergenerational Decision Making Partnerships*, National Democratic Institute, 2004, https://tinyurl.com/ztz3nx5.

39. "Tokenism is participation 'for show' where young people have little or no influence. Even among well-intentioned agencies, tokenism is common when engaging underrepresented groups—including youth. It can be difficult to avoid when adult-led organizations elicit input from youth without em-powering them as decision-makers. When youth are given opportunities to engage only in marginal roles, the chance of tokenism multiplies." C4 Inno-vations, "Avoiding Tokenism When Engaging Young People," https://tinyurl.com/zc2x447r, accessed December 30, 2022.

40. For more information about this school and their unique hiring pro-cess, see *Voice of San Diego*, "High Tech's Hiring 'Bonanza,'" February 20, 2009, https://tinyurl.com/29hpjjmw.

41. "Intergenerational partnerships are not only about creating the leaders of tomorrow, they are about supporting the young engaged citizens of today. They are about recognizing that marginalization of young people is real, that ageism is real, and that we collectively are able to do something about it." Dougherty, *Intergenerational Decision Making Partnerships*.

42. "Research provides some evidence . . . that partnering with youth and respecting their ability to contribute may provide important protective factors for young people. The Innovation Center for Community and Youth Development (a division of National 4-H Council) conducted one of the few existing studies on the effect of youth-adult partnerships. The study showed that 'involving young people in decision making provides them with the essential opportunities and supports (i.e. challenge, relevancy, voice, cause based action, skill building, adult structure, and affirmation) that are consistently shown to help young people achieve mastery, compassion, and health.'" Jane Norman, "Building Effective Youth-Adult Partnerships," Advocates for Youth, *Transitions* 14, no. 1 (October 2001), https://tinyurl.com/5cnwsrsy.

43. "Research has identified many factors that help young people resist stress and negative situations. These factors . . . are produced and facilitated by effective youth-adult partnerships." Norman, "Building Effective Youth-Adult Partnerships."

44. "Research identifies an internal locus of control, or the feeling of being able to have an impact on one's environment and on others, as a key protective factor possessed by resilient youth. In this regard, opportunities for meaningful involvement and participation—such as are found in youth-adult partnerships—may provide youth with opportunities to develop and/or strengthen his/her internal locus of control." Norman, "Building Effective Youth-Adult Partnerships."

45. "Research shows that contributing to one's community has many positive outcomes. One study found that college students who provided community service for credit significantly increased their belief that people can make a difference and that people should be involved in community service and advocacy. They showed significantly increased commitment to performing volunteer service. Finally, they became less likely to blame social services clients for their misfortunes and more likely to stress a need for equal opportunities." Norman, "Building Effective Youth-Adult Partnerships."

46. Berk, *Child Development*, 11.

47. Here are some resources for best practices: Joy Thornburg Melton, *Safe Sanctuaries: Reducing the Risk of Child Abuse in the Church* (Nashville: Discipleship Resources, 1998); Jeanette Harder, *Let the Children Come: Preparing Faith Communities to End Child Abuse and Neglect* (Scottdale: Herald Press, 2010); Boz Tchividjian, *Protecting Children from Abuse in the Church* (Greensboro: New Growth Press, 2013); and Boz Tchividjian and Shira M. Berkovits, *The Child Safeguarding Policy Guide for Churches and Ministries* (Greensboro: New Growth Press, 2017).

Chapter Twelve

1. Patrick McKinley Brennan, "Children Play with God: A Contemporary Thomistic Understanding of the Child," in *The Vocation of the Child*, ed. Patrick McKinley Brennan (Grand Rapids: Eerdmans, 2008), 190.

2. "Christians have no problem seeing themselves honoring God through their work. . . . Play, on the other hand, gets no respect in the Christian tradition. The assumption is that for adults at least—and even children, to some degree—play is selfish, serving no good purpose in the world, something that should be undertaken only in moderation. Too much play distracts from one's proper purpose in the world and can hinder one in serving the neighbor. Play

is at cross purposes with work, and the former is often seen as a threat to the latter. No one has ever been canonized by excelling at play!" Kristin Johnston Largen, *Baby Krishna, Infant Christ: A Comparative Theology of Salvation* (Maryknoll: Orbis Books, 2011), 201.

3. Robert K. Johnston, *The Christian at Play* (Grand Rapids: Eerdmans, 1983), 67.

4. David Naugle, "A Serious Theology of Play," *Q Ideas*, https://tinyurl.com/2kh77969, accessed November 2, 2015.

5. Naugle, "Serious Theology of Play."

6. Nimi Wariboko, "Grace Is Play: Our Magazine Interview with Nimi Wariboko," *Mockingbird*, May 6, 2015, https://tinyurl.com/d8t28kx3.

7. Nimi Wariboko, *The Pentecostal Principle: Ethical Methodology in New Spirit* (Grand Rapids: Eerdmans, 2011), 183–84.

8. Dietrich Bonhoeffer, *Letters and Papers from Prison*, ed. Eberhard Bethge (New York: Macmillan, 1971), 198, emphasis original.

9. "When a child plays they are living in 'kairos,' or God's time. It is only in kairos that we can become what we were meant to be as human beings, participating with God in the wonder of His creation." Vivian L. Houk, *Parenting by Developmental Design* (Eugene: Resource Publications, 2010), 109.

10. David Heller, *The Children's God* (Chicago: University of Chicago Press, 1986), 43.

11. Heller, *Children's God*, 15.

12. John N. Briere and Catherine Scott, *Principles of Trauma Therapy: A Guide to Symptoms, Evaluation, and Treatment* (Thousand Oaks: SAGE Publications, 2015), 38.

13. "Play helps buffer the life stress on children. It helps them deal with all those things that go wrong in their young lives." Houk, *Parenting by Developmental Design*, 112.

14. Jerome W. Berryman, *Godly Play* (Minneapolis: Augsburg Fortress, 1995), 1.

15. Berryman, *Godly Play*, ix.

16. Berryman, *Godly Play*, 60.

17. Berryman, *Godly Play*, 30.

18. Houk, *Parenting by Developmental Design*, 98.

19. Marjorie J. Thompson, *Family the Forming Center: A Vision of the Role of Family in Spiritual Formation* (Nashville: Upper Room Books, 1996), 88.

20. Berryman, *Godly Play*, 94.

21. "This 'talking back to [the Bible]' is a skill that has been lost in evangelicalism today. One reason is because we have lost the freedom to ask questions of the Bible." Kelly Edmiston, "Talking Back to the Bible," *Christianity Today*, August 19, 2020, https://tinyurl.com/mt399acj.

22. Reimagining and pushing back against sacred texts is deeply important to the task of liberation. Emerson B. Powery and Rodney S. Sadler Jr. document how enslaved and formerly enslaved Black Americans used the Bible for liberatory purposes. They explain, "Biblical literacy allowed these black interpreters to 'talk back' to [the Bible] and thereby to engage in a critical hermeneutical challenge to the widespread oppressive use of Scripture on the side of [slavery]." *The Genesis of Liberation* (Louisville: Westminster John Knox Press, 2016), 29.

23. Houk, *Parenting by Developmental Design*, 113.

24. R. L. Stollar, "Job, Reimagined," November 27, 2014, https://tinyurl.com/4svnhf4j.

25. Elaine A. Heath explains, "Often [child abuse survivors] are internally if not outwardly disconnected from Christianity, the church, the Bible, and clergy. Much of their alienation has to do with how the Bible is read and interpreted in the church. Some of it has to do with excessively gendered language for God in hymnody, prayers, and the liturgy." *We Were the Least of These* (Grand Rapids: Brazos, 2011), 4.

26. Largen, *Baby Krishna, Infant Christ*, 202.

27. Largen, *Baby Krishna, Infant Christ*, 138.

28. Largen, *Baby Krishna, Infant Christ*, 201.

29. Houk, *Parenting by Developmental Design*, 100.

30. Marcia J. Bunge, "The Vocation of the Child: Theological Perspectives on the Particular and Paradoxical Roles and Responsibilities of Children," in *The Vocation of Children*, ed. Patrick McKinley Brennan (Grand Rapids: Eerdmans, 2008), 50.

31. bell hooks, *Teaching to Transgress: Education as the Practice of Freedom* (New York: Routledge, 1994), 5.

32. hooks, *Teaching to Transgress*, 40.

33. Gregory C. Carlson and John K. Crupper, "Instructional-Analytic Model," in *Perspectives on Children's Spiritual Formation*, ed. Michael J. Anthony (Nashville: Broadman & Holman, 2006), 136.

34. Carlson and Crupper, "Instructional-Analytic Model," 106.

35. Carlson and Crupper, "Instructional-Analytic Model," 104.

36. Carlson and Crupper, "Instructional-Analytic Model," 124.

37. Joyce Ann Mercer, *Welcoming Children: A Practical Theology of Childhood* (St. Louis: Chalice Press, 2005), 167–68.

38. Scottie May, "Instructional-Analytic Model," in *Perspectives on Children's Spiritual Formation*, ed. Michael J. Anthony (Nashville: Broadman & Holman, 2006), 150, emphasis original.

39. Mercer, *Welcoming Children*, 168.

40. Mercer, *Welcoming Children*, 167.

41. Dr. Maria Montessori developed the Montessori method in the late 1800s and early 1900s. Montessori described children as "naturally eager for knowledge and capable of initiating learning in a supportive, thoughtfully prepared learning environment." See American Montessori Society, "Introduction to Montessori Method," https://tinyurl.com/2r5p544c, accessed November 2, 2015. As an application of the Montessori method to Christian education, Godly Play emphasizes the importance of children actively "exploring the mystery of God's presence in our lives." See Godly Play Foundation, https://tinyurl.com/mr2azwax, accessed November 2, 2015.

42. Emily A. Mullens, "What Is Godly Play? Our Review & Introduction," Ministry-To-Children, https://tinyurl.com/wa3zrjhr, accessed November 2, 2015, emphasis added.

43. A few examples from leaders in the conservative evangelical child training industry: James Dobson compares child training to beating a dog in his book *The Strong-Willed Child*; Michael Pearl compares child training to training mules and horses in *To Train Up a Child*; and Voddie Baucham compares child training to getting a viper under control in his 2007 Hardin Baptist Church sermon "Child Training." See R. L. Stollar, "The Child as Viper: How Voddie Baucham's Theology of Children Promotes Abuse," Homeschoolers Anonymous, January 16, 2015, https://tinyurl.com/4kfefc8w.

44. "The same principles the Amish use to train their stubborn mules [are] the same technique God uses to train His children." Michael Pearl, "Introduction," *To Train Up a Child* (Pleasantville: No Greater Joy Ministries, 2006).

45. We can find this idea in each of their books: Michael Pearl declares, "The parent's role is not that of policemen, but more like that of the Holy Spirit." *To Train Up a Child*, 18. Tedd Tripp tells parents, "You exercise authority as God's agent. . . . You must direct your children on God's behalf." *Shep-*

herding a Child's Heart (Wapwallopen: Shepherd Press, 2005), xix. J. Richard Fugate writes, "Parents are the symbol and representative of God's authority to their children." *What the Bible Says about . . . Child Training* (Tempe: Aletheia, 1980), 41. John MacArthur says, "The parents stand in the place of the Lord." *What the Bible Says about Parenting* (Nashville: W Publishing Group, 2000), 121. Larry Tomczak claims, "The father is the priest of the home" who "represents his family to God." *God, the Rod, and Your Child's Bod* (Old Tappan: Fleming H. Revell Company, 1982), 59.

46. Fugate, *Child Training*, 158–59.

47. Yoshiharu Nakagawa, "The Child as Compassionate Bodhisattva and as Human Sufferer/Spiritual Seeker: Intertwined Buddhist Images," in *Nurturing Child and Adolescent Spirituality: Perspectives from the World's Religious Traditions*, ed. Karen Marie Yust, Aostre N. Johnson, Sandy Eisenberg Sasso, and Eugene C. Roehlkepartain (Lanham: Rowman and Littlefield, 2006), 41.

48. Tripp, *Shepherding a Child's Heart*, xx.

49. Mullens, "What Is Godly Play?"

50. Jerome Berryman, "Q&A: Jerome Berryman," *Premier Childrenswork*, June/July 2015, https://tinyurl.com/586ts88c.

51. Berryman, "Q&A: Jerome Berryman," emphasis added.

52. In Daoism, the concept of empty space is described by the Chinese word *wu*, translated as "emptiness" or "nothingness." This emptiness is an active, life-giving force. In chapter 11 of the *Dao De Jing*, emptiness is talked of positively: "We throw clay to shape a pot, but the utility of the clay pot is a function of the nothingness inside it." *Dao De Jing: A Philosophical Translation*, trans. Roger T. Ames and David L. Hall (New York: Ballantine Books, 2003), 91. In the Daoist worldview, it is a sign of good leadership when a leader creates empty spaces for people to self-determine.

53. Joyce Ann Mercer, "Play and Theology," July 16, 2013, https://tinyurl.com/2wv84ksh.

54. Johnston, *Christian at Play*, 75–77.

55. Josef Pieper, *Leisure: The Basis of Culture* (New York: Pantheon Books, 1963), 40–42.

56. Marcia J. Bunge, "The Dignity and Complexity of Children: Constructing Christian Theologies of Childhood," in Yust et al., *Nurturing Child and Adolescent*, 54.

57. Michael J. Anthony, "Putting Children's Spirituality in Perspective," in

Perspectives on Children's Spiritual Formation, ed. Michael J. Anthony (Nashville: Broadman & Holman, 2006), 33.

58. Anthony, "Putting Children's Spirituality in Perspective," 31.

59. Heller, *Children's God*, 134.

60. Heller, *Children's God*, 135.

61. Heller, *Children's God*, 136.

62. Heller, *Children's God*, 140.

63. Eric J. Mash and David A. Wolfe, *Abnormal Child Psychology* (Boston: Cengage Learning, 2016), 465.

Chapter Thirteen

1. Karl Rahner, as quoted by Karen Marie Yust, *Real Kids, Real Faith: Practices for Nurturing Children's Spiritual Lives* (San Francisco: Jossey-Bass, 2004), 124.

2. Yust, *Real Kids, Real Faith*, 7.

3. The main parachurch organization promoting this movement is the National Center for Family-Integrated Churches (NCFIC). See their website at https://tinyurl.com/yc6ucv58. Vision Forum, a now-defunct homeschooling ministry that promoted patriarchal gender roles, founded NCFIC. For more information about the connection between Vision Forum and NCFIC, see Doug Phillips, Vision Forum, "Church Leaders Discuss Family-Integrated Churches," September 25, 2001, https://tinyurl.com/34t83s6x.

4. Shawn Mathis, "Scott Brown's New Family Integrated Church Declaration and Why You Should Care," August 30, 2015, https://tinyurl.com/ypnxvaxx.

5. Judith A. Cohen, Anthony P. Mannarino, and Esther Deblinger, *Treating Trauma and Traumatic Grief in Children and Adolescents* (New York: Guilford Press, 2006), 7.

6. David Ng and Virginia Thomas, *Children in the Worshiping Community* (Louisville: John Knox, 1981), 31.

7. For more information about Erik Erickson's psychosocial stages, see Laura E. Berk, *Child Development* (London: Pearson Education, 2013), 15–17. This table is my summary of the information presented there.

8. Yust, *Real Kids, Real Faith*, 44.

9. Vivian L. Houk, *Parenting by Developmental Design* (Eugene: Resource Publications, 2010), 66.

10. Ng and Thomas, *Children in the Worshiping Community*, 37.

11. Berk, *Child Development*, 228.

12. Berk, *Child Development*, 239.

13. Berk, *Child Development*, 239.

14. Berk, *Child Development*, 249.

15. "Between ages 7 and 10, children pass Piaget's *class inclusion problem*. This indicates they are more aware of classification hierarchies and can focus on relations between a general and two specific categories at the same time— that is, on three relations at once." Berk, *Child Development*, 250, emphasis in original.

16. Berk, *Child Development*, 253.

17. "A second important characteristic of Piaget's formal operational stage is propositional thought—adolescents' ability to evaluate the logic of propositions (verbal statements) without referring to real-world circumstances. In contrast, children can evaluate the logic of statements only by considering them against concrete evidence in the real world." Berk, *Child Development*, 254.

18. "I believe that Piaget's view of childhood was a limited one, and that these limitations can have a seriously damaging or at least impoverishing effect on our educational practice. . . . The starting point of all Piaget's thought about childhood is the incapacity of children to see the world as adults see it. . . . He seems always to assume that reality is the way adults see it, and that if children do not see it that way they are victims of 'deceptive figurative appearances.' Where in fact there is a difference of opinion, adults are right and children are wrong. Of course, under proper adult influence, children get better all the time, but this development is best measured in their relative incapacity to see this adult 'reality.'" Edward Robinson, *The Original Vision: A Study of the Religious Experience of Childhood* (New York: Seabury Press, 1983), 9.

19. Robinson, *Original Vision*, opening page.

20. Robinson, *Original Vision*, 11.

21. Yust, *Real Kids, Real Faith*, 11.

22. David Heller, *The Children's God* (Chicago: University of Chicago Press, 1986), 39–41. Hereafter page citations will be in the text.

23. Yust, *Real Kids, Real Faith*, 10.

24. Houk, *Parenting by Developmental Design*, 111.

25. Ng and Thomas, *Children in the Worshiping Community*, 10.

26. John Calvin, *Institutes of the Christian Religion*, ed. John T. McNeill (Louisville: Westminster, 1960), 1281.

27. Ng and Thomas, *Children in the Worshiping Community*, 30.

28. David Ng and Virginia Thomas have many more helpful ideas in their book *Children in the Worshiping Community*, which I highly recommend.

29. Ng and Thomas, *Children in the Worshiping Community*, 127.

30. Play is not only a spiritual necessity; it is also a human right. Article 31 of the UN Convention on the Rights of the Child acknowledges "the right of the child to rest and leisure, to engage in play and recreational activities appropriate to the age of the child and to participate freely in cultural life and the arts." Amnesty International explains why it is important to protect children's right to play: "At the heart of children's lives everywhere is the right to play, including games, sports, and the creative arts, such as drama, dance, art, music, and poetry. It supports your right to a voice and to agency and it is vital to your health and well-being. The right to play helps your development in every way—physical, intellectual, social, and emotional—and is a form of self-expression." *Know Your Rights and Claim Them* (Minneapolis: Zest Books, 2021), 155.

31. Boz Tchividjian, in the foreword to Victor Vieth's *On This Rock: A Call to Center the Christian Response to Child Abuse on the Life and Words of Jesus* (Eugene: Wipf and Stock, 2018), xi–xii.

32. Ng and Thomas, *Children in the Worshiping Community*, 21–22.

Chapter Fourteen

1. Joyce Ann Mercer, *Welcoming Children: A Practical Theology of Childhood* (St. Louis: Chalice Press, 2005), 111.

2. "Our care of children—our 'welcoming' of them among us—is a direct reflection of our love for and obedience to God. As the sweet nursery song teaches, Jesus loves the little children, and one of the most important works any church can undertake—to love God—is to love the children in its care." Boz Tchividjian and Shira M. Berkovits, *The Child Safeguarding Policy Guide for Churches and Ministries* (Greensboro: New Growth Press, 2017). While I agree with Tchividjian and Berkovits on the importance of welcoming children, I disagree with their portrayal of the song as "sweet." The traditional lyrics to "Jesus Loves the Little Children" include racial slurs (referring to Native people and Asian people as "reds" and "yellows"). See Libby Anne,

"Red and Yellow, Black and White: Evangelicals Miss a Wakeup Call on Race," *Patheos*, December 14, 2017, https://tinyurl.com/2dwkhpct.

3. "We simply do not have the luxury of building social movements that are not intersectional, nor can we believe we are doing intersectional work just by saying words." Kimberlé Crenshaw, "Why Intersectionality Can't Wait," *Washington Post*, September 24, 2015, https://tinyurl.com/43me8b7b.

4. Kelly Brown Douglas, "Teaching Womanist Theology," in *Living the Intersection: Womanism and Afrocentrism in Theology*, ed. Cheryl J. Sanders (Minneapolis: Fortress Press, 1995), 151.

5. "What womanist theology says about God, Christ, and the church must make sense, must ring true, to these women in the context of their daily struggles." Douglas, "Teaching Womanist Theology," 155. What Douglas says about womanist theology applies equally to child liberation theology in reference to children.

6. While I will use data about Black children as my primary examples in this section, many of my conclusions and suggestions are equally applicable for other children of color. I will try to be clear in distinguishing when I talking about Black children specifically versus all children of color.

7. Dorothy Roberts, *Shattered Bonds: The Color of Child Welfare* (New York: Basic Civitas Books, 2002), 10, viii.

8. Roberts, *Shattered Bonds*, vi.

9. Roberts, *Shattered Bonds*, 8.

10. "White children are the least likely of any group to be supervised by child protective services. Black children make up more than two-fifths of the foster care population, though they represent less than one-fifth of the nation's children. Latino and Native American children are also in the system in disproportionate numbers." Dorothy Roberts, "Race and Class in the Child Welfare System," PBS, 2003, https://tinyurl.com/ht8mh5s.

11. "Only about 17% of children removed from their homes nationwide are in foster care because of allegations of physical or sexual abuse. . . . The vast majority of children in foster care are there on allegations of parental neglect." Dorothy Roberts, as cited by Janell Ross, "One in Ten Black Children in America Are Separated from Their Parents by the Child-Welfare System. A New Book Argues That's No Accident," *Time*, April 20, 2022, https://tinyurl.com/8yrmtzme.

12. Roberts, *Shattered Bonds*, 35, emphasis original.

13. Roberts, *Shattered Bonds*, 6.

14. Michelle Alexander, *The New Jim Crow: Mass Incarceration in the Age of Colorblindness* (New York: The New Press, 2012), 6.

15. Elisabeth Young-Bruehl, *Childism: Confronting Prejudice against Children* (New Haven: Yale University Press, 2012), 2.

16. Alexander, *New Jim Crow*, 118, emphasis added.

17. "Black juveniles were more than four times as likely to be committed as white juveniles, American Indian juveniles were more than three times as likely, and Hispanic juveniles were 61 percent more likely." Joshua Rovner, "Racial Disparities in Youth Commitments and Arrests," April 1, 2016, https://tinyurl.com/2xvvrwrm.

18. Sabrina Tavernise, "Rise in Suicide by Black Children Surprises Researchers," *New York Times*, May 18, 2015, https://tinyurl.com/4jansm3s.

19. Sari Horwitz, "The Hard Lives—and High Suicide Rate—of Native American Children on Reservations," *Washington Post*, March 9, 2014, https://tinyurl.com/bdzd7xjj.

20. Ludmila Leiva, "Latina Suicide Rates of Control—Here's Why," *Refinery 29*, October 15, 2018, https://tinyurl.com/4bu6dp96.

21. When applied to discussions about race, "colorblindness" is an ableist term (a term that contributes to prejudice and discrimination against people with disabilities) so I will avoid it henceforth. However, I am calling attention to the term itself because it is a popular term.

22. Children's Assessment Center, "Child Sexual Abuse Facts," https://tinyurl.com/yc4dz6np, accessed March 6, 2017.

23. Children's Assessment Center, "Child Sexual Abuse Facts."

24. Stephanie Hargrove, "What's Hidden in Plain Sight: A Look at Child Sexual Abuse in the Black Community," American Psychological Association, November 2014, https://tinyurl.com/y27nczdz.

25. Horwitz, "Hard Lives."

26. Children's Assessment Center, "Child Sexual Abuse Facts."

27. World Health Organization, "Violence against Adults and Children with Disabilities," https://tinyurl.com/5n76pypc, accessed March 6, 2017.

28. Hilary Brown, "Sexual Abuse of Children with Disabilities," Council of Europe, https://tinyurl.com/2p8jjm2b, accessed March 6, 2017.

29. US Office for Victims of Crime, "Responding to Transgender Victims of Sexual Assault," June 2014, https://tinyurl.com/ywhua58a.

30. Regarding the mainstreaming of white supremacists, see Simon Clark, "How White Supremacy Returned to Mainstream Politics," Center for American Progress, July 1, 2020, https://tinyurl.com/36f6na2f. Regarding the mainstreaming of white nationalists, see Molly Olmstead, "'Christian Nationalism' Used to Be Taboo. Now It's All the Rage," *Slate*, August 5, 2022, https://tinyurl.com/59d3jaft.

31. "To effectively defeat systemic racism—racism embedded as normal practice in institutions like education and law enforcement—you've got to be continually working towards equality for all races, striving to undo racism in your mind, your personal environment and the wider world. In other words, you've got to be anti-racist." Eric Deggans, "'Not Racist' Is Not Enough: Putting in the Work to Be Anti-Racist," NPR, August 25, 2020, https://tinyurl.com/2p83wmbp.

32. Amanda Armstrong, "Bias Starts as Early as Preschool, but Can Be Unlearned," *Edutopia*, June 4, 2019, https://tinyurl.com/n4ndhmwm.

33. Melissa Kuipers, "Jesus in Color: Toward an Anti-Racist Children's Ministry," *The Banner*, December 25, 2020, https://tinyurl.com/2mf3k7a6.

34. "Most children's ministries and children's ministry curricula do not address race at all. By this I mean there's a scarcity of discussion, materials, and lessons in children's ministries that bring up a person's race. There's even less that broach topics like racial discrimination and racism. There's also a lack of resources that equip leaders to address race and meanings of race with children at church." Henry Zonio, "Why We Must Start Talking about Race in Our Children's Ministries," *Children's Ministry Magazine*, February 25, 2022, https://tinyurl.com/ycyx6s4u.

35. Kuipers, "Jesus in Color."

36. "White saviorism still influences child welfare practice. In 2018, writing on the death of Devonte Hart, Stacey Patton wrote, 'It seems that America cannot see or hear black children's tears unless they are framed in the context of white redemption or white saviorism.'" Sharon L. McDaniel, "White Privilege in Child Welfare: What Racism Looks Like," *The Imprint*, June 23, 2020, https://tinyurl.com/53kb5tbw.

37. "I sort of liken someone who's engaged in white saviorism to a person who rushes into the emergency room wanting to help, but if they don't have training as a nurse or a doctor, they may actually end up doing more harm than good." Savala Nolan as cited by Colleen Murphy, "What Is White Sav-

ior Complex—And Why Is It Harmful?," *Health*, October 24, 2022, https://tinyurl.com/2p8k4sfb.

38. People with disabilities prefer person-first language (i.e., "*people* with disabilities") rather than identity-first language (i.e., "*disabled* people"). See Kevin Timpe, *Disability and Inclusive Communities* (Grand Rapids: Calvin College Press, 2018), 69: "'Person with a disability' is an instance of person-first language. It is a way of focusing on a person's humanity and individuality rather than leading with their disability. . . . Many people with disabilities think person-first language is preferable to identity-first language. It is a good default we should work to foster."

39. While this section focuses on children with disabilities, it is important to note that most people with disabilities are adults. In fact, "over 90% of Americans with disabilities are adults." Timpe, *Disability and Inclusive Communities*, 27.

40. As quoted in Erik W. Carter's book *Including People with Disabilities in Faith Communities: A Guide for Service Providers, Families, and Congregations* (Baltimore: Paul H. Brookes, 2007), 19.

41. "Just as the term *racism* refers to behaviors or policies that discriminate against or devalue individuals on the basis of their race and the term *sexism* refers to behaviors or policies that discriminate against or devalue individuals on the basis of their sex, the term *ableism* refers to behaviors or policies that discriminate against or devalue people on the basis of disability." Timpe, *Disability and Inclusive Communities*, 29.

42. Timpe, *Disability and Inclusive Communities*, 39–40.

43. Steve Silberman, *NeuroTribes: The Legacy of Autism and the Future of Neurodiversity* (New York: Avery, 2016), 51.

44. Silberman, *NeuroTribes*, 113–16.

45. Timpe, *Disability and Inclusive Communities*, 43.

46. Sara Luterman, "31 States Have Laws That Allow Forced Sterilizations, New Report Shows," *The 19th*, February 4, 2022, https://tinyurl.com/mve5v8um.

47. Silberman, *NeuroTribes*, 116.

48. Timpe, *Disability and Inclusive Communities*, 106.

49. Susan Richardson, *Child by Child: Supporting Children with Learning Differences and Their Families* (New York: Morehouse Publishing, 2011), xii.

50. "Families refuse to take back their children for often complex and emotionally fraught reasons; many have struggled to get their kids psychiatric help early because of a lack of availability of outpatient care. The child

might have difficult or dangerous behaviors that could put their siblings at risk. Some have intellectual or developmental disabilities and their families are unsure how to care for them." Hannah Furfaro, "Abandoned in the ER: When Kids Are Left at Hospitals, the State Is No Longer Taking Charge of Their Care," *Seattle Times*, February 21, 2022, https://tinyurl.com/mwndk64r.

51. Naomi Larsson, "Out of Sight: The Orphanages Where Disabled Children Are Abandoned," *The Guardian*, September 26, 2016, https://tinyurl.com/yc49fpm3.

52. Chris Kaposy, "The Ethical Case for Having a Baby with Down Syndrome," *New York Times*, April 16, 2018, https://tinyurl.com/4rv5n7t8.

53. Ruth Graham, "Choosing Life with Down Syndrome," *Slate*, May 31, 2018, https://tinyurl.com/4ysensmf.

54. Emily Flores, "The #MeToo Movement Hasn't Been Inclusive of the Disability Community," *Teen Vogue*, April 24, 2018, https://tinyurl.com/3t6bu9m4.

55. Shannon Dingle, "Inaccessible Justice Movements Aren't Just," *BMP Voices*, https://tinyurl.com/5vyub56z, accessed May 16, 2019.

56. Timpe, *Disability and Inclusive Communities*, 91–92.

57. Rebecca S. Chopp, in the foreword to Nancy L. Eiesland, *The Disabled God: Toward a Liberatory Theology of Disability* (Nashville: Abingdon, 1994), 11: "The disabling theology of most Christian traditions has equated disabilities with sin. From codes of purity to acts of Jesus' healing, the implicit theological assumption has equated perfect bodies with wholeness of the spirit."

58. Timpe, *Disability and Inclusive Communities*, 38.

59. Timpe, *Disability and Inclusive Communities*, 57.

60. For more about these barriers, see Carter, *Including People with Disabilities*, 8–16.

61. For more information on the image of Jesus as disabled, see Eiesland, *Disabled God*, 100: "In presenting his impaired hands and feet to his startled friends, the resurrected Jesus is revealed as the disabled God. Jesus, the resurrected Savior, calls for his frightened companions to recognize in the marks of impairment their own connection with God, their own salvation."

62. "Inclusion is much more than just being present in the same building. Rather, it is evidenced when children worship, learn, serve, and fellowship side-by-side." Carter, *Including People with Disabilities*, 92.

63. "Injustice against persons with disabilities is surely sin; our bodies,

however, are not artifacts of sin, original or otherwise. Our bodies participate in the imago Dei, not in spite of our impairments and contingencies, but through them." Eiesland, *Disabled God*, 101.

64. "Think broadly about what it really means for a child to participate *fully* in your congregation and brainstorm strategies for supporting this type of participation. Although inclusion in Sunday/Sabbath school classes often receives the most attention, consider how you will help each child participate in the many other activities of your congregation, such as children's time during the worship service, choirs and musical groups, holiday pageants, summer programs, day trips, service projects, and other ceremonies and rites of passage (e.g., baptism, bar/bat mitzvah, confirmation, Shabbat services)." Carter, *Including People with Disabilities*, 99, emphasis original.

65. Timpe, *Disability and Inclusive Communities*, 74.

66. Timpe, *Disability and Inclusive Communities*, 101.

67. Carter, *Including People with Disabilities*, 9.

68. "Congregations must do more than passively affirm the rights of people with disabilities, but should also advocate for changes in society to ensure those rights are supported. Such actions might include encouraging passage of favorable laws, standing up against ineffective or oppressive service systems that stifle community participation, or advocating on behalf of people whose voice often is not heard." Carter, *Including People with Disabilities*, 18.

69. "Sensory experience in liturgy is important to all of us, but especially to children, elderly people, and persons with disabilities. It should be considered in our planning of corporate worship and its setting. Many elements of worship are non-verbal, and we can be more intentional about how we incorporate them to enhance the service for everyone." Carter, *Including People with Disabilities*, 79, citing the World Council of Churches' 2003 statement, "A Church of All and for All."

70. "The church finds its identity as the body of Christ only by being a community of faith and witness, a coalition of struggle and justice, and a fellowship of hope. This mission necessitates that people with disabilities be incorporated into all levels of participation and decision making." Eiesland, *Disabled God*, 104.

71. Dingle, "Inaccessible Justice Movements Aren't Just."

72. Carter, *Including People with Disabilities*, 9–10.

73. While the concept of neurodiversity was first embraced by autists, it

has come to apply to other developmental conditions as well, such as ADHD, dyslexia, and Tourette syndrome, or mental health conditions such as bipolarity, schizophrenia, or OCD.

74. Silberman, *NeuroTribes*, 14–15.

75. "Many Deaf individuals, for whom their deafness is part of their culture and language, prefer to be called Deaf rather than 'a person with a hearing impairment'. . . . Many people with an autism diagnosis prefer to be called 'autistic' rather than 'a person with autism,' given how they see their autism as part of their identity." Timpe, *Disability and Inclusive Communities*, 70.

76. Temple Grandin, as quoted in Lamar Hardwick, *I Am Strong: The Life and Journey of an Autistic Pastor* (Little Elm: eLectio Publishing, 2017), viii.

77. "Many autistics are proud of their autism and see it as a form of neurodiversity rather than a disability." Timpe, *Disability and Inclusive Communities*, 70.

78. Richardson, *Child by Child*, 30.

79. Steve Silberman, "The Geek Syndrome," *Wired*, December 1, 2001, https://tinyurl.com/28anyjcy.

80. Silberman, *NeuroTribes*, 41.

81. Richardson, *Child by Child*, 30–31.

82. Jessica Flynn, "Why Autism Functioning Labels Are Harmful—and What to Say Instead," *The Mighty*, July 22, 2018, https://tinyurl.com/bdhk7vub.

83. Emily Sohn, "How Abuse Mars the Lives of Autistic People," *Spectrum News*, February 5, 2020, https://tinyurl.com/n94ddmu3.

84. Fabienne Cazalis, Elisabeth Reyes, Séverine Leduc, and David Gourion, "Evidence That Nine Autistic Women Out of Ten Have Been Victims of Sexual Violence," *Frontiers in Behavioral Neuroscience*, April 26, 2022, https://tinyurl.com/2n459wam.

85. Edith Sheffer, "The Nazi History behind 'Asperger,'" *New York Times*, March 31, 2018, https://tinyurl.com/y3jtkr8h.

86. "Making peace with autism—by viewing it as a lifelong disability that deserves support, rather than as a disease of children that can be cured—seemed like a new and radical idea. In fact, it was the oldest idea in autism research." Silberman, *NeuroTribes*, 81.

87. David Briggs, "Study: US Churches Exclude Children with Autism, ADD/ADHD," *Christianity Today*, July 20, 2018, https://tinyurl.com/3k5y5j5v.

88. Kerry Magro, in the foreword to Lamar Hardwick, *I Am Strong: The Life and Journey of an Autistic Pastor* (Little Elm: eLectio Publishing, 2017), v.

89. Carter, *Including People with Disabilities*, 97.

90. Carter, *Including People with Disabilities*, 124.

91. For information about how to help children include children with differences and disabilities, see Barbara Newman's book *Helping Kids Include Kids with Disabilities* (Grand Rapids: Faith Alive Christian Resources, 2001).

92. Richardson, *Child by Child*, 32.

93. Oregon Zoo, "Oregon Zoo Launches New Sensory-Inclusive Program," April 9, 2019, https://tinyurl.com/amzz3d6s, accessed April 25, 2019.

94. "We need to help those with autism get a diagnosis as early as possible. Early intervention is key to help our loved ones across the lifespan regardless of autism or another special need. One way we can do this is teaching people about the early signs of autism." Magro, in the foreword to Hardwick, *I Am Strong*, vi.

95. "The popular image of autism is with children. With that we must understand that children with autism will become adults with autism and we must be ready for them. Autism and other disabilities don't just stop in childhood." Magro, in the foreword to Hardwick, *I Am Strong*, v.

96. "Some researchers deployed ABA towards other conditions. A particularly famous example was the 'Feminine Boy Project', an attempt to preemptively 'cure' those male children considered at risk of becoming gay or transvestites. The leaders of the project sought advice from Lovaas, and used an approach strongly influenced by ABA, indicating Lovaas' status in the field." Patrick Kirkham, "'The Line between Intervention and Abuse' —Autism and Applied Behaviour Analysis," *History of the Human Sciences* (2017): 112.

97. "Lovaas began to use such 'aversives' regularly, initially through beatings and later through shocks and the withholding of food." Kirkham, "'Line between Intervention and Abuse,'" 111.

98. While accommodating and supporting an autistic child is not the same as accommodating and supporting a left-handed child, I think it is fruitful to compare the two in terms of how society has reacted to both sets of differences. For centuries, left-handed people were considered demonic, they were beaten as children by their teachers until they wrote with their right hands, and they were even excluded from religious leadership. In short, they were treated much like autistic children have been treated: with suspicion,

discrimination, and abuse. For more information on the mistreatment of left-handed people, see Lily Rothman, "How Lefties First Gained Acceptance," *Time*, August 13, 2015, https://tinyurl.com/yhav3fbm; *Time*, "Lefty Liberation," January 7, 1974, https://tinyurl.com/mr4auhyn; and Joshua Goodman, "The Wages of Sinistrality: Handedness, Brain Structure, and Human Capital Accumulation," *The Journal of Economic Perspectives* 28, no. 4 (Fall 2014): 193–212, https://tinyurl.com/9hj6vjp4.

Conclusion

1. Brett Webb-Mitchell, *God Plays Piano, Too: The Spiritual Lives of Disabled Children* (New York: Crossroad Publishing Company, 1993), 57.

2. Rebecca Stevens-Walter, "Children Are Living in Biblical Times," *Medium*, February 23, 2022, https://tinyurl.com/yhnab9xx.

3. David Dark, *Everyday Apocalypse: The Sacred Revealed in Radiohead, the Simpsons, and Other Pop Culture Icons* (Grand Rapids: Brazos, 2002), 10.

4. Dark, *Everyday Apocalypse*, 10.

Selected Bibliography

Alexander, Michelle. *The New Jim Crow: Mass Incarceration in the Age of Colorblindness*. New York: The New Press, 2012.

Ali, Abdullah Yusuf. *The Holy Qur'an*. New Delhi: Kitab Bhavan, 1996.

Amazzone, Laura. *Goddess Durga and Sacred Female Power*. Lanham: Hamilton Books, 2010.

Amnesty International. *Know Your Rights and Claim Them*. Minneapolis: Zest Books, 2021.

Anthony, Michael J. "Putting Children's Spirituality in Perspective." In *Perspectives on Children's Spiritual Formation*, ed. Michael J. Anthony, 1–43. Nashville: Broadman & Holman, 2006.

Assmann, Hugo. *Theology for a Nomad Church*. Maryknoll: Orbis Books, 1975.

Ateek, Naim Stifan. *Justice and Only Justice: A Palestinian Theology of Liberation*. Maryknoll: Orbis Books, 2003.

Aune, David E. *Prophecy in Early Christianity and the Ancient Mediterranean World*. Grand Rapids: Eerdmans, 1983.

Baucham, Voddie. *Family Shepherds*. Wheaton: Crossway, 2011.

Beck, John A. *The Baker Illustrated Guide to Everyday Life in Bible Times*. Ada: Baker Books, 2013.

Berger, Peter L. *The Sacred Canopy: Elements of a Sociological Theory of Religion*. New York: Anchor Books, 1967.

Berk, Laura E. *Child Development*. London: Pearson Education, 2013.

Berryman, Jerome W. *Godly Play*. Minneapolis: Augsburg Fortress, 1995.

Betsworth, Sharon. *Children in Early Christian Narratives*. London: Bloomsbury, 2015.

Bonhoeffer, Dietrich. *Letters and Papers from Prison*. Edited by Eberhard Bethge. New York: Macmillan, 1971.

Bradley, Reb. *Child Training Tips: What I Wish I Knew When My Children Were Young*. Fair Oaks: Family Ministries Publishing, 1996.

Brandt, Cindy Wang. *Parenting Forward: How to Raise Children with Justice, Mercy, and Kindness*. Grand Rapids: Eerdmans, 2019.

Brennan, Patrick McKinley. "Children Play with God: A Contemporary Thomistic Understanding of the Child." In *The Vocation of the Child*, ed. Patrick McKinley Brennan, 189–214. Grand Rapids: Eerdmans, 2008.

———. "Introduction." In *The Vocation of the Child*, ed. Patrick McKinley Brennan, 1–28. Grand Rapids: Eerdmans, 2008.

Briere, John N., and Catherine Scott. *Principles of Trauma Therapy: A Guide to Symptoms, Evaluation, and Treatment*. Thousand Oaks: SAGE Publications, 2015.

Brown, Sheila. *Understanding Youth and Crime: Listening to Youth?* New York: McGraw-Hill Education, 2005.

Bunge, Marcia J. "The Dignity and Complexity of Children: Constructing Christian Theologies of Childhood." In *Nurturing Child and Adolescent Spirituality: Perspectives from the World's Religious Traditions*, ed. Karen Marie Yust, Aostre N. Johnson, Sandy Eisenberg Sasso, and Eugene C. Roehlkepartain, 53–68. Lanham: Rowman and Littlefield, 2006.

———. "The Vocation of the Child: Theological Perspectives on the Particular and Paradoxical Roles and Responsibilities of Children." In *The Vocation of Children*, ed. Patrick McKinley Brennan, 31–52. Grand Rapids: Eerdmans, 2008.

Calvin, John. *Institutes of the Christian Religion*. Edited by John T. McNeill. Louisville: Westminster Press, 1960.

Carlson, Gregory C., and John K. Crupper. "Instructional-Analytic Model." In *Perspectives on Children's Spiritual Formation*, ed. Michael J. Anthony, 103–47. Nashville: Broadman & Holman, 2006.

Carter, Erik W. *Including People with Disabilities in Faith Communities: A Guide for Service Providers, Families, and Congregations*. Baltimore: Paul H. Brookes, 2007.

Chung, Hyun Kyung. "Following Naked Dancing and Long Dreaming." In *Inheriting Our Mothers' Gardens: Feminist Theology in Third World Per-*

spective, ed. Letty M. Russell, Kwok Pui-lan, Ada María Isasi-Díaz, and Katie Geneva Cannon, 54–72. Louisville: Westminster Press, 1988.

Cohen, Judith A., Anthony P. Mannarino, and Esther Deblinger. *Treating Trauma and Traumatic Grief in Children and Adolescents*. New York: Guilford Press, 2006.

Coles, Robert. *The Spiritual Life of Children*. Boston: Houghton Mifflin, 1990.

Collins, Billy. *Sailing Alone around the Room*. New York: Random House, 2001.

Cone, James H. *Black Power and Black Theology*. Maryknoll: Orbis Books, 1997.

———. *The Cross and the Lynching Tree*. Maryknoll: Orbis Books, 2011.

Dao De Jing: A Philosophical Translation. Translated by Roger T. Ames and David L. Hall. New York: Ballantine Books, 2003.

Dark, David. *Everyday Apocalypse: The Sacred Revealed in Radiohead, the Simpsons, and Other Pop Culture Icons*. Grand Rapids: Brazos, 2002.

Delaney, Carol. *Abraham on Trial: The Social Legacy of Biblical Myth*. Princeton: Princeton University Press, 2020.

Dixon, C. Madeleine. *Children Are Like That*. Omaha: John Day, 1930.

Dobson, James. *The New Strong-Willed Child*. Carol Stream: Tyndale House, 2004.

Douglas, Kelly Brown. "Teaching Womanist Theology." In *Living the Intersection: Womanism and Afrocentrism in Theology*, ed. Cheryl J. Sanders, 147–55. Minneapolis: Fortress Press, 1995.

Edwards, Jonathan. *Thoughts on the Revival of Religion in New England*. 1742.

Ehrman, Bart. *Lost Scriptures: Books That Did Not Make It into the New Testament*. Oxford: Oxford University Press, 2003.

Eiesland, Nancy L. *The Disabled God: Toward a Liberatory Theology of Disability*. Nashville: Abingdon, 1994.

Elkins, Kathleen Gallagher, and Julie Faith Parker. "Children in Biblical Narrative and Childist Interpretation." In *The Oxford Handbook of Biblical Narrative*, ed. Danna Nolan Fewell, 422–33. Oxford: Oxford University Press, 2016.

Eusebius of Caesarea. *Ecclesiastical History*. Translated by Arthur Cushman McGiffert. *Nicene and Post-Nicene Fathers*. 2nd ser., vol. 1. Edited by Philip Schaff and Henry Wace. 28 vols. in 2 series. Repr., Buffalo: Christian Literature Publishing, 1890.

Farris, Michael. *The Joshua Generation: Restoring the Heritage of Christian Leadership*. Nashville: B&H Publishing Group, 2005.

Fewell, Danna Nolan. *The Children of Israel: Reading the Bible for the Sake of Our Children*. Nashville: Abingdon, 2003.

Fretheim, Terence E. "'God Was with the Boy' (Genesis 21:20): Children in the Book of Genesis." In *The Child in the Bible*, ed. Marcia J. Bunge, 3–23. Grand Rapids: Eerdmans, 2008.

Fugate, J. Richard. *What the Bible Says about . . . Child Training*. Tempe: Aletheia, 1980.

Grant, George. *Bringing in the Sheaves*. Powder Springs: American Vision Press, 1985.

———. *The Changing of the Guard: Biblical Blueprints for Political Action*. Fort Worth: Dominion Press, 1987.

Greven, Philip. *Spare the Rod: The Religious Roots of Punishment and the Psychological Impact of Physical Abuse*. New York: Vintage Books, 1992.

Gundry-Volf, Judith M. "The Least and the Greatest: Children in the New Testament." In *The Child in Christian Thought*, ed. Marcia J. Bunge, 29–60. Grand Rapids: Eerdmans, 2001.

Gutiérrez, Gustavo. *A Theology of Liberation*. Maryknoll: Orbis Books, 2014.

Haight, Wendy L. *African-American Children at Church: A Sociocultural Perspective*. Cambridge: Cambridge University Press, 2002.

Harder, Jeanette. *Let the Children Come: Preparing Faith Communities to End Child Abuse and Neglect*. Scottdale: Herald Press, 2010.

Harding, Nick, and Sandra Millar. *Ready to Share One Bread: Preparing Children for Holy Communion*. London: Society for Promoting Christian Knowledge, 2015.

Hardwick, Lamar. *I Am Strong: The Life and Journey of an Autistic Pastor*. Little Elm: eLectio Publishing, 2017.

Havighurst, R., and B. Keating. "The Religion of Youth." In *Research on Religious Development*, ed. M. Strommen, 686–723. New York: Hawthorn Books, 1971.

Hazleton, Lesley. *The First Muslim: The Story of Muhammad*. New York: Riverhead Books, 2013.

Heath, Elaine A. *We Were the Least of These*. Grand Rapids: Brazos, 2011.

Heimlich, Janet. *Breaking Their Will: Shedding Light on Religious Child Maltreatment*. Amherst: Prometheus Books, 2011.

Heller, David. *The Children's God*. Chicago: University of Chicago Press, 1986.

Holcomb, Justin, and Lindsey Holcomb. *God Made All of Me: A Book to Help Children Protect Their Bodies*. Greensboro: New Growth Press, 2015.

hooks, bell. *Feminism Is for Everybody*. Cambridge: South End Press, 2000.

———. *Teaching to Transgress: Education as the Practice of Freedom*. New York: Routledge, 1994.

Houk, Vivian L. *Parenting by Developmental Design*. Eugene: Resource Publications, 2010.

Ingersoll, Julie. *Building God's Kingdom: Inside the World of Christian Reconstructionism*. Oxford: Oxford University Press, 2015.

Isasi-Díaz, Ada María. *Mujerista Theology: A Theology for the Twenty-First Century*. Maryknoll: Orbis Books, 1996.

Jarl, Ann-Cathrin. *In Justice: Women and Global Economics*. Minneapolis: Fortress Press, 2003.

Johnson, Elizabeth A. *Dangerous Memories: A Mosaic of Mary in Scripture*. New York: Bloomsbury, 2004.

Johnston, Robert K. *The Christian at Play*. Grand Rapids: Eerdmans, 1983.

Josephus. *Jewish Antiquities*. In *The New Complete Works of Josephus*. Translated by William Whiston. Grand Rapids: Kregel Academic, 1999.

Keener, Craig S. *The Gospel of Matthew: A Socio-Rhetorical Commentary*. Grand Rapids: Eerdmans, 2009.

Klein, Linda Kay. *Pure: Inside the Evangelical Movement That Shamed a Generation of Young Women and How I Broke Free*. New York: Touchstone, 2018.

Koepf, Laurel. "Inside Out: The Othered Child in the Bible for Children." In *Text, Image, and Otherness in Children's Bibles: What Is in the Picture?*, ed. Caroline Vander Stichele and Hugh S. Pyper, 11–30. Atlanta: Society of Biblical Literature, 2012.

Kwok, Pui-lan. "Mothers and Daughters, Writers and Fighters." In *Inheriting Our Mothers' Gardens: Feminist Theology in Third World Perspective*, ed. Letty M. Russell, Kwok Pui-lan, Ada María Isasi-Díaz, and Katie Geneva Cannon, 21–34. Louisville: Westminster Press, 1988.

Laffey, Alice L. *An Introduction to the Old Testament: A Feminist Perspective*. Minneapolis: Fortress Press, 1988.

Lancaster, Philip. *Family Man, Family Leader*. San Antonio: Vision Forum, 2011.

Lapsley, Jacqueline E. "'Look! The Children and I Are as Signs and Portents in Israel': Children in Israel." In *The Child in the Bible*, ed. Marcia J. Bunge, 82–102. Grand Rapids: Eerdmans, 2008.

Largen, Kristin Johnston. *Baby Krishna, Infant Christ: A Comparative Theology of Salvation*. Maryknoll: Orbis Books, 2011.

Lockyer, Herbert. *All the Women of the Bible*. Grand Rapids: Zondervan, 1988.

MacArthur, John. *What the Bible Says about Parenting*. Nashville: W Publishing Group, 2000.

Mash, Eric J., and David A. Wolfe. *Abnormal Child Psychology*. Boston: Cengage Learning, 2016.

Mather, Cotton. *A Family Well-Ordered, or, AN ESSAY to Render PARENTS AND CHILDREN Happy in One Another*. 1699.

May, Scottie. "Instructional-Analytic Model." In *Perspectives on Children's Spiritual Formation*, ed. Michael J. Anthony, 147–53. Nashville: Broadman & Holman, 2006.

Mercer, Joyce Ann. *Welcoming Children: A Practical Theology of Childhood*. St. Louis: Chalice Press, 2005.

Michel, Andreas. "Sexual Violence against Children in the Bible." In *The Structured Betrayal of Trust*, ed. R. Ammicht-Quinn, H. Haker, and M. Junker-Kenny, 51–59. London: SCM, 2004.

Miller, Alice. *The Truth Will Set You Free*. New York: Basic Books, 2001.

Miller-McLemore, Bonnie J. *Let the Children Come*. San Francisco: Jossey-Bass, 2003.

Minns, Denis. *Irenaeus*. Washington, DC: Georgetown University Press, 1994.

Nakagawa, Yoshiharu. "The Child as Compassionate Bodhisattva and as Human Sufferer/Spiritual Seeker: Intertwined Buddhist Images." In *Nurturing Child and Adolescent Spirituality: Perspectives from the World's Religious Traditions*, ed. Karen Marie Yust, Aostre N. Johnson, Sandy Eisenberg Sasso, and Eugene C. Roehlkepartain, 33–42. Lanham: Rowman and Littlefield, 2006.

Ng, David, and Virginia Thomas. *Children in the Worshiping Community*. Louisville: John Knox, 1981.

Nhat Hanh, Thich. *The Heart of the Buddha's Teaching: Transforming Suffering into Peace, Joy, and Liberation*. New York: Broadway Books, 1999.

——. *Living Buddha, Living Christ*. New York: Riverhead Books, 1995.

——. *Touching Peace: Practicing the Art of Mindful Living*. Berkeley: Parallax Press, 1992.

Oduyoye, Mercy Amba. "Be a Woman, and Africa Will Be Strong." In *Inheriting Our Mothers' Gardens: Feminist Theology in Third World Perspective*, ed. Letty M. Russell, Kwok Pui-lan, Ada María Isasi-Díaz, and Katie Geneva Cannon, 35–53. Louisville: Westminster Press, 1988.

Pais, Janet. *Suffer the Children: A Theology of Liberation by a Victim of Child Abuse*. Mahwah: Paulist Press, 1991.

Pearl, Michael, and Debi Pearl. *To Train Up a Child*. Pleasantville: No Greater Joy Ministries, 2006.

Perry, Marvin, and Frederick M. Schweitzer. *Antisemitism*. New York: Palgrave Macmillan, 2002.

Philip, Tarja S. *Menstruation and Childbirth in the Bible: Fertility and Impurity*. Frankfurt: Peter Lang, 2006.

Pieper, Josef. *Leisure, the Basis of Culture*. New York: Pantheon Books, 1963.

Plantinga, Alvin. *God, Freedom, and Evil*. Grand Rapids: Eerdmans, 1974.

Polanyi, Michael. *Personal Knowledge*. Chicago: University of Chicago Press, 1974.

Powery, Emerson B., and Rodney S. Sadler Jr. *The Genesis of Liberation*. Louisville: Westminster John Knox, 2016.

Pride, Mary. *The Way Home: Beyond Feminism, Back to Reality*. Fenton: Home Life Books, 2010.

Provan, Charles D. *The Bible and Birth Control*. Monongahela: Zimmer Printing, 1989.

Reid, Charles J., Jr. "The Rights of Children in Medieval Canon Law." In *The Vocation of the Child*, ed. Patrick McKinley Brennan, 243–65. Grand Rapids: Eerdmans, 2008.

Richardson, Susan. *Child by Child: Supporting Children with Learning Differences and Their Families*. New York: Morehouse Publishing, 2011.

Roberts, Dorothy. *Shattered Bonds: The Color of Child Welfare*. New York: Basic Civitas Books, 2002.

Robinson, Edward. *The Original Vision: A Study of the Religious Experience of Childhood*. New York: Seabury Press, 1983.

Ruether, Rosemary Radford. "Religion and Society: Sacred Canopy vs. Prophetic Critique." In *The Future of Liberation Theology: Essays in Honor of Gustavo Gutiérrez*, ed. Marc H. Ellis and Otto Maduro, 172–76. Maryknoll: Orbis Books, 1989.

———. *Sexism and God-Talk*. Boston: Beacon Press, 1993.

Shaffer, David. R. *Social and Personality Development*. Boston: Cengage Learning, 2009.

Shire, Michael. "Learning to Be Righteous: A Jewish Theology of Childhood." In *Nurturing Child and Adolescent Spirituality: Perspectives from the World's Religious Traditions*, ed. Karen Marie Yus, Aostre N. Johnson, Sandy Eisenberg Sasso, and Eugene C. Roehlkepartain, 43–52. Oxford: Rowman & Littlefield, 2005.

Silberman, Steve. *NeuroTribes: The Legacy of Autism and the Future of Neurodiversity*. New York: Avery, 2016.

Stortz, Martha Ellen. "'Where or When Was Your Servant Innocent?' Augustine on Childhood." In *The Child in Christian Thought*, 78–102. Grand Rapids: Eerdmans, 2001.

Strohl, Jane E. "The Child in Luther's Theology: 'For What Purpose Do We Older Folks Exist, Other Than to Care for . . . the Young?'" In *The Child in Christian Thought*, ed. Marcia J. Bunge, 134–59. Grand Rapids: Eerdmans, 2001.

Tchividjian, Boz. *Protecting Children from Abuse in the Church*. Greensboro: New Growth Press, 2013.

Tchividjian, Boz, and Shira M. Berkovits. *The Child Safeguarding Policy Guide for Churches and Ministries*. Greensboro: New Growth Press, 2017.

Thatcher, Adrian. *Theology and Families*. Hoboken: John Wiley & Sons, 2008.

Thompson, Marjorie J. *Family the Forming Center: A Vision of the Role of Family in Spiritual Formation*. Nashville: Upper Room Books, 1996.

Timpe, Kevin. *Disability and Inclusive Communities*. Grand Rapids: Calvin College Press, 2018.

Tomczak, Larry. *God, The Rod, and Your Child's Bod*. Old Tappan: Fleming H. Revell Company, 1982.

Traina, Cristina L. H. "A Person in the Making: Thomas Aquinas on Children and Childhood." In *The Child in Christian Thought*, ed. Marcia J. Bunge, 103–33. Grand Rapids: Eerdmans, 2001.

Tripp, Tedd. *Shepherding a Child's Heart*. Wapwallopen: Shepherd Press, 2005.

Vieth, Victor. *On This Rock: A Call to Center the Christian Response to Child Abuse on the Life and Words of Jesus*. Eugene: Wipf and Stock, 2018.

Walker, Alice. *In Search of Our Mothers' Gardens*. San Diego: HBJ Publishers, 1983.

Wariboko, Nimi. *The Pentecostal Principle: Ethical Methodology in New Spirit.* Grand Rapids: Eerdmans, 2011.

Webb-Mitchell, Brett. *God Plays Piano, Too: The Spiritual Lives of Disabled Children.* New York: Crossroad Publishing Company, 1993.

Weren, W. J. C. *Studies in Matthew's Gospel: Literary Design, Intertextuality, and Social Setting.* Leiden: Brill, 2014.

Werpehowski, William. "In Search of Real Children: Innocence, Absence, and Becoming a Self in Christ." In *The Vocation of the Child*, ed. Patrick McKinley Brennan, 53–74. Grand Rapids: Eerdmans, 2008.

———. "Reading Karl Barth on Children." In *The Child in Christian Thought*, ed. Marcia J. Bunge, 386–405. Grand Rapids: Eerdmans, 2001.

White, Keith J. "'He Placed a Little Child in the Midst': Jesus, the Kingdom, and Children." In *The Child in the Bible*, ed. Marcia J. Bunge, 353–74. Grand Rapids: Eerdmans, 2008.

White, Keith J., and Haddon Willmer. *An Introduction to Child Theology.* The Child Theology Movement Limited, 2006.

Whitehouse, Maggy. *A Woman's Worth: The Divine Feminine in the Hebrew Bible.* Winchester: John Hunt, 2013.

Wilson, Lois. *Stories Seldom Told: Biblical Stories Retold for Children and Adults.* Kelowna: Wood Lake Publishing, 1997.

Young-Bruehl, Elisabeth. *Childism: Confronting Prejudice against Children.* New Haven: Yale University Press, 2012.

Yust, Karen Marie. *Real Kids, Real Faith: Practices for Nurturing Children's Spiritual Lives.* San Francisco: Jossey-Bass, 2004.

Index of Authors

Index of Subjects